A Journey to Unlearn and Learn in Multicultural Education

PETER LANG
New York • Washington, D.C./Baltimore • Bern
Frankfurt am Main • Berlin • Brussels • Vienna • Oxford

A Journey to Unlearn and Learn in Multicultural Education

EDITED BY

Hongyu Wang & Nadine Olson

PETER LANG
New York • Washington, D.C./Baltimore • Bern
Frankfurt am Main • Berlin • Brussels • Vienna • Oxford

Library of Congress Cataloging-in-Publication Data

A journey to unlearn and learn in multicultural education /
edited by Hongyu Wang, Nadine Olson.
p. cm.
Includes bibliographical references.
1. Multicultural education. 2. Multiculturalism in literature.
3. Racism in education. 4. Sexism in education. 5. Teachers—Training of.
6. Teaching—Philosophy. I. Olson, Nadine. II. Title.
LC1099.W355   370.117—dc22   2009003813
ISBN 978-1-4331-0446-6

Bibliographic information published by **Die Deutsche Bibliothek**.
Die Deutsche Bibliothek lists this publication in the "Deutsche
Nationalbibliografie"; detailed bibliographic data is available
on the Internet at http://dnb.ddb.de/.

Cover photo by Shanedra Nowell
Cover design by Clear Point Designs

The paper in this book meets the guidelines for permanence and durability
of the Committee on Production Guidelines for Book Longevity
of the Council of Library Resources.

© 2009 Peter Lang Publishing, Inc., New York
29 Broadway, 18th floor, New York, NY 10006
www.peterlang.com

Printed in the United States of America

Table of Contents

Part VI: Perspectives, Visions, and Praxis

Acknowledgments

A book like this cannot be born without many people's support. First, we thank all of our students and especially the contributors to this book for their courage to unlearn and learn and for what they have taught us about education. Second, our thanks go to Christine Ormsbee, Head of the School of Teaching and Curriculum Leadership, for her support of this book project, and particularly for granting Hongyu Wang a course release to finish the book proposal. Third, we are indebted to Frances Griffin's timely and excellent professional editing, along with Robin Fuxa's and Miriam Ward's thoughtful reading and editing of some chapters. Our special thanks go to Jill Martin, who has done a marvelous job tracking down all the references and polishing many chapters. Fourth, we are thankful to Chris Myers for welcoming this book and to Sophie Appel and Valerie Best, along with other Peter Lang staff, for their tremendous help in turning this manuscript into a book. Last but not least, we are deeply honored and most grateful that Sonia Nieto and Wendy Kohli gracefully and generously wrote endorsements for this book on a very short notice.

Hongyu is also grateful to her colleagues in the Curriculum Studies Project who warmly and unwaveringly support her work, including Kathryn Castle, Pam Brown, and Gretchen Schwarz. These wonderful colleagues' commitment and humor in difficult times are such an inspiration to her. She thanks William F. Pinar for his encouragement and insights into the link between her multicultural education and her scholarship. She also thanks James A. Banks for his helpful suggestions. Grateful to Tianlong Yu's advice on her book proposal, she thanks him for his enthusiastic support of this work. Her conversation with Lucy Bailey on the book has also been helpful. Special thanks go to Mechelle Brown at the Greenwood Cultural Center who sacrificed her weekend time to guide students' visit to the center and to offer inspiring teachings during the past several years. She is also indebted to Shanedra Nowell and Jon Smthye for their generous help in selecting a cover photo for this book.

As the journey of students in multicultural education is unfinished, so is our effort to teach multicultural education. This collection serves as an invitation to all educators to travel along winding paths towards nonviolence and social equity with commitment, care, and creativity.

Introduction

Hongyu Wang

The trauma of racism is, for the racist and the victim, the severe fragmentation of the self…

> —Toni Morrison, "Unspeakable Things Unspoken"

The river of diversity offers both dangers and delights to those of us who choose to ply its ever-changing waters.

> —Gary Howard, *We Can't Teach What We Don't Know*

If racism, sexism, and other forms of social injustice deform all of us in different ways (Morrison, 1988; Pinar, 1993), can we work through denial, shame, guilt, and anger to create new identities that embrace a more integrative and fuller vision of life, subjectivity, and education? Such effort is an upward journey against the mainstream of what is taken for granted, a journey of climbing to reach the top of the mountain for a broader view of the landscape, a journey of uprooting from the comfortable to reach new awareness and new relationships. This collection of writings depicts such journeys, the unfinished work of teachers, teachers-to-be, and teacher educators who engage the difficult yet exciting work of multicultural education. What are highlighted in this book are students' journeys in teacher education toward transforming their professional and personal identities for educational and social change.

Although the additive approach to multicultural education has been criticized extensively in the field (Banks, 2008; Edgerton, 1996; Nieto, 1999; Rothenberg, 2000), teacher education in many universities has hardly gone beyond this model. Related to this "safe" strategy of keeping differences at bay is teaching about different racial and ethnic groups in the U.S. to make students familiar with "other cultures" as if these groups have static characteristics that, once understood, can be mastered. While dynamic and historical analyses of each different social group are essential to cultivating multicultural awareness, what teachers-to-be usually expect is to learn recipes for what to do in their own classroom to "click" with cultural minority students. Such attention to technique and procedure is embedded in the belief that multicultural education is for other people's children and that the knowledge of "others" can produce effective teaching for other people's children.

As a result, what is left untouched is the privileged site of the self, and what is left unquestioned is the desire for mastery and control, the desire underlying racial, gendered, and class hierarchies both historically and contemporarily. It is this neglected area that this collection of writings attempts to address. The central assumption of this book is that multicultural education must attend to and transform teachers' subjectivity as much as it must attend to creating new strategies for educating students from diverse backgrounds. Howard (2006) argues that our task is two-fold, including the inner work of multicultural teaching and the outer work of social transformation. This collection demonstrates a dynamic interaction between the inner and the outer, the personal and the cultural, the individual and the structural. Here a structural analysis of, for instance, racism, is blended with a personal reflection of one's own responsibility for anti-racism. While acknowledging this step in itself does not guarantee the success of individual and communal efforts to change the larger social and economic structure, it is a transformation starting from the root and branching out to enable educational and pedagogical capacities for effective teaching in a multicultural and global society. In this sense, the inner work and the outer work are integrated rather than separate efforts.

Looking back on the self is a difficult journey, necessarily involving the complexity of working through intellectual and emotional blocks, a journey difficult to accomplish by individuals alone. While many multicultural education books discuss what we need to achieve, not many books demonstrate the process of working through resistance to question one's own deeply cherished assumptions and beliefs in order to unpack socially sanctioned values and perspectives. Particularly missing are students' own points of view in their struggles. This book adopts a process-oriented approach and illuminates learners' perspectives through their own voices. It promises to fill in a gap and provide necessary companionship for those who also travel in multicultural education. In sharing these intimate moments of awakening, authors invite readers to join in the journey. This collection of writings not only speaks to those who have started their journey of learning but also invites teacher educators to tune in to the inner landscapes of their students in order to create a more democratic classroom for the democratization of both self and society.

To Unlearn in Order to Learn

> Our own re-education means not only learning new things but also *un*learning some of the old.
>
> —Nieto & Bode, 2008, p. 425

There is a popular Zen story about unlearning. A Japanese master during the Meiji era received a university professor who came to inquire about Zen. The professor talked about Zen while the master quietly served tea. He poured his visitor's cup full, and then kept on pouring. The professor watched the overflow until he no longer could hold back. "It is overfull. No more will go in!"

"Like this cup," the master said, "you are full of your own opinions and speculations. How can I show you Zen unless you first empty your cup?" This is an intriguing metaphor for learning about diversity issues in education. Students (and instructors) come into the classroom full of their own opinions, assumptions, and perspectives: how can they learn anything new without first emptying previous understandings that may be covered by "the cold mist of bias and ignorance" (Delpit, 2006/1995, p. xxiii)?

Even though many of my White students have not taken any multicultural education classes as undergraduate students, they seldom come to the class with empty minds. Some students feel that "we have heard enough" about minority struggles (Yu, in Wang &Yu, 2006); some students are intimidated by the topics of the class, even afraid to say the word "race"; quite a few perceive multicultural education as a faulty conception and practice. For those who have less resistance and who are more open to new knowledge, what they usually expect to learn is how to teach minority students in the classroom. They expect to learn what is African American culture, Native American culture, Hispanic culture, Asian American culture, and so on and so forth so that they can effectively teach students from cultures different from their own, as if each culture has some core characteristics that once mastered brings the magic of successfully teaching in multiracial schools. They expect to receive a "how to" package so that they can handle situations that they are not familiar with. But they are at least willing to learn *about* others.

Not surprisingly, least of all do my White students expect to meet the challenge of questioning their own fundamental assumptions, perceptions, beliefs, and understandings in order to transform educational, curricular, and pedagogical praxis. Their refusal to think about deeper issues, a refusal to unlearn in order to learn, usually comes with the complaint that the class should teach what to do in a multicultural classroom and should not offer so much social and political critique without practical values. But the issue is: How can students know what to do without examining their basic orientations toward teaching in the context of diversity, equity, and social justice? As Christine E. Sleeter (2000) argues, how can one understand the cultural contexts of teaching and connect with students from different cultures without understanding oneself as a cultural being?

As our society is increasingly diverse, many universities especially in the middle part of the U.S. are still predominately White, middle class, ethnocentric institutions. It is widely acknowledged that the cultural backgrounds of the majority of pre-service teachers cannot meet the needs of increasingly diverse K-12 students from different racial, social class, and linguistic backgrounds (Howard, 2006; Ladson-Billlings, 2001; Sleeter, 2005). The task of reaching all children through heart, mind, and soul becomes even more imperative. Lisa Delpit's (2006/1995) call for "basic understandings of who we are and how we are connected to and disconnected from one another" (p. xxv) remains an unfulfilled plea in teacher education. The superficial way of nodding the head to non-mainstream cultures can hardly meet the challenge. Now it is time to empty the cup in order to see, hear, smell, taste, and make sense of the world differently.

Unlearning involves the capacity to step out of oneself, to look at the self from a distance in a new light. This process is not possible without engaging others' lenses to examine one's own worldviews. Engagement with both others' worlds and others' understandings of the (White) self is necessary. Studies of White identity from minority perspectives (Fine, 2004; Tatum, 1997) provide an avenue for examining "the institutional, ideological, and material triple of production, embodiment, and denial [of Whiteness] in the everyday practices of schooling" (Fine, 2004, p. 246) that Whites usually have a difficult time seeing. At the same time, the recent studies on Whiteness, White privilege, and White identity re-formation by White scholars/practitioners pave new pathways for Whites' self-understanding. Intercultural conversation and cross-cultural dialogues (Lawrence & Tatum, 2004) also facilitate different positioning of racial identification. The engagement with the other and the engagement of the self go hand in hand. This collection demonstrates such a simultaneous process of mutual engagement.

Minority students also need to engage in a critical encounter with the self. For a handful of racial minority students I have taught in teacher education classes, unlearning is also a condition for learning, although in a different sense. Although not as "self-shattering" (Pinar, 2004) as Whites need to experience, self-affirmation of minority students who embrace rather than erase cultural differences does not come easily. Due to internalized racism, minority students sometimes also advocate colorblind approaches, and it is a struggle for them to de-naturalize what is filtered by the mainstream culture in order to reclaim their own sense of history and culture. Native American students, for instance, growing up in a White society, usually have to grapple with their own internalized Whiteness in their efforts to embrace their Native American roots. More often than not, students with Native American heritages have a mixture of racial backgrounds, which makes the task of self-understanding even more complicated. Unlearning and learning are two sides of one coin for all learners with different patterns on both sides. As our society becomes more and more like a borderland (Anzaldúa, 1999), continuous dialogue and conversation is essential to generating intercultural knowledge, awakening moments, and multicultural pedagogy.

Creating Multicultural Diversity Experiences

What can teacher educators do to facilitate such a challenging process of unlearning in order to learn? Most likely, unlearning is not a voluntary act. Sleeter (2005) argues that multiracial groups in which Whites are present but not the majority usually produce livelier and richer discussions about race and anti-racist teaching than predominately White groups. Such a diverse group in teacher education classes in many universities in the Midwest, however, is more the exception than the rule. In my own classes, there are times when the instructor is the only racial minority member. While structured immersion experiences are ideal for students to engage another culture, they are not always available. One way to deal with this challenge is to create multicultural diversity experiences in the classroom through various activities, along with critical readings of multicultural education theories. These activities are designed for students to engage with others, but such an engagement must, at the same time, come back to engaging the self.

Our pedagogical efforts in critically and engagingly using narratives, videos and films, local investigation, historical memory work, and self-study intend to stretch students' imagination beyond the usual landscape and expand their limited exposures to diverse cultures. Creating experiences here is understood as engaging both activity and reflection so that intellect and emotion are integrated to enable movement away from the given social structure and culturally sanctioned identity. Unlearning through experiencing is a heart-felt process rather than an imposed outcome; it is a complicated process that does not follow straight lines but works through curves.

In multicultural education it is generally acknowledged that autobiography, fiction, and films can effectively bring students to other people's lives to experience the impact of racism, sexism, poverty, and other forms of social inequality and inspire students to join in a collective struggle for social justice. Teachers' stories (Chan & Boone, 2001; Obidah & Teel, 2001; Paley, 2000/1979) are also effective in initiating a desire for change. However, as Ann C. Berlak (1996) points out, learning about cultural diversity issues through the lens of narrative does not necessarily lead to the critique of dominant storylines but works through silences, gaps, masks, and ambiguities with uncertain outcomes. *The*

Color of Fear, which she used in her class and is also used in my classes, produces both resistance and insights at the same time. But this uncertainty of teaching through narratives provides a productive site for engaging students' understandings, desires, and personhood. Not intending to reproduce any linear storyline of from not knowing to reaching enlightenment (Miller, 2005), students' writings in this collection demonstrate the power of critical narrative in enabling personal transformation through getting in touch with other people's lives imaginatively, emotionally, and intellectually.

Memory work is not valued in the mainstream future-oriented "progressive" plot; however, historical memory work is precisely what we need in order to confront the legacy of racism, sexism, and classism, among other forms of social injustice. As William Ayers (2001) points out, we desire to forget the past, but this relationship with the past is different for the majority and minority racial groups: "White people can never quite remember the scope and scale of the slavocracy and of rule by lynching, while Black people can never quite afford to forget" (p. 213). The opening of students' eyes to the hidden history of the Tulsa Race Riot of 1921 had a dramatic impact on them. The majority of them knew little about it, and they were shocked to know the extent of this horror and were outraged with the fact that only when they came to graduate school and in this multicultural education class were they encouraged to know more fully about what happened. They began to understand how the past Tulsa had impacted the present Tulsa in a way that was not accessible to them before. Since this had happened in their own backyard, many of them responded to it intensely. They had a firsthand experiencing and understanding of a relationship to suffering other than amnesia: "Once suffering is acknowledged, it can be dealt with. If left repressed or denied, however, suffering only festers and pushes the pain ever deeper" (Howard, 2006, p. 83). Historical trauma is usually pushed under the rug in many places, not just in Oklahoma; investigating local resources and using them educationally in other places can also deepen students' understanding of what they tend to push aside as "old" tales.

The efforts to encounter a collective past pushed behind the selective remembering are also enhanced by reading James W. Loewen's (1995) provocative book, *Lies My Teacher Told Me.* The sections on the treatment of Native Americans in the school textbooks were particularly astonishing to students. Much of what Loewen discusses was news to them, while they had assumed that they "knew" as Oklahomans. The combination of intellectual experience and firsthand historical encounters characterizes what I mean by creating multicultural education experiences on a predominantly White campus. Experience is created here, not ready-made.

As a Native American state, Oklahoma has a lot of resources on American Indian cultures. When students engage in local investigation projects, many of them choose to undertake projects related to American Indians' lives in Oklahoma, both historically and contemporarily. These investigations are refreshing because they give students new lenses through which to read, discuss, and critically understand multicultural theories. For instance, along with reading Sandy Grande's (2004) *Red Pedagogy*, some students chose to go to the Museum of the Five Civilized Nations, the Muskogee Tribe College that was in a process of being established, or various Native American tribes for their projects. They learned things that they had not learned from books, but such learning was also enabled by reading books that they would not have picked up by themselves.

Self-study conducted either systematically or voluntarily is another major thread in creating experiences for students. Readings, experiences, and discussions encourage students to understand the self differently, not just in the sense of seeking their own ethnic identity, but also in the sense of acknowledging and integrating what has been excluded in their socially constructed sense of the self. While privilege is analyzed and discussed, understanding the role of power needs to serve for enhancing interconnections both inside and outside of the self so that students feel more encouraged to take personal responsibility for contesting social hierarchy. Students from the cultural minority groups and the majority group have different relationships with such a complicated study of the self, but their ongoing engagement with reconstructing their professional and personal identity is crucial to multicultural education and cannot be trivialized into celebrating holidays or sharing ethnic food even though such activities can be part of a bigger project.

When students connect learning through experiencing differences both inside and outside of the self—intellectually, emotionally, socially, and spiritually—they are more willing to take on the necessary yet difficult work of unlearning. Creating multicultural diversity experiences in a predominantly White classroom is possible, and this possibility is also enhanced by multiple layers of social differences other than race and ethnicity. The interrelationship of race/ethnicity with gender, sexuality, poverty, and global issues highlights multiplicity within experience and complicates multicultural conversations. Students bring their own multiple identities, acknowledged or unacknowledged, into the classroom, and my hope is that they leave the class with an enriched and expanded sense of the self and that they are committed to enriching their own students' lives in a similar way.

Student's Voices

The uneasiness of teaching and learning uncomfortable topics related to race, gender, class, and sexuality has been acknowledged by many scholars from a variety of disciplines (Chan & Treacy, 1996; Chizhik, 2003; Jakubowski, 2001; Pipino, 2005; Rhone, 2002; Roberts & Smith, 2002). Pedagogical strategies for responding to this issue are also elaborated, such as a pedagogy of discomfort (Boler, 1999; Boler & Zembylas, 2003), action-oriented strategy (Jakubowski, 2001), ethnic literature teaching strategies (Pipino, 2005), case study approach (Chan & Treacy, 1996), and other specific teaching techniques (Chan and Treacy, 1996; Pipino, 2005; Rhone, 2002). What has made these strategies effective, at least to a certain degree, is instructors' increasing understanding of students and their efforts to make teaching relevant to students' lived experiences, including their lack of experiences in diversity issues. These educators painstakingly attempt to understand the reasons for students' resistance and to build bridges to work productively through it rather than simply denouncing it. Such efforts, I would prefer to phrase as teaching "in a third space" (Wang, 2004), promote intercultural dynamics for transformative education.

In dealing with this issue, however, students' own struggles with uncomfortable truths in their own voices are relatively absent. What we usually hear is the teacher's account of students' resistance; students' words, when presented, are mediated through the teacher's own theoretical analysis. This collection of writings is different, foregrounding students' own accounts of what it is like to engage in an ongoing process of multicultural learning. These students either currently work in the field of education or are prospective educators. Both the process-oriented narrations and the strong personal touch of these writings can directly speak to both students and professors of teacher education as they co-travel on uneasy paths. This approach also invites a shift in the teacher-student relationship from an authoritarian approach to a dialogic approach (Freire, 2005/1970), an approach that many multicultural educators advocate for meaningful and empowering learning.

A few books (Lesage, Ferber, Storrs, & Wong, 2002; Garrod & Larimore, 1997) that bring out students' voices usually highlight cultural minority students' perspectives. While it is absolutely important to bring into light what has been neglected, this collection not only provides minority students' writings but also includes a substantial part of White students' writings, as well as interracial dialogues. In a sense, it depicts a "typical" multicultural classroom on a "typical" university campus, demonstrating the power of multicultural and intercultural education despite its difficulty. Because of the makeup of the student body at our university, White students' writings compose a large part of the collection, and their struggles with Whiteness are highlighted in different sections. This highlighting of understanding and transforming Whiteness from White students' own work-in-progress efforts makes this book unique, especially appealing to many universities (and communities) with a predominantly White student body.

These students' writings are courageous, and their journeys are brave. With all the obstacles of teaching multicultural education classes, it is students' courage and willingness to take this journey that has sustained my own courage to teach and to teach against the grain. I am often profoundly touched by my students at the end of the class in looking back on how far we can go as both individual persons and a community. If students can accomplish so much in one semester, it demonstrates that multicultural education can make a dramatic difference, inspiring dynamic intercultural creativity against an age of standardized conformity, offering hope against an age of despair in public education. Students' own voices speak the loudest.

Certainly, these writings only indicate students' starting points and invite readers to critically engage them for transformative learning. As the majority of essays are experiential, thoughtful writings of modest length, teacher educators can use this book creatively and flexibly according to their students' needs and their curriculum design.

Climbing the Sky City Together:
The Call for Teacher Educators' Joint Journey

Nadine and I drove to New Mexico during the hot summer of 2004. We had co-taught a doctoral seminar on diversity and equity issues in 2002 when I had just been at OSU for a year. I was one of the few whose faces are marked as "different" in the college of education. By the end of the class, we had become good friends. Our backgrounds, experiences, and teaching styles are quite different, sometimes forming dramatic contrasts; yet we worked together so well. Our mutual respect for each other, the meals we shared to discuss the class, and our willingness to listen and learn led to a lasting friendship after the class ended. This cross-cultural collaboration not only provided different perspectives to students but also set up an example of working across differences. Team teaching is not a new concept or practice, but successful joint journeys (Obidah & Teel, 2001; Rothenberg, 2000) through both the difficulty and the possibility of collaborating across racial and cultural differences can demonstrate what we teach about through how we teach. Since our first team teaching, we had learned about the Native American and Hispanic cultures together in Oklahoma, and when we were choosing a site for a vacation trip, New Mexico was a natural spot.

What was most impressive to us during that trip was the tour to the Sky City of Acoma Pueblo. The city was built on a huge mesa about 7,000 feet above sea level centuries ago. Ideal for defending against enemy attacks in the old days, the city is still an inhabited village. Climbing to the top in a bus, we saw the Pueblo's mission church, San Esteban del Rey. Our tour guide explained that although forced to build a Catholic church, Native Americans introduced their own traditions in the way they set up the church, traditions that were not understood by the colonists but were recognized by their own people. These wise and subtle ways of subversion fascinated me. Today people who live in the sky city do not enjoy "modern" luxuries, but they choose to live their own traditions. On the top of the massive rock, we viewed the enchanting surrounding mesas and felt the magical power of the whole area in an unforgettable way.

To tell this story is not to provide any superficial, romantic, tourist tale but to borrow the metaphor of upwardness to echo students' upward journeys: to climb to the top to see the world differently. Multicultural teacher educators also need to work through our own resistance and go to places where we have not been before (Ladson-Billlings, 2001), co-traveling with our students to reach new awareness and renew our educational commitment.

At a personal level, no other class has challenged so intensely my own identity as an international faculty member from China working at an American university (Wang, 2005). Aware that Chinese and Chinese Americans are located differently in American racial dynamics, worrying that students' attention to my own national and cultural backgrounds may divert the discussions about racism, I initially tried not to encourage their curiosity about Chinese culture. Even when I selected multicultural literature for students, I intentionally selected books written by and about other Asian and Asian American minority groups. After the first few years of teaching, however, I realized the paradox of my own approach: How can I encourage my students to see themselves as cultural beings (Sleeter, 2000) while not actively positioning myself as a cultural being? There were times when students directly asked me to share my own heritage, which questioned my cultural and gendered habits of remaining invisible and not appearing self-serving. Leaving China and living as a foreigner in another land is more or less a loss, self-chosen but a loss nevertheless: Did my good pedagogical intention cover up a defensive gesture of not working through this loss? As a result of this reflection, I changed my strategy. When I discuss Chinese culture, I try to complicate the issues and challenge students to critically reflect on racial, gender, and social class issues in American society through critically reflecting on my own privilege and disadvantage in my own culture. This is just an example of how engaged teaching can influence the instructor's personal and professional identity. While students acknowledge that the learning in our multicultural class has life-changing effects, teaching this class has also brought me astonishing revelations about my own life.

In this sense, this collection is also an invitation to teacher educators to engage their own personal transformation for social transformation. We need to listen to students' voices, whether or not those voices coincide with our own visions and hopes. Imposing our own notion of what multicultural education should be, despite self-perceived good intentions, replicates the transmission mode of teaching and oppressive education. Truly listening to students, we must be open to our own change, both pedagogically and personally. Coupled with our dialogical relationship with students, shared commitment and collaborative work among teacher educators is also important. Both reliance on minority faculty alone and refusal to diversify the faculty body have serious limitations. Only a community of committed educators with intercultural and cross-cultural collaborative relationships can make a difference.

Outline of the Book

This book is composed of an introduction, six thematically organized parts, and an afterword. Each part, except the last, ends with a pedagogical reflection, with students' own writings as the major component. This introduction chapter provides an overview of the book, situating it in the context of multicultural teacher education with an emphasis on the necessity of unlearning in order to learn.

Part I focuses on students' learning through reading and writing autobiography. It includes six students' essays. Part II focuses on the encounter with the Tulsa Race Riots of 1921. It includes five students' essays written from various angles. Part III focuses on minority students coming to terms with their own heritages in three essays. Part IV includes three essays on global issues reflected by both American and international students. Part V includes six students' essays on White identity development. The last part, Part VI, contains five essays providing a more systematic viewpoint on multicultural education, especially students' renewed commitment to daily multicultural praxis as educators. In this last part, the students' voices are heard without the instructors' pedagogical narrations.

Part I

Autobiography
and Social Difference

1. Two Perspectives on Race and Gender

Ben Mortensen

Paula Rothenberg's (2000) *Invisible Privilege* and Maya Angelou's (1997/1969) *I Know Why the Caged Bird Sings* offer two distinctly different backgrounds from which to observe racism and sexism. Maya Angelou tells of her experiences growing up as a Black girl in rural Arkansas, while Paula Rothenberg speaks of her ordeals as a Jewish girl in New York City. Both women highlight the disadvantages of being female, but they also complicate gender issues through other layers of social difference. Angelou tells her story mainly from the perspective of the child, and Rothenberg analyzes her experiences through the lens of the present. Angelou's sense of being a woman is constructed around her Black identity, while Paula Rothenberg has come to understand that her privilege in class and race provides more possibilities to overcome the obstacles of gender. In this essay, I discuss what I've learned from Angelou's and Rothenberg's different perspectives on race, gender, and social class in American society and I address how I plan to share these lessons in the classroom.

Gender Tales

Both Rothenberg and Angelou were avid readers from a young age. Despite the distinct differences in their backgrounds, their reactions to the *great* authors were similar. Both felt that the truly great authors and their heroes always coincided with being male. As a result, they both began to reject their own femininity. For Angelou (1997/1969), the trauma of being raped amplified the feeling that being female meant being helpless and powerless, and she wished that she "had been born a boy" (p. 75). In fifth grade, Rothenberg (2000) already lamented about the choices available for girls: "either you were attractive, sexual, and stupid, or you were ugly, smart, and thought like a boy. I decided to be smart" (p. 81). While both women thoroughly enjoyed literature, they felt painfully at odds with the ideals for women presented in the great works.

Angelou was luckier than Rothenberg in that Angelou had much stronger female role models. Momma (her grandma) was probably one of the most successful Blacks in Stamps, Arkansas, and Momma was a pillar of strength in the face of adversity. Angelou looked up to Momma, who provided so much inspiration for Angelou's life. Although Mother Dear did not raise her during much of her childhood, she supported Angelou through some of the crises. When Angelou was pregnant as a teenager, Mother Dear was there to help her stay strong. Mother Dear also encouraged her to finish school and to believe that she could do anything she put her mind to. Angelou (1997/1969) attributed African American women's strength to their struggles:

> The black female is assaulted in her tender years by all those common forces of nature at the same time that she is caught in the tripartite crossfire of masculine prejudice, white illogical hate and black lack of power. The fact that the adult American Negro female emerges a formidable character is often met with amazement, distaste and even belligerence. It is seldom accepted as an inevitable outcome of the struggle won by survivors and deserves respect if not enthusiastic acceptance. (p. 273)

Rothenberg, on the other hand, had very weak female role models. Her mother presented the biggest accomplishment of a woman as marrying rich instead of as anything that she could accomplish on her own. Rothenberg's mother felt "powerless in all her privilege" to the point where she was unable to confront supposed slights from her Black housekeepers (p. 27). Just like many of her friends, Rothenberg's mother "traded empowerment for dependency rationalized by gender stereotypes" (pp. 53–54). Ironically, Rothenberg's mother did back her up as she discussed going to college, while Rothenberg's father hesitated. Perhaps her mother intuitively did not want her daughter to follow the same path.

Rothenberg resolved to be different from her mother. Her mother's life was like an image in a mirror that reminded Rothenberg of what she refused to become. Although Rothenberg noticed that males were given privilege and authority in classrooms, both as students and as professors, she did not let this stop her pursuit. She did drop out of the University of Chicago but quickly rebounded. Rothenberg completed her education at New York University and eventually became a successful professor.

After reading these two women's stories, I confess that it never crossed my mind that one's gender or/and race could instantly disqualify one from getting a job (as it did in Angelou's ordeal of becoming a conducterette on the trolley). Neither did I realize that something besides my intellect could have been responsible for the favorable reactions I have almost always received from teachers over the years. In contrast, Rothenberg faced supercilious and condescending contempt from many professors and male classmates. Enjoying the advantages of being part of the powerful White male group is a concept I am still processing. Nevertheless, imagining these situations has a powerful impact on me. This understanding will be a challenge to the psyche of most White males. However, realizing that males still receive more attention than their female counterparts is an important first step in changing the culture of the classroom (Sadker & Sadker, 1986). We, as teachers, must not overvalue our male students at the expense of female students. Moreover, it is our calling as teachers to construct a curriculum that encourages female students to pursue what they wish to become.

Deeper Than the Skin

While struggling with gender issues, Paula Rothenberg gradually realized how her privileged upbringing gave her many opportunities that others did not have. For instance, she was able to get a mortgage for her house while others from minority backgrounds were under suspicion. Initially she was told her gender would exclude her income from calculations the bank uses to determine whether or not she and her partner would qualify for a mortgage. But Rothenberg was able to overcome her gendered disadvantages in the bank's eyes by her social position and race. Realtors hinted, or joked outright, about the advantages Rothenberg experienced because of her race.

Angelou experienced some privileges in her Black community due to her social class. Momma was financially successful as the owner of the Store and did not have to struggle like the cotton pickers. Mother Dear was also respected in her community and no one dared to mess with her. However, these advantages of class were tempered by the color of Angelou's skin. Angelou (1997/1969) tells how, as a child, she often fantasized about being White: "I was going to look like one of the sweet little white girls who were everybody's dream of what was right with the world" (p. 2).

Growing up in the fully segregated rural community of Stamps, Arkansas, Angelou had very little exposure to the White side of town or to White people in general. Angelou's first steady exposure to *Whitefolks* came when she started working for Mrs. Viola Cullinan. Although Mrs. Cullinan seemed to think she was gracious towards the Blacks who worked for her, Mrs. Cullinan refused to call Angelou by her name, "Marguerite," but gave her a White name, first as "Margaret" and then "Mary" to make the name simple. Angelou (1997/1969) resented the implications of Mrs. Cullinan's naming practice: "It was a danger-ous practice to call a Negro anything that could be loosely construed as insult-ing because of the centuries of their having been called niggers, jigs, dinges, blackbirds, crows, boots and spooks" (p. 109). Angelou had to wait until she was fourteen to meet the first White person who treated her with respect. She was shocked when Miss Kirwin, her teacher, treated her equally to White classmates, and Angelou realized that not all White people were automatically opposed to every Black person.

Angelou had a hard time finding role models within her race. The only Blacks presented as role models were male athletes. She wondered what place was left for her or her slightly-built brother Bailey. The attitude, that all that Black students could aspire to was to be famous athletes, was expressed by the White speaker at Maya Angelou's Black high school graduation and had a crushing effect on Angelou and her classmates:

> He went on to praise us. He went on to say how he had bragged that "one of the best basketball players at Fisk sank his first ball right here at Lafayette County Training School." The white kids were going to have a chance to become Galileos and Madame Curies and Edisons and Gauguins, and our boys (the girls weren't even in on it) would try to be Jesse Owenses and Joe Louises. …Graduation, the hush-hush magic time of frills and gifts and congratulations and diplomas, was finished for me before my name was called. …It was brutal to be young and already trained to sit quietly and listen to charges brought against my color with no chance of defense. (Angelou, 1997/1969, pp. 179–80)

Sadly, to some extent, athletics today are still advertised as *the* way out of the ghetto for Blacks. In addition to recognizing Black athletes, most people educated in America can now identify, and maybe even expound momentarily about the accomplishments of Black heroes and heroines such as Harriet Tubman, Rosa Parks, and Martin Luther King, Jr. Why are the numerous examples of successful Black scientists, educators, musicians, political leaders, artists, writers, entertainers, and activists not acknowledged as readily? Unfortunately we have a tendency to compartmentalize minorities' accomplishments (i.e., Black History month) as opposed to presenting minorities as always being an important part of the fabric of our culture.

Rothenberg's privilege made her experiences quite different from Angelou's. Rothenberg explained how, even though her test scores were not high enough, her father pulled some strings from his business network to help her enter the University of Chicago. When Rothenberg's car broke down, her mother didn't understand why Rothenberg would try to fix it instead of simply buying a new one. It is interesting to examine the way Rothenberg's ideas evolved. When she was in high school, she did not talk to any non-Whites in her school. Her first impression of non-Whites was: "I felt sorry for them—just as I pitied those born poor or with physical disabilities" (Rothenberg, 2000, p. 15). Over time, in the larger context of social movements, Rothenberg was able to transform her pity into compassion and social activism.

Rothenberg's journey opened my eyes about how those who have privileges and use those privileges in their daily lives often fail to recognize they are doing so. This became more obvious to me as students in a class I attended began discussing this book, *Invisible Privilege*. Almost everyone in our predominantly White class took issue with the way Rothenberg addressed White privilege. Rather than tackling how we can play a role in dismantling the power structures implicit in our educational system, we became defensive about the very notion that we had enjoyed privileges due to the color of our skin and that we might be part of the discrimination problem. One of the most difficult and, therefore, most important steps for me as a White male is to accept the ownership of this problem. Recognizing the benefits or preferential treatment received is an essential first step in moving beyond the refusal to accept responsibility and in finding ways to be part of the solution. My own perspective remains a work in progress, but as I analyze my interaction with the world through the lens of invisible privilege, a new dimension opens for me. I did not grow up with the financial or social class privilege that Rothenberg did; but, I cannot deny my White privilege, and I am willing to take on White responsibility, as she calls us to do:

> Racism is a white problem and that white people have a special responsibility for undoing the damage that has been done in our name and to our advantage. This means that white people must talk about race. The real issue for us is not whether but how to do so. (Rothenberg, 2000, p. 2)

Although difficult, I begin to understand that those who hold privileges must actively seek to change the power structure in collaboration with minority groups, to eliminate glass ceilings in corporations and other facets of our lives for women and non-Whites. Not opposing minority groups who seek a university education is not enough. Merely saying one does not approve of "something" is not the same as making efforts to change it. Being actively involved in antiracism requires those who stay at the center to confront the problem at personal and structural levels and to accept responsibility for changing social reality, even when change requires a willingness of the privileged to give up part of their privilege for the welfare of more people. Rothenberg poignantly points out the irony of the White liberal ideal as minority residents are excluded from her city's swimming pool:

> What allowed those public school teachers to spend their summers at swim clubs that excluded half the children in their classrooms because of the color of their skin? Why didn't they see a problem with doing so?...As a white person, I feel both anger and shame when I think about the role that so many well-meaning white liberals play in maintaining the color line, and I need to understand what allows them to live this way. (Rothenberg, 2000, p. 198)

The line of questioning Rothenberg uses parallels the challenge a young Black woman raised in class the first time Rothenberg team-taught a racism/sexism course at college. The student said she had enrolled in the course because she wanted to understand what is wrong with White people; why White people committed crimes against Blacks, for instance, during slavery. Her question turned "Whiteness" into a problem, shifting the attention from seeing racial minority as a problem to the construction of racial majority as a problem. This shifting of perspective is what educators must also confront.

Lessons for Education

Teaching students to be cognizant of the power structures that exist in American society and directing their awareness to the possible influence they might have will hopefully help students think critically about the world we live in. Students need to ask, "How do power relationships ultimately affect my own perceptions?"

As Rothenberg observed in her own teaching practice, teaching is often conducted under the guise of neutrality and universality, but in fact only one particular way of thinking is regarded as the model for intelligence. Rothenberg further argues that many teachers are the products of a Eurocentric curriculum and, as a result, an inclusive curriculum is more or less perceived and practiced as some kind of "charity work" rather than an essential curriculum for all students. It took years for Rothenberg to go beyond the failure of her own educational background to finally recognize the Eurocentric nature of American education. When Rothenberg's minority students confronted her with how Descartes, Locke, and other philosophers sounded alien and did not "speak" to them, she responded that, as college students, they did not have to believe or internalize what they were reading. She encouraged them to question the authors' beliefs and to ask why they felt the way they did about the author's work:

> Instead of beginning with the assumption that some of my colleagues adopted, that my students' difficulties were a sign of their inadequacy, I decided to operate from the premise that their discomfort was a sign of Descartes' inadequacy. I decided to ask the students to make allowances for his limitations, and, in order to do so, I spent more time discussing the context out of which Descartes' writings and worldview emerged.... Along with my students, I asked why someone might end up posing the kinds of questions that Descartes did. (p. 122)

Educators need to bring Rothenberg's approach to their classrooms. As Descartes' privileged upbringing was brought to the fore, Rothenberg's students developed a new appreciation of Descartes rather than dismissing his ideas as merely whims of fancy. Rothenberg felt liberated by the realization that "I could encourage my students to see ideas as weapons in a political struggle as well as puzzles in an intellectual tradition." (p. 124).

If minority students can make sense of Descartes, mainstream students can be taught to appreciate, for instance, the power of Toni Morrison's imaginative literature. It is up to us, as teachers, to offer diverse experiences for our students and to provide them the opportunity to see that people of other ethnic backgrounds, as well as that of women, have played an important part in making our society what it is today.

As Rothenberg observes, "because we are encouraged to think about diversity and tolerance rather than racism and privilege, it is easy for many of us who are white to take comfort in our good intentions" (p. 212). But good intentions do little to right the wrongs of our educational system. Many well-intentioned educational programs do little to challenge the dominant power structure of race, gender, and class. If we, as teachers, aren't willing to actively identify problems and search for ways of understanding and further transforming the whitewashed social, cultural, and personal reality, we are tacitly condoning the way things are. We obviously are not going to cure all societal problems alone, but if we can give our students a more balanced view of the world, those students are better equipped to do their part in creating a better future. We as teachers must not worry about "opening old wounds" when we educate our students about our country's racist past in order to go beyond racism. Reviewing historical and current race relations as well as many other issues in this country can be horrifying; but, it is necessary for teachers to develop an awareness of what has shaped the prevailing attitudes in our culture.

One of our goals as teachers should be to help our students develop an understanding of cultures different from their own, and this, in turn, can enhance the students' critical self-understandings. Lack of knowledge or understanding of other groups lessens human possibilities and potentials. Angelou poignantly displayed how a lack of understanding between races allowed abhorrent treatment of one race by another. Angelou reports that after Bailey was forced to help move the body of a Black man who had been lynched, he asked: "Uncle Willie, why do they hate us so much?" Uncle Willie muttered, "They don't really hate us. They don't know us. How can they hate us? They are mostly scared" (p. 197). Angelou further complicates the necessity for understanding by pointing out the lack of empathy toward the Asian Americans as they were being hauled off to internment camps in the 1940s:

> A person unaware of all the factors that make up oppression might have expected sympathy or even support from the Negro newcomers for the dislodged Japanese. Especially in view of the fact that [the Blacks] had themselves undergone concentration-

camp living for centuries in slavery's plantations and later in sharecroppers' cabins. But the sensations of common relationship were missing. (p. 211)

Too often in our curriculum we educators are so embarrassed by the horrible misdeeds of the powerful over the powerless that we simply ignore the misdeeds entirely. We educators cannot foster appropriate attitudes in our students if we ignore what we find objectionable in history. When teachers gloss over controversial topics and when discussions of discrimination and prejudice are avoided, students are denied the necessary information to recognize, understand, and perhaps solve the dilemmas that plague our society. It is not easy to present a well-balanced curriculum considering the male-dominated, Eurocentric, authoritative tone of our textbooks; but, as teachers, we must find opportunities to do so. Students frequently find sources with alternative frames of reference more interesting than textbooks, and we need to use those sources.

We, as teachers, have a crucial role in assisting students to learn to question unequal social reality. Multicultural education must be more than the window-dressing that often parades in today's diversity programs. Fostering students' awareness and understanding of social difference and student commitment to cultural transformation is much more important than merely teaching to make people feel good. By giving our students multiple perspectives of the world we live in, we teachers can do our small part in creating a better, more equitable future for all people.

2. Power and Privilege

Juliana Utley and Betsy Showalter

In a scene from the movie *Pretty Woman,* the saleswomen in the exclusive Rodeo Drive dress shop looked down on Vivian Ward because of her street-walker and low-class appearance. In the saleswomen's judgment, Vivian did not have the social capital to be in their shop nor the financial capital to make a purchase. They snubbed Vivian, hoping that she would leave before her presence discouraged the patronage of more desirable customers. Vivian, sensitive to this treatment, was made to feel inadequate and out of place, but rich and powerful Edward Lewis intervened to help her. Edward holds the power due to his gender and class. Has a situation like this ever happened to you? Have you ever felt that you were in a position where, due to your race, class or gender, you were powerless—or powerful?

In *Invisible Privilege: A Memoir about Race, Class, and Gender,* Paula Rothenberg (2000) uses examples from her own life to illustrate the invisible privilege that exists in our society and to "uncover the forces that often render [privilege] invisible to those who benefit from it most" (p. 1). Growing up in a privileged, upper-middle-class Jewish household in New York City, Rothenberg lived through the social movements of the sixties both as a student and a college instructor. In her writing, she is very open about her own naiveté about her social class status and her revelations about inequities that she experienced throughout her career due to her gender. She also claims, provocatively, that racism is a White problem and that Whites must take a special responsibility for anti-racism. As one reads the book, a picture emerges of how power and privilege influenced and shaped her life. Rothenberg reflects thoughtfully on her life and her discovery of self, other, and invisible privilege in the societal contexts of her time.

Rothenberg's book and other readings on multiculturalism (e.g., McIntosh, 1998) reveal that with privilege comes power and that White, upper-class males possess the ultimate cultural capital of power and privilege. "Power is inseparable from the social domain" (Steinberg & Kincheloe, 2001, p. 9), and is present in all human relationships. According to Apple (1990), the hegemony exerted by upper-class, White males enables "social control to be maintained without the necessity of this dominant group having to resort to overt mechanisms of domination" (p. 204).

Rothenberg argues that morality is defined by the behavior of those with power and privilege (the culturally dominant class, race, and gender). Because of this invisible privilege, our country perpetuates a double standard. For example, she points out, an unmarried pregnant woman from the lower socio-economic class or of a non-White ethnic group is labeled "unwed," while an unmarried pregnant woman from the upper socio-economic class, such as a celebrity, is labeled a "single mom." What can an individual within our society do to stop this double standard? Self-reflection is a valuable activity through which one can begin to question the status quo and effect change.

As one reads a book like Rothenberg's or an article like McIntosh's, one cannot help but reflect upon one's own life and how invisible privilege has had an impact. In this paper, we will rethink about those incidents in our pasts when power and privilege played a role in shaping our own life experiences. We will tell our stories one by one and then come together in our conclusion.

Mothers and Daughters

Although Rothenberg (2000) wrote *Invisible Privilege* as a chronicle of the dawning awareness of her early position of privilege due to class status and as an examination of the hidden curriculum dominated by White male thought, she would perhaps be intrigued to find out that a third aspect of her book arrested my interest: Rothenberg's mother and mine attended the same Julia Richmond High School, and according to the information she provides about the ages of her parents, our mothers could have been at Julia Richmond at the same time. Her mother was perhaps a year or two younger than mine. Our mothers were contemporaries and perhaps schoolmates, but their adulthoods were as different as night and day, up to a point.

Although my mother was Jewish, her parents were not Orthodox, but Reformed. My grandfather owned a pharmacy but lost it in the stock market crash, and the family was forced to move in with my grandmother's relatives. Eventually my grandparents divorced and my mother and grandmother moved to an apartment and lived together until my grandmother's death. After high school, my mother worked and attended art school. After my grandmother's death, my mother enlisted in the U. S. Army, drove across the country with two people she met through an ad for traveling companions that she had placed in the newspaper, and shipped out to serve in the Pacific Theater during WWII. She later served in the Korean conflict, where she met my father, a soon-to-be-divorced (and excommunicated) Catholic. They came back to the United States to be married and found (after going through the Yellow Pages) that the only religious representative who would accept the challenge of uniting two such diverse people was the Unitarian minister. Neither her marriage nor the birth of her first and only child kept my mother home. My parents eventually found themselves in Midwest City, Oklahoma, where both were employed in the Civilian Service at Tinker Air Force Base. My mother worked in the male-dominated drafting/engineering section, and although she received many commendations from the U.S. Air Force, her civilian rank (and hence, her salary) was lower than that of her male coworkers who performed the same tasks as she. I was in day-care (it was called nursery school at that time) from the time I was six months old through sixth grade, when I became a latchkey child.

When I was in college, my mother retired from the Civil Service in response to pressure from my already-retired father but much earlier than she would have liked. At this point, the two mothers' lives come full circle. Rothenberg holds up her mother as an example of a woman who accepted the traditional marriage arrangement in exchange for financial and emotional security but ended up having neither and who took opportunities to ameliorate her situation by reading, going to museums and concerts, and spending summers in the "country" but remained bound by commitment. My mother refused to fulfill the traditional role of wife and mother. She did not have a happy marriage; the ameliorating factor was her work. She had financial security, but it was of her own making. She had no time for cultural events; she had no desire to practice her faith in the Baptist Bible Belt. However, she remained bound in her marriage. I wonder how my mother (if she were still alive) would respond to Rothenberg's notion of invisible privilege. Would she also find this layer of invisibility in her own life despite her refusal to fulfill a traditional woman's role?

I had sensed my own "invisible privilege," but could not attach a name to it until Rothenberg named it. I first came face to face with my privileged status when I was with my sons in San Antonio a few summers ago. We were there because my boys were in the local boys' choir, and the group had been invited to perform at the Texas Choral Directors Convention. Since our days began early and I like to run in the morning, I got up before dawn in order to be ready on time for the day's activities. Therefore, I found myself running in downtown San Antonio in the dark (my mother would have been "worried sick" had she known). I was proud of myself for being up so early while other parents were still abed. I saw many people who were also up early and would cheerfully greet them, imagining that we had some connectedness by being out together at what many would term "an ungodly hour." Nevertheless, the men and women whom I so blithely acknowledged were not out running for their "health"; they were hurrying to catch the city bus to go to work for their "life." They would make sure that restaurants, offices, and motels were cleaned, food was prepared, trash was removed, trucks were unloaded, and whatever else that was needed to be done was done so that people like myself could go about our self-important business. I was quite taken aback by this flash of insight, and now I see this "luxury" of compassion for others constantly in my and my friends' attitudes.

A second epiphany about my privileged status came when I read the book *Yo, Little Brother* by Davis and Jackson (1998). While I might have been concerned for my safety while running at that time of day, I had no fear that I would be viewed with suspicion. On the other hand, Davis and Jackson warn young Black men:

> Don't run at night unless being chased.... If the cops see you running at night, you will probably be stopped and questioned.... If you feel the need to run, do it during the daytime, or get yourself a treadmill. Go to a gym. Even if you are late for curfew, don't run home at night if you can help it. You don't want to be mistaken for a criminal. (p. 10)

Thus, even the dark, which often has the effect of diminishing contrast and creating the illusion of making black and white become gray, cannot erase the inequity between those who have the status of privilege and those who don't.

Although our mothers were contemporaries, Rothenberg is actually eleven years older than I am, and given what was happening in the decade between our respective adolescent periods, I am uncertain that her revelations about her secondary and post-secondary educational experiences say anything about my own. I must confess that I was not a questioning teenager or young adult, and my memory of that time fails me. I did choose math as my field of study, with certification in secondary education as an option. I suspect male students dominated my math classes, and I recall only two female mathematics professors. I also suspect that female students dominated my education classes, and I recall nothing about the education professors, which probably speaks more to the nature of the classes at that time than to my faulty memory. I have no idea whether I was evaluated any differently in my math classes than my male peers, but I have wanted to believe that all of us were evaluated equally rigorously. However, reading Rothenberg's account of university education has heightened my awareness of inequities that existed in academia during that period. I am wondering whether, if I could time travel back as an observer, I would see issues, similar to those of Rothenberg's, to which I had been blind.

School Years

Reading Rothenberg's personal experiences caused me to reflect upon my own life experiences. For this paper, I will focus on my school experiences while growing up in a very small, rural town in southern Oklahoma. I lived in a community that consisted of one small mom-and-pop grocery store, a single-pump, full-service gas station (gas and repairs), and several churches. At the time, my graduating class of twenty-one was considered a "big" class. My classmates did not vary much from year to year; essentially the same students started first grade and graduated together in twelfth grade. There were five African American students and the rest of the class would be classified as either White or Native American. All of the African American residents lived as a community in one rural area outside of town. I never thought this arrangement was noteworthy until I was an adult. As a child, I accepted it as just the way things were. Looking back on this arrangement, I now wonder, "Were they not allowed to buy houses or live in town?" I know that even today this is an unwritten, unspoken code in some rural communities.

As I look back upon my own school experiences, I realize that there were numerous incidents where power and privilege were prevalent. Similar to Rothenberg, I can see my own naiveté about my world as a schoolgirl. Reflecting on my years of schooling during the 1960s and 1970s in rural Oklahoma, I see the color line that I did not consciously acknowledge at the time. For example, being from such a small town, I had the same friends each school year. All the parents knew each other, thus making it much easier when we wanted to go to each other's houses to play as kids or to socialize as teenagers. As I read Rothenberg's book, I remembered those times and how the White kids spent time at each other's houses, but I don't ever remember any of the African American kids' spending time at my house or friends' houses. During the school day, they were part of our various groups and never excluded, but this apparent bias outside of school now appalls me. I do recall that around the time of middle school, I asked my mom if Josey, an African American girl, could come over after school to visit, and she agreed. However, when Josey asked her mom, she said I had to come to their house first. I remember that my mom took me to Josey's house one afternoon, but she was still not allowed to visit my home. This was after we had been in school together since second grade. Josey and I were teammates in basketball, and our parents saw each other at games and various school functions, but the issue of race was obviously a problem. Rothenberg also tells a similar story of the immense difficulty of her daughter Andrea's interracial friendship with an African American girl, Jewel. What does it take to overcome such obstacles on both sides? I am glad that my own son has had many African American friends over the years and that he and his friends did spend time in each other's homes. I hope this is a sign of progress.

Another instance that stands out for me pertains to a very sweet African American woman, Bonita, who was an aide in the Headstart program. Bonita began working as an aide when I was in early elementary school; her son was in my class. She was a single mom whose income would put her in a low-income bracket. As the years passed, several Headstart directors quit, and although Bonita would be suggested for the position, she was repeatedly passed over. Did the powerful and privileged, the White, upper social class for this community influence those who ignored Bonita's qualifications to be the director? Did Bonita feel powerless to do anything to help her situation? Did the views of those in power change when in the late 1970s Bonita was made director? Was the change due to societal norms changing or just to the views of those in power?

At a homecoming dance during my senior year, I recall how some of us "white" girls danced with a couple of African American boys at the dance. Tyson, Bonita's son, had been in school with our class since first grade and the other young man was from a nearby town. I remember watching the faces of the adult chaperones when the first White girl danced with an African American boy. I could tell that they were not sure what to do, but they decided not to say anything. Of course, there was gossip among the adults and teachers the next day. While the adults saw the dance as a breach of the invisible color line, the young people saw it as friends having fun. Even now I still hear many comments about mixed-race couples. A friend has commented that she needs to remain in a metropolitan area where there is more tolerance to her mixed marriage, particularly for the sake of her children. Is rural America still intolerant when it comes to racial issues? Do racial minorities in rural America still perceive that they take a backseat to their White counterparts?

Gender issues are not as prevalent in my memory as race issues, but one instance does stand out. When it came to math and science in school, the boys were expected to do better than girls. Since I was always extremely good at math, this inequity in expectations bothered me. One situation in particular occurred in my physics class. There were only four students, two girls and two boys. The instructor took great pleasure in pitting the boys against the girls. The other female and I always complained that our teacher favored the boys. Of course he denied it but seemed to enjoy the gendered rivalry that he instigated. He would make comments like, "Well, these are ideas that guys just know because they are guys." Such comments were upsetting to us and made us work harder. Looking back, I realize that this male teacher was perpetuating the notion that with maleness comes a certain amount of assumed privilege and power.

In addition to race and gender, I now see class and social status as another polarizing factor within schools. In my school, as well as many rural schools today, the school board members tended to be people within the community who were members of the middle or upper class. During my school years, my mother mentioned that she felt some school board members made decisions that were good for their children but not necessarily good for all children. Having taught in several rural schools, I still see this situation happening today. School board members as well as community members in the upper social class use their powered and privileged status to affect decisions that pertain to the running of the school or even a particular classroom.

In my childhood community, class and social status were important when it came to leadership roles, awards, and events such as the crowning of the home-coming queen. Those who were chosen for homecoming queen or those who were elected president of the class were students whose family held a privileged role within our community based on their social status. Their social status may have been determined by their class or by their families' roots within the community. In many rural communities, social status does not always coincide with having money but with the ancestral roots within a community. For example, when a student moved into our community, the student and his/her family were welcomed but not fully accepted within the social structure of the community. Of course the situation changed if the family brought money and power.

These few childhood memories bring up as many questions about the perceived power and privilege within my school and community as they do answers. However, are the answers really important? I believe that in order to truly effect change in our society, members of our society need to be encouraged to read books such as Rothenberg's or articles such as McIntosh's, which reveal the power and invisible privilege within our society.

Concluding Comments

Both Rothenberg and, previously, McIntosh (1998), whom Rothenberg referenced in her book, examined the privilege they experienced due to their Whiteness and, correspondingly, the privilege they had been denied due to their gender. In her article, McIntosh enumerated the daily benefits of White privilege, while Davis and Jackson (1998) enumerated the rules of survival for young African American males. While acknowledging that young Black men are unfairly profiled, in writing their list of survival tactics, they intended to enable African American youth to be victorious "over the anomie, crime, lack of consciousness, and mental slavery that exist in our cities" (p. vii).

The school-years vignettes reveal how the denial of privilege to females and people of color decreases their political and social status, while in many of the mothers-and-daughters vignettes, we see the denial of privilege and the proactive overcoming of oppression as a strengthening agent that ultimately increases one's social and political status. McIntosh (1988) states:

Those who do not depend on conferred dominance have traits and qualities that may never develop in those who do....In some groups, those dominated have actually become strong through *not* having all of these unearned advantages, and this gives them a great deal to teach the others. (p. 101)

We see this in many of our students, particularly those young men who have survived the gang culture in the inner city or those young women who have a child or children and must balance child care, job, and school. These students have much to teach their fellow students who have come from suburbia, stable families, and adequately staffed and equipped schools. Additionally, they serve as reminders to their professors, who may have become too comfortable in their privileged status, that issues of inequity, the struggle against inequality, and the resultant building of character are still very much part of the everyday lives of the underrepresented young and not so young.

Literary works such as Rothenberg's book can serve as tools to help individuals think about and reflect upon power and privilege in their personal lives. Only through this sort of reflective awareness can change begin to happen.

3. Lessons in an Unspoken Language

Sue Rankin

Feminists have argued that language is a masculine construction and, therefore, limited in its ability to define a woman's experience, resulting in a representation that is "subjugated or repressed" (Munro, 1998, p. 34). Undoubtedly, Mary Aswell Doll would agree. Doll's (1995) four-part essay, *Mother Matters* in her book *To the Lighthouse and Back: Writings on Teaching and Living*, articulates the struggle with her mother's disease and death and the intimate healing process. However, it is not words that repair and reclaim the fractured relationship with her mother but rather gestures and experiencing.

In Doll's mind, "sin and daughters and mothers were intertwined" (p. 19). The sin is resentment fueled not just by her mother's lack of interest in Doll's life, work, and successes but by the bottomless emptiness that forms around her mother's ignorance of Doll. Doll is haunted by memories of her mother's omissions:

> Once, when she tucked me into bed she had left the room without turning out the light. Not turning out the light became, in my mind, synonymous with being on another side of her awareness. Dark mother: do you see only my light side? (p. 19)

Doll is not a "doctrine Catholic" (p. 23). She attended Quaker meeting with her mother; her father was an atheist and her step-mother a skeptic. Her Catholicism, a gift to her husband, does not rise from a biblical query but rather has metastasized from the ponderings and yearnings for symbols and ritual within a "daughter of an iconless world" (p. 23). This symbolism led Doll to begin her journey of healing in an act of confession, a litany of words and sentences; but, it is her unspoken words, her tone, that communicate her need to connect with mother. She employs a metaphor of stones to convey the burden of her bitterness, frustrations, and accusations, the sins that tangle her daughter-mother relationship. "Sitting in the parlor of my priest's confession room, I could feel how my mother's nonactions had turned a part of me to stone" (p. 19). In confession, Doll chips at that part and throws out stone after stone "trying to understand a relationship of mutual negativity" (p. 19). Doll nervously expects the obvious but unasked question, "Why don't you confront your mother?" (p. 20). The young priest, however, neither picks up nor carries her burden but instead rakes the stones, planting rather than burying, creating a space for transformation. Doll believes that the priest's unspoken question and unassigned penance are an acknowledgment of her yet unrecognized need to "meet [her] mother on non-worded ground" (p. 20). It is on this non-worded ground that Doll finds absolution and healing.

I began building my Ebenezer when I was ten. My mother and grandmother dropped me off at Girl Scout camp—two weeks of swimming, horseback riding, campfires, and s'mores. At 2:00 each afternoon, our unit hiked to the camp store where we could purchase postcards and camp souvenirs and receive mail from home. The councilors called the names of campers while waving and tossing letters about the circle of anxious girls. By the end of the first week, everyone had received mail except me. Where were my letters? Did Mom even miss me? Finally, the day before camp ended, my name was called. My tent mates were excited for me. I tentatively opened the envelope and pulled out a slip of ruled paper: "I'll pick you up on Sunday. Love, Dad." Where was Mom?

I do not remember how I was told that my mother was in the hospital. She left me at camp, my brothers with relatives, and committed herself to a mental hospital—the first of several confinements. I only remember the abandonment, a wound that festers beneath the skin of daily busyness and explodes like a tornado in the silent spaces of my mind.

Doll's mother suffers from Sezary Syndrome, a disease in which cells of the lymph system become malignant and affect the skin. Dark patches develop on the skin, the skin itches, tumors develop on the skin, and large numbers of tumor cells are found in the blood:

> The disease dried [mother's] skin, causing it to lose its out layer. Dust-like particles of skin could be found everywhere she went and on every thing she touched. The floors of her home were covered with a permanent film, her clothes were dusted, the sheets and bedboards had skindust on them. (p. 24)

During a Christmas visit, mother and daughter talk about dying when they "so seldom talked about her living: her life and [Doll's] life and the way [they] experienced earth" (p. 56). As her mother talks of dying, the "stone of [their] silence" (p. 58) is passed between mother and daughter. "I rejoiced in the feel of the imaginary stone passing from her hand to mine, imagining the scales of my eyes lifting as the scales of her skin drifted" (p. 58). Doll begins to wear her mother's clothes. The seemingly mundane exchange of clothes is an important junction in Doll's progression: "I used to reject her hand-me-down clothes" (p. 84). Doll realizes that to her mother she has been the "unobtainable daughter" (p. 83), creating a separation that bars the close mother-daughter relationship that Doll desperately seeks. She had been perfect, "perfectly married, perfectly content, complete with husband and adorable son" (p. 83), where her mother had failed. Wearing a white cashmere sweater with a bow in front, Doll reflects "what makes it [mother's] is for all its quality and good taste, the thing is riddled with moth holes....It seems that moths were everywhere around my mother (my moth-er), biting little holes into the garments of her self" (p. 59). The stones raked and planted in her non-worded ground are covered by the fabric that once enveloped her mother's skin. This means of wrapping the mother around the daughter is a gesture of connection in which Doll can feel the warmth, texture, and fit of her mother. Similarly, in her otherwise colorless hospital room, Doll's mother wrapped herself in an afghan with "seventy squares of her favorite shades of pink, one square for each year of her life" (p. 85). Doll made this afghan for her mother's seventieth birthday. Mother experienced the warmth, texture, and tension of the yarn that had been pulled, knotted, and caressed by her daughter's fingers. The intimacy allowed two women to not only see their mirrored images, but also to feel what the other had felt: a bond forged through experiencing not through words.

When I was about six, I wanted animal mittens with wiggly eyes. These mittens could not be purchased; someone had to knit them. Grandma knitted and purled until a pair of lions with loopy manes and wiggly eyes warmed my hands. Years later she confessed that she really did not know how to knit; she had learned it just for me. Yarns, fabrics, and laces are my passion. I stroke the cloth, pull and rub the fibers between my fingers, and examine the stitching. The materials I select will be fashioned into garments for my daughters and granddaughters. I can see the girl-child in the dress before the first snip. Each stitch is placed with her image in my inner eye. Often the dresses mark a special occasion—baptisms, birthdays, or wedding—but sometimes they just let me communicate how much I love this child.

Mother's disease progresses and she is hospitalized. Several times each day, daughter travels between mother's home and mother's hospital room, journeys similar to those of the Sumer goddess Inanna, who represents the numerous facets of womanhood and the myriad roles that women play. Like Inanna, Doll is the gift bearer: "I could bring her the gift of her former self in the clothes of her younger years; she could bring me the gift of mother earth: passive, waiting, not done, just there, in the 'matter' of her body" (p. 86). Clothes dress the feminine body and protect against "underworldly female truths" (p. 86). Sleeping in mother's bed, Doll dreams of being draped in her grandmother's gown. The gown is fashioned from two long heavy panels that hang from the shoulders. The fabric does not provide warmth and comfort but rather a cumbersome and, perhaps, embarrassing burden. The imagery provides a different understanding and interpretation of the wearing of others' clothes. Doll sees the ugly, old-fashioned material as the "unwanted gifts from the foremothers" (p. 86), the social prejudices, expectations, and etiquettes that defined and restrained her. In another dream, Doll sees herself as a bride wearing secondhand clothes and shiny brown loafers. Her marriage partner is a princess. Doll's juxtaposition with "a princess Diana figure" (p. 87) presents a conflict between her and the beautiful, virginal, princess image, the male perspective of womanhood. Through the interpretation of her dreams, Doll comes to a different knowledge, a knowledge derived from the subconscious, non-worded in the daylight: The shroud of "patriarchal imagination" (p. 87) presents women as "surfaces without depth." The depth of *mother matters* rebels against the surface and invites daughter's journey. To learn the lesson of Inanna is to leave behind the blanket of the father-world to become immersed in the transformational space of the mother-world.

Throughout Doll's narrative, unspoken gestures guided peace-making between daughter and mother. The priest heard unspoken words and sensed from Doll's tone her need to connect with her mother. He did not respond to her confession with penance but rather with minimal words, "Expect nothing" (p. 20). Wrapped in "psychic textures of relationship" (p. 89), the women grant forgiveness "the new dress of old memory" (p. 59). Then, Doll reveals the "unspoken stuff of dreams and myths and repressions—unspoken, but a language nonetheless" (p. 89).

With her mother's death imminent and with Doll feeling overwhelmed by the caretaking tasks before her, Doll's last visit with her mother begins with resentment and dread and culminates in the physical work that allows mother to communicate her terms of dying. Doll's anxiety is compounded by the perceived competition with her mother's care staff. "I wanted more from her....The seven homecare providers seemed, like the dwarves, better able to anticipate her needs than I, the daughter....Now I had seven daughters to compete against....Even in her dying I felt at the edge of her consciousness" (p. 114). Doll describes her mother's room:

> She was as usual at her TV, watching "Days of Our Lives." Beautiful women and beautiful men were raping each other. The care provider on duty was in a back room, absorbed in a book. Agi was sitting in a broken chair, bad tempered. No one spoke. (p. 115)

The four women are silent and have submitted to the false reality of daytime television drama. "Tuned into a different kind of speaking, as that, say, of a draped arm or a half-averted gaze" (p. 115), Doll sets out to create a living space in this room of dying. This transformation requires physical action and strength. The television is turned off and replaced with music; living room chairs are moved in; rainbows are projected by crystals; the bed sheets are changed; mother is lifted and attended to; the daughter's muscles ache in response to strain. Through physical strain Doll "was learning that her [mother's] joy, pain, sorrow, disgust could become [Doll's] joy, pain, sorrow, disgust" (p.

116). This new experience echoes the wrapping in second-hand clothes that enabled Doll to see and feel as her mother. Doll's resentment became "re-sentiment," not through speaking, but through experiencing care.

During my first readings of Mother Matters *and drafts of this essay, I shrank from including personal reflections of my relationship with my mother. Since that first encounter with Doll's writings, my mother was diagnosed with a tumor that wrapped itself around her optic nerve. She told everyone that she did not know how she could have a mass when she wasn't even Catholic. My mother loves jokes, clean or naughty; she basks in delight when anyone tells her she is funny. My brother flew in from Utah a few days ahead of my drive home from Oklahoma. It's good that he was home; both my mother and I missed him. Catching up with my brother's happenings delayed talk about the impending surgery. My mother had given her power of attorney to my cousin, Liz, and me. Originally, Liz and I and Mother's accountant shared equally in making decisions regarding Mother's care. I understood my cousin's inclusion; Mom considers Liz to be smart. But Mother's accountant? How can a mother even think of replacing a daughter with an accountant? Her rejection formed another cancer within the black hole of my resentment. After a week of sleepless nights, I sat with my mother and told her that I was not comfortable with her decision to include her accountant in what I perceived to be intimate family matters. She shrugged and said, "OK, I'll change it." The discussion was finished. I did not feel triumphant; my mother had not heard my pain.*

My mother expected to wake up dead from the surgery. She did not. Her eyesight is still impaired; a stroke left her weak; she no longer drives and should not live alone. My brother now lives with her. We unequally share her care; he keeps up with the day-to-day tasks, and I pay her bills and send the tax information to her accountant. Doll's struggle for her intimacy with mother is more poignant to me now than the first time when I read her book. I, too, long for the healing of my fractured relationship.

In the introduction of *To the Lighthouse and Back*, Pinar (1995) states "per-haps the greatest praise I can make regarding a colleague's work: that I take notes, that I learn from it. And I have always learned from Mary Aswell Doll" (p. ix). What is it that I should learn from these essays, *Mother Matters*? First, to be limited by the patriarchal image, a fairy-tale, fantasy image, is to be isolated within femininity and to fear that which mother offers:

> Our earliest fantasy images, read to us by our mothers in our beds, warn us of the terror of being daughters of the mother! The mother is hideous in every way: a witch, a hag, a step-mother whose soul purpose is to eat us or hide us away. (Doll, 1995, p. 111)

Women are not bound by or to the flat, substance-less images of the forefathers. Women experience their lives through the traditions and imaginations handed down by their mothers as well. The legacy of mother provides connection to be tried on, a wrapping in womanhood. Likewise education needs to embrace maternal legacy and be open to different perspectives through imagination.

Second, women meet on non-worded ground. The language is one of gestures and actions. A friendship can begin with a shared cup of coffee. It's not the conversation but the giving and receiving of warmth that forms the bond. Since I first began teaching, I have found all kinds of ways to appreciate students' efforts and to share a sense of connectedness and warmth with them. Even though I often feel overwhelmed by the responsibilities of being a teacher, I am overjoyed when a former student returns to share progress or even to ask for help in new studies. I do not believe that it is my perfectly constructed and executed lesson plans that bring the student back but, rather, the small gestures and actions that assure the student that his/her success is important.

Third, women have the knowledge and strength to transform. These transformations are not the result of logical, linear argument but the outcome of physical and emotional efforts and connections. Actions, such as an embrace or the physical work of helping another complete a disagreeable chore, may seem mundane and trivial, but are connecting forces that lead to new images. In education too, the actions of teachers often have more impact than teachers' words. Recently, I had an opportunity to work with soon-to-be-ninth-graders. The first day of the session, one of the young men announced that he would not be "doing high school." I knelt down in front of his desk and folded my arms in front of his work. I told him that he was smart; I told him I thought he was doing amazing work; I told him that he could easily do high school. His ear-to-ear grin told me that he heard me. I do not believe that my words alone would make a difference in his desire to continue his education but my willingness to believe in him just might.

Lastly, women and educators must be attentive to and trusting of the language of the unconscious. I do not presume to be able to ascribe meaning to dreams as Doll does. But, through the process of reading, reflecting, and writing, I have heard a different voice and found comfort in its message. Doll and her writing are the unspoken stuff, the depth in which women find continuity and language and teachers find transformative power.

4. Opening Up
Intellectual and Emotional Gates

Yan Yang

Studies have shown that using autobiography to engage students with lived experiences in multicultural diversity education can be effective (Gallavan, 2006; Hesford, 1999; Pinar, 2004; Wang & Yu, 2006). According to Wang and Yu (2006), "Good autobiographies usually evoke strong responses from readers, whether positive or negative, or both" (p. 32). These responses, when worked through pedagogically, provide an emotional and intellectual site for cultivating multicultural awareness and commitment. In this essay, I narrate my own paths and struggles in engaging autobiography through *currere* writing.

Currere (Pinar & Grumet, 1976), an autobiographical method originally designed for understanding educational experiences, was used (and modified) as a writing assignment for a multicultural education class. Students were asked to make the connection between life histories and diversity issues in education. *Currere* includes four stages. The first stage is regressive writing in which we focused on the past and remembered those life situations when we were positioned as somebody different or we encountered somebody different. The memories could be pleasant or unpleasant. Next, in the progressive stage, we pondered the future to uncover our aspirations through imagining and narrating new life situations. In the third, analytic, stage, we looked at the regressive and progressive writings to see both connections and disjunctions between the past and the future as they inhere in the present. The last stage is about putting things together and re-entering the educational present in a different way. The focus of our writing was on what social differences meant to us through examining the past, envisioning the future, and reconstructing the present.

In the beginning, I was a little skeptical about how this whole writing would develop and how it would turn out. My doubts were further enhanced when, in the regressive stage, I had great difficulty remembering the events of my past. I was born in a happy family in rural China, have been an academically successful student, and am pursuing my doctoral degree in this foreign country: All these were happy memories, but they did not seem to be related to "diversity." I was aware that I had been intentionally avoiding unpleasant memories, but as I struggled, I began to loosen my emotional gate. It was not an easy job. I was quite frustrated when I tried to put some of my feelings and experiences into words. I did not know if I was even on the right track. When the age-old memories of being a poor country girl in China came back, however, I had another pain—the pain of digging out all those miseries and struggles I once had and experiencing them for a second time. In addition, so many things were going through my mind that I did not know where to start and where to stand.

However, this process has not only opened doors inside of me that I may have never really seen before, but it has at the same time opened me up. It has been an invigorating and enlightening experience, bringing me to awareness that I would have never acquired otherwise. The process has been transformative, and I feel like a totally different person now because I have a new understanding of the world and the self, an understanding that I would not have if I had not faced my past and reflected on it with courage and insight.

I was born in a poor rural area in China and grew up there until I was 13 years old. I still remember the days when food was not adequate, so my father was the only person eating regular rice meals as he was the breadwinner in the family. My mother and the rest of the family had to take other types of food as needed. Even as a child, I understood that there were bound to be things that we had to give up due to circumstances, whether material or spiritual. My childhood experiences taught me the lesson of moderation and hard working.

After finishing elementary school, I was admitted to a local key middle school where the majority of the students were from upper-class families who equipped them with a wide range of knowledge outside the textbooks. As a result, my ignorance of a more luxurious daily life as well as my difficulty of socializing with peers made me feel inferior to them. Most of my peers, who were city folks, looked down upon me as a poor country girl who was not up to their level. Thankfully, one of my teachers was kind to me, inviting me over to dinner, together with her family, during some weekends. She might not have known what was going on in my life, but she could see my poor family background through my clothes. Her loving care, along with my drive to succeed, saved me from that horrible situation. The social isolation intensified my eagerness to stand out from my peers academically, an eagerness supported by my teacher's compassion. I spent most of the time studying in the classroom and became a top student. Eventually, this achievement helped me out of the predicament, as my classmates started to treat me with special respect due to my high academic standing. But this luck by no means indicates that those were happy experiences for a teenager.

I am tremendously grateful that my teacher made a difference with her inclusion of me in her family activities so that I did not feel completely excluded from the world around me. She definitely played a big role in reducing my pain, and her kindness contributed to my resilience. Otherwise I would have very likely dropped out of school. Now looking back, I realize how important a teacher can be in helping a child deal with the adversities and setbacks in life. Aside from having a good heart, a teacher can make a difference by being better equipped with knowledge about students from poverty and low social economic status. By showing particular respect toward rural experience or trying to integrate rural knowledge into classroom activities, teachers can at least let students know that life is a lot more than snacks and brands and that knowledge about agriculture is also valuable. Unfortunately, in my school time teachers rarely paid attention to the experience gap among students, let alone dealt with the subsequent discrimination. Worse still, the disrespect many city residents showed to the rural people when I was a teenager has not changed much today but has been further intensified by the widening gap between the rich and the poor in China.

Gender prejudice is another issue. Although aware of it, I did not realize its pervasive impact until I returned to those memories. For instance, at that time, all the students graduating from junior high were advised to go to either a senior high school or a vocational school. More often than not, the advice was based on gender stereotypes rather than a student's academic potential. Many male students in my class were advised to continue with senior high schooling. In contrast, many teachers and my father strongly urged me to go to a vocational school despite my strong academic performance. They told me, "We don't want you to lag behind in senior high school. Though you have a fairly good standing in your grade now, a higher level of school is a lot tougher. The risk is too high." I was not alone: almost all the female students were expected to go to a vocational school. It was believed that the older girls get, the less intelligent they become. Moreover, it was pointless for a girl to receive too much education, as her major task was to be a good housewife. Luckily, my math teacher saved me, insisting that I was an exception and should receive higher education and that my parents would regret it if they did otherwise.

Racial diversity is the toughest issue for me to work on. I cannot help but wonder why in the U.S., a country that claims freedom and equality, race has been such an issue for so long. However, it was an astonishing experience for me to watch *The Color of Fear* (Lee, 1994) and witness David's stubborn refusal to see racial discrimination in front of his eyes. The heated class discussions on race and racism made me reflect on the Chinese situation more critically. In China, race is much less of an issue, but we do have ethnic minorities—making up only a very small percentage of the population. Since I am from the dominant ethnicity of Han, I might have been biased in what I saw and felt when I was in China. What I observed at the time was that the government's policies gave ethnic minorities favorable considerations in their access to public goods.

These policies might be equivalent to affirmative action policies in the United States. As we discussed different reactions to affirmative action in the class, I began to question myself and think more about ethnic issues in China. What are those aspects of ethnic prejudice and discrimination that I might have been blind to as a privileged ethnic Han Chinese? If the U. S. has struggled for racial equality for so long and still has a long way to go, then what is beneath the ethnic harmony, as officially depicted in China, needs to be brought to the foreground. The power of education to transform racial and ethnic relationships towards equality and equity can be released only if inequality and inequity are recognized.

Apart from the issues of poverty, gender, and race/ethnicity, I also remembered those occasions when my classmates were excluded due to their sexual orientations or religious belief, which I do not discuss in detail here. In short, I think that diversity means any possible difference in students brought about by their unique backgrounds and personal experiences. An ideal multicultural education should respect and value differences. With the rapid speed of globalization, more and more students of diverse backgrounds are being brought together. They have different skin colors, hair colors, and perhaps eye colors. They have different beliefs—Buddhism, Christianity, Islam, Taoism, Confucianism, Judaism, or atheism. Some of these students are from affluent families, some are from middle-class families, and some are from poverty-stricken families, even homeless. A successful educational system should try to address all these differences in a comprehensive way. We are born differently but as equals. Students should have equal opportunities to be successful at school, and no student should be excluded due to any difference. Even though difference might cause trouble at times, often difference is the engine that drives human progress.

To sum up, *currere* writing has been a great journey for me and an effective means to open up the intellectual and emotional gates that would have otherwise been kept shut. The regressive stage helped me recall my distant past with its many painful memories. The progressive stage helped me see the hope in multicultural education by envisioning the future. The analytic stage enabled me to analyze the gap between what I desire and what is in reality. And the synthetic stage provided a great platform for putting my dreams, past memories, and possible futures together. This process has enabled me to access the painful past, imagine the promising future, and re-enter the progressing present. Such a powerful experience of engaging in *currere* speaks compellingly for its use to promote multicultural education.

5. Invisible Boundaries, Soul-Awakening Moments

Sylvia Muse

Signs that directed "colored" to another entrance to a restaurant…or bathroom is [*sic*] a vivid memory to me. I saw those signs in my community and everywhere I was willing to travel in my boyhood.…I say willing to travel because blacks in the Deep South knew they were taking certain risks each time they ventured beyond both the visible and invisible borders that had been placed there by those wanting to separate the races.
—William E. Cox, 2004, p. xvii

As a child I grew up in the midst of an "invisibly" segregated community. I use the term "invisibly segregated" because at that time the segregation was more covert than overt. While there were obvious signs of how much race and class separated out African Americans from the so-called mainstream, there were also subtle ways in which Whites expressed their disdain for Blacks. Land (2005) uses the term "microaggression" to define "unconscious and subtle forms of racism…[which]…have a major impact on the lives of African Americans" (p. 119). Such was the case during my childhood, and even today I recognize subtle forms of "microaggression" being played out as I live, breathe, and move throughout various spaces of my life. Usually, they take the form of off-hand comments, racial or gender insensitive attempts at humor, or purposeful slights in public accommodations. Sadly, though, on most occasions I am either expected or asked outright to ignore the incident or get over my "heightened sensitivity" to such blunders. And on each occasion, I find neither option acceptable.

I do realize that as a child I was somewhat shielded from the realities of racial prejudice, but when I reached a certain age, I came face to face with outright racial bigotry from my peers and classmates. Now I understand more clearly how the foundation of my existence was molded by my family, my community, and my schooling. There was a certain sense of security that I felt (and still feel) from having both of my parents in the home and an extended family that supported me, particularly in my efforts to pursue education. We were by no means wealthy, and there were times when my parents sacrificed their own needs to provide me with an educational advantage. Ultimately they provided a life that transcended what society dictated we were entitled to based on race and class. Much of this I did not realize until I became an adult and, in essence, married myself to becoming a *well-educated* Black woman. My mother, for example, filled our home with books, most of them second-hand and many with tattered covers and worn pages. But each book was treated as a treasure, and I came to love learning for the sake of learning itself. She also filled her children with the possibility that all six of us could go on to college and pursue our dreams without limits. Society said we were "too black and too poor." My mother said, "I believe in you beyond what any words can express and your heart can imagine." And so I stepped out into my possibility, strengthened by my mother's belief that the world was mine to embrace. Today, I continue on that journey, empowered by the voices of where I've been *en route* to where I am going.

Coming to an Understanding

It is as if the past were a transparent veil over the present, fine enough to be over-looked, but consequential enough to skew our perception not only of the present but also of the future and the past.

—William Pinar, 1975, p. 15

Gradually, I am coming to a deeper realization of who I am, both inwardly and outwardly. The boundaries placed about my existence are not only formed by race and class issues, but by gender issues as well. As a little girl, I was trained to only speak when spoken to. (This training came mainly from God-fearing aunts and from teachers and other matriarchal figures in the community.) As a little *Black* girl, I was on the cusp of understanding what role race played in my everyday experiences. Thus, I was to maintain a balance between what was proper as a *female* and what was expected as a member of the Black community receiving my education against the backdrop of the Civil Rights Movement. As I grew older, maintaining this balance became more of a challenge. My personal experiences with negative racial attitudes often intersected with the role I was expected to play as a submissive and silent female. I recall an incident from my childhood that demonstrated the isolation I sometimes felt. The incident relates to my first experience with school integration:

The next year, 4th grade, brought early morning bus rides to the new school. It felt cold and lonely. Such a long ride everyday to a strange place. There were no "welcome" signs or warm hugs. Just cold, drab loneliness. Teachers and students did not look like me anymore. Most of them went out of their way to point this out. I sat next to a White girl with flaming red hair and a spotted, freckled face. She whispered hateful things to me, mostly when the teacher was not attending to the class. But sometimes her tactics were open and obvious. I did not feel I had an ally in anyone, including the teacher. No one was there to come to my rescue. Each time the red-haired girl accidentally brushed up against my dark skin she would panic as if some leprous disease had overtaken her body. Her actions made me feel small, dirty, and unwelcome. I was alone in an unfriendly environment. I was silenced and felt I could complain to no one. (Excerpt from *Currere* writings, Regressive Stage)

It was not "proper" to challenge traditional practice, even if such practice served to push one to the margins of invisibility. In my schooling (especially in predominately White school systems), I was often objectified by teachers and classmates as less than others. My social role was to be graceful to the point of non-resistance. My soul, however, cried out to be emancipated from the place of isolation and loneliness. That cry has not completely subsided, as on occasion it erupts from the depths of fresh experiences which challenge my sensibilities relating to who I am as an *empowered* Black woman. As I did in my childhood, I draw on the words of African American poets and scholars to encourage myself. In particular, I was drawn to Angelou's (1994) poem, "Still I Rise." Even today those words inspire me because they speak of an enduring capacity to rise valiantly and triumphantly above the depths of oppression.

My first exposure to this poem was at the age of nine or ten when I came across a book of poetry. I was unaware at the time that from the musty back room of one of my elementary classrooms I had retrieved a priceless gem. A very small collection of books in our classroom made some reference to African Americans, but these books were never integrated into our curriculum and our everyday learning. They were tossed aside as irrelevant and unimportant, fit only to collect dust in a dark and forgotten space. Apple (1999) talks about how textbooks are often the result of "hegemonic and counterhegemonic relations and social movements involving multiple power relations, including, but not limited to race, class, gender/sexuality, and religion" (p. 170). Given their potentially powerful impact, how we make certain books visible or invisible in the classroom can directly affect the messages a child receives about his/her own identity. Even in my own community school, as in many schools today, awareness of diversity and difference can easily be diminished to nothingness. The message for me in that moment was a confused signal about what role race actually played (or did not play) in the classroom environment.

I believe that the words of Dr. Angelou's poem still speak to women of color today. It is unfortunate that sometimes we, as women of color, must extract our identities from the wreckage of education's failed attempts to address its own shortcomings. The lessons that I have learned from exploring my own path continually resonate in my heart and consume my soul as I experience the metamorphosis of becoming an *awakened* Black woman. They are lessons which must be conveyed to women who find themselves on similar paths in pursuit of the fullness of who they are in creation. Perhaps they are lessons which can be fully cultivated in the classroom setting, but they are also evocative lessons which should have a place within the course of everyday living. I have found the expression of one such lesson embodied in my own writings, "Soul Awakening: In Two Parts":

Part One:
nappy head, never go straight
eyes dark, can never be blue
skin like leather, brown from the sun
that beats down on your parched soul.

tongue slow, doesn't sound like ours
"be's" and "ain'ts" meaningless, strange
talk right and you'll be right
'cause WHITE is RIGHT in our world

eyes dark, but I see inside
your ancestors, from long ago
did they make you, into this being, this creature
that stands before me, face so strong

i am drenched with the passion to re-name you
i am consumed by the lust that wants to claim you
as a thing to be possessed.
i want to put my mark on the soles of your feet
and brand you with the searing iron of oppression.
as I breathe my hot breath into your ear
and clench my sweaty hand across your mouth
i want you never to be able to speak again...

Part Two:
I hear you but the Ocean drowns out the sound of your voice
The same Ocean that carried my Ancestors,
Sweeps now over my Awakened Soul.
You see, I cried out for freedom and Sister Earth
bowed Her ear and bared Her breasts
It was She who nurtured me back to health and strength

In my Womanhood the tangled mass branded a "Nappy Head"
are the extensions of life that coil around my Humanity
and envelope my Dignity. As I smooth the Oil of Healing

over my bleeding, cracked, brown skin
the fragrance of Peace rises to my nostrils

Springing forth from my Womb is the seed of Possibility.
Even you could not abort this Divine appointment.
I reach down and gently kiss the forehead
of my Awakening and look into the eyes of my Reality.

I speak into that Soul and I say,
"Walk boldly into the dawn of your existence.
May You and your Sisters dance with unfettered feet
Synchronized by the rhythm of all your
Beautiful Tomorrow
And I breathe it in slowly, deeply.

I penned the poem as a representation of an interchange between the "oppressor" and the "oppressed." It attests to the hegemonic nature of power and control that dehumanizes and devalues the "other" in an attempt to weaken and eventually silence the voice of the "other." It especially speaks to the issue of gender, and in particular, White male dominance over the Black female body (e.g. during the time of slavery). There is a moment when even the "oppressor" realizes the presence of an unknown source of strength that resonates in the countenance of his "victim." The "oppressed" knows that victimization is not her ultimate end. Her soul is awakened by the strength of her ancestors, and she is moved by this strength to deny the voice that desires to crush her spirit. It is in these moments that the female body must be "reclaimed…as a site of power and possibility" (hooks, 1994, p. 73). Such moments can be the impetus for a radical breaking away from oppressive traditions. hooks notes such a transformation within contemporary feminist beliefs:

> We believed that women would never be free, if we did not have the right to recover our bodies from sexual slavery, from the prison of patriarchy. We were not taking back the night; we were claiming it, claiming the dark in resistance to the bourgeois sexist world of repression, order, boredom and fixed social roles. In the dark, we were finding new ways to see ourselves as women. We were charting a journey from slavery to freedom. (p. 74)

Visions of the Soul

This essay is a result of engaging the *currere* writing project which has helped me come to realize a sense of purpose in the movement of my life. As I infuse my writing and my teaching with purpose, my focus tends to become more vivid and intense. I also understand more clearly that what I do is much bigger than myself. Throughout the process of *currere*, my writings have led me on a journey. Part of this journey calls me out into broader terrain where I must sometimes challenge myself to take risks. I also must envision my future as the promise of possibility begins to emerge. One particular excerpt from my *currere* writings captured a glimpse of that vision:

> *My words are a gift and I share that gift with the world....They must be shared because that is a part of my journey. When I share my words then I am fulfilled. I have brought myself to a deeper place of knowing who I am because I have allowed others to know me....My works speak to women who have thought themselves oppressed and without hope. My work leads them out of the hopelessness and embraces them. Then they begin to realize their greatest potential and move toward their God-given purpose....I make change and I work to empower those who have thought themselves powerless. I work to give voice to those who have been silenced. I find more of my own voice. It is a voice of possibility, of strength, a voice that brings together the disjointed and disconnected places.* (Excerpt from *Currere* writings, Progressive stage)

So the vision of my future also draws me to infuse hope into the situations I encounter. Particularly I feel that my call as an educator is to challenge the status quo and push against boundaries of stagnation. A *re*-visioning, of sorts, calls complacency out of its deep sleep and awakens the soul to life.

Close to completing this essay, I was drawn to the words of Dwayne Huebner (1975) with an intensely thought-provoking challenge to his "fellow educators." I also challenge my own fellow educators with Huebner's words:

> Oh yes, we are for the urban black, if he is not angry and will speak in moderate tones, accept our middle-class behaviors, and affirm our future, thus perhaps giving up his. Oh yes, we are for the American Indian if he will give up his past and accept our future and our last forty-five years of public policy. Oh yes, we are for the homosexual if he will stay in the closet and not let his peculiarities stain our image of the future. Oh yes, we are for women, if they will accept their female role in our male future. Oh yes, we are for the Asian Marxist or Maoist if they will recognize that the way to the future is by maintaining present power balances. We are for those individuals who will protect and maintain our image of the future, but what of their imagined futures? If their tomorrow requires that we give up some of our privileges, will we still be for those individuals? (p. 275)

A Deeper Gaze

People often question our sanity when we engage in discussion with ourselves. I believe that even discussion with oneself can be fruitful in introspection. As human beings, we are prone to finding moments that give us reason to gaze more intimately at what moves us, shakes us, and inspires us. As educators, this process is especially important. Every day I realize the potential impact I could have upon those who are drawn into my circle of influence. My desire is for that influence to be positive and lasting. In whatever form that influence may come, I realize that where I have come from remains a part of where I am now and where I am traveling to. I am also by no means a static being, but dynamic, complex, and ever changing. This project of *currere* has brought me to a point of essentially meeting myself face to face; this meeting at times has been difficult. But difficulties aside, I know that it was also a necessary task to examine what has somewhat haunted me. I was haunted by feelings of being pushed aside by those whom I believed considered me less than others. In some ways I carried those feelings into adulthood. The intent has been to bring them into awareness, to enable awakening moments, and to make peace out of the place of alienation that resided in a corner of my life. I believe, though, that all things are meaningful because I have brought light to the possibility of who I am. There is the possibility of myself as an educator, as a writer, as a researcher, as a leader, and as a woman who embraces the challenge of moving into a new realm of *all* that I am. I feel that this is the jumping off point where I can look out over the vastness of what next awaits me. With every new revelation of who I am, jumping seems less frightening.

6. My Son Is a Gay: A Mother's Story

Miriam Ward

July 4th…Independence Day! Our family was preparing hamburgers and brats with all the trimmings for an outdoor barbeque with special friends. The sun shone brightly in the clear morning sky. The freshly cut lawn provided not only a plush green carpet for our gathering but also filled the yard with a clean, natural aroma. The warm air offered buoyancy which lifted our spirits.

Brian, our oldest son and a pilot living in a large city in the neighboring state, had some off-duty time and was visiting for the weekend. July 5th was Brian's 23rd birthday and since special friends were to attend our barbeque, we planned to combine our July 4th observance with Brian's birthday celebration. Brian's younger brother, Justin (soon to be a high school senior) was using the summer to recover from major back surgery and was recovering remarkably well. All in all, our family had a variety of reasons to be happy and festive.

Midmorning on that July 4th day, Brian walked spryly down the stairs and into the living room. I was preparing food when he sat on our burnt orange love seat that was in ear shot of the kitchen. I set my cooking aside and walked through the dining area to sit beside Brian. For a couple months, Brian had told me that he wanted to visit privately with his father and me about *something*. His father and I had inquired about the subject of that *something*, but to no avail. Brian was insistent about not telling us over the phone and was equally persistent about being with us when he spoke about the *something*.

I quietly asked Brian what was on his mind. Brian started to shake; he took a deep breath, and blurted out, "***I'm gay.***" Brian's chest was heaving as though he was drawing in his last breath of freedom. I panicked. I was shocked; nevertheless, I instinctively leaned over, hugged him and said, "I love you." After those three words, I was speechless for a time. Brian's father was standing nearby and, for a few seconds, seemed to quietly process what he had just heard. He thanked Brian for telling us about being gay and remarked that he believed that knowledge of Brian's sexual orientation was "just one more piece of information" we have about who Brian is and that *it* [being gay] was "not a big deal." Since I did not know how to respond further, I was relieved that Brian's father affirmed Brian's identity.

Quietness filled the room. I did not know where to proceed with the conversation. Fear and millions of questions flooded my mind, but I was too dazed to move the questions out of my mind and into the vernacular. Growing up in a rural Bible Belt community in the Bread Basket of America impacted my perceptions of gay individuals. I knew nothing about homosexuality until I was in high school, and information I learned at that time was biased. Until I left home at age 18, I knew of only two homosexuals, both men and both, as I recall, very talented. It was after I moved into a dormitory at college when the word *lesbian* entered my vocabulary. Two females living on the same hall of the dorm as me were identified as *lesbian*. I was extremely cautious about associating with them, and thought homosexuals were mentally sick and needed professional help. Imagine my shock at Brian's "coming out"!

At the same time, I suddenly became aware of my sensitivities, especially my compassion for the marginalized people in our society. I abruptly felt connected with those who had been and who currently are merely on the borders of "living in full communion" with their neighbors in a country where "life, liberty, and the pursuit of happiness" are implied as accessible to all inhabitants. I realized now what it must feel like to be left out, ostracized, and unseen because of an identity one does not choose, but an identity that defines an individual. It was obvious to me that although the individuals outside the orthodox borders of society chose to be neither invisible nor inaudible, the established society attempts to silence and conceal those who do not transmit conventional ideologies.

Genuine acceptance of Brian's homosexuality was going to require time for me. On the July 4th day that Brian "came out," I tried to act as "normal" as possible, not ready to disclose further what I had just learned. Before our friends arrived, I tried to relax with a LONG warm shower. The shower temporarily isolated me from family members, and I could reflect about the impact of Brian's gayness on his and on our lives. The shower was also a place where my tears could be washed away, tears that seemed to be released from every cell in my body. I was probably trying to use the shower to wash away the reality and guilt I had to face. The Independence Day celebration now seemed liked an oxymoron. Where was freedom? Brian had lost the freedom to be honest about part of his identity. Freedoms Brian lost were entwined with insecurity and danger. I had lost the freedom to believe my son would be physically and emotionally safe as he went about daily activities.

In the evening after our special friends had gone home, Brian and I talked until the wee hours of the following morning. I was particularly worried about his safety. Homosexuals, especially gay men, have been targets of hate crimes that range from verbal abuse and harassment to physical injury and death. Gay men have been kicked, beaten, and sometimes violently killed. It seemed that a gay man must be extremely aware of physical surroundings and be aptly perceptive about whom to trust. Being alert at all times is crucial for safety and survival. Youth, suspected of being gay or having come out as gay, also suffer from cruel actions of peers. Peers tease, mimic, push, shove, fight with, and bully gay youth.

Fortunately, Brian came home prepared with literature for me to read. Some of the literature explained homosexuality, some were stories from families with a gay son or daughter, and some was information from the American Psychological Association. That was the beginning for me to learn what being the mother of a gay son entails and to learn how to deal with the myriad issues surrounding homosexuality.

While searching for answers, I wondered if I was on a solo expedition in my community or if there were other explorers like me who were also in the midst of self reflection and self doubt, explorers searching for truths and support, companionship and understanding, confidence and courage. Later in the summer after Brian had "come out" to me, a most unusual event happened that helped me realize that I *was not* alone. A friend I cherished wanted to talk about *something* and asked if we could go to lunch. We met at a cozy little cafe in the center of town and sat in one of the semi-private booths. My friend initiated conversation about her family and promptly disclosed that her youngest daughter had said: "Mom, I think I am lesbian." What a relief...someone I highly respected and felt comfortable with was dealing with the same basic question as I: How do I, as a parent, support my gay adult child?

I knew that I had to learn *from* homosexuals and not just *about* homosexuals. I began observing other people, especially younger people, and yearning to know other individuals who were gay. I listened carefully to remarks, casual and formal, that other people made about homosexuality. I watched and read news items that addressed issues surrounding homosexuality. I also tried to determine how others in my closer circles of acquaintances perceived homosexuality. I was, in my own way, analyzing how the community, the state, and society dealt with homosexuality.

It saddened me to conclude that Oklahoma is not a gay-friendly place. Attitudes toward gays are not usually welcoming, and discrimination against gays is sometimes subtle, passive, and covert. I conducted a study in 2003 (Ward, 2005), looking at the perceptions incoming college freshmen at Oklahoma State University have of gays and lesbians and at the language the students use to describe gays and lesbians. Only 32 percent of students reported positive perceptions of gays and 25 percent reported positive perceptions of lesbians. When expressing severe, judgmental, and negative impressions of gays and lesbians, students used words such as *weird, confused, gross, nasty, wrong, sinful,* and *immoral.*

Because of what I heard and read, I felt insecure revealing my identity as the mother of a gay son. When negative comments about homosexuality were made, I wanted to respond but I was too reticent. I feared not only the person's reaction, but also the possibility that my revelation would reach boundaries I was not ready to explore. I felt guilty for not speaking out, but I felt unprepared to defend myself and I believed that if I spoke insecurely, I would "lose the battle" or pass on incomplete or inaccurate information. I put a lot of pressure on myself to be knowledgeable and confident.

I also realized it was important that my positive and negative emotions about a homosexual are based on the "whole" person and not exclusively on the "gay" feature of the person. Individuals should not be liked or reprimanded merely because of their sexual orientation. I do not believe homosexuals want "special" rights, but prefer equitable, fair, and just rights. Being seen as a human being is much more important than being seen as a homosexual.

I further questioned why "sex" was such a crucial topic when thinking about homosexuality, but not so important when referring to heterosexuals. What about the need for a confidant, a companion, in good times and in bad? Isn't that relationship as important as is sex for both hetero- and homosexuals? Does the heterosexual feel as guarded as the homosexual does from serving in the armed service, displaying "couple" photos at work, talking about the week-end, commenting about vacation plans, going to church with a spouse, applying for housing, visiting a spouse in the hospital, adopting a child, working with children?

Eventually, I realized that I was *not* on the *outside* looking *at* a group (homo-sexuals) that I had mostly ignored and merely tolerated (and a group that I had previously considered "the other"). I was actually a branch of the group's identity as well as a link to those outside the group. It was time to look more intensely *within myself*. I had reached the point where I needed to identify and confront my own beliefs, beliefs that I had absorbed over years of living in a society that does not accept homosexuals. I knew that before I could relate to others, I had to know myself. I needed interior knowledge, belief, and courage before I could approach the exterior. I felt that after wrestling with society's perceptions of homosexuality, I should return to the question of my own identity, the mother of a son who is gay. Although, this transition would be a process with no time limits and probably no finish line, I wanted to reach the point where I could get on with my life without the constant need to justify the reality and morality of homosexuality.

With all my questions, only a few of my concerns could be answered solely on an intellectual plain. It was the emotional aspects of dealing with homosexu-ality that were most perplexing and difficult for me. My head and my heart did not always connect, especially since elements of society said one thing and my heart kept reminding me of affective needs of humanity. Channeling my energy into action helped me connect intellect and emotion. I worked with an international friend to develop a handbook for the local junior high school. The topics in the handbook ranged from statistical information and journal articles about homosexuality to how organizations and hotlines provide support for gay individuals and their families. Not only did this project open my eyes to various possibilities for assisting homosexuals, but it also was therapeutic. I was channeling my search for identity into efforts to assist others. Also beneficial to me was training I received at work so that my office could be designated a Safe Zone for students or others who needed someone to visit with about their own or another's sexual orientation. Being trained taught me how to listen and respond compassionately.

For nearly two years I internalized the reality of Brian's homosexuality and read almost every article I found about gay individuals, gay couples, parents of gays, and additional material Brian sent. I read fiction and non-fiction. I read books by and about gay individuals. FINALLY, I decided that I was ready to go beyond printed information and get in touch with the local PFLAG (Parents, Family, & Friends of Lesbians and Gays). When I dialed the contact number, I was surprised to learn that the voice on the other end of the line was that of a lady who lived only four blocks from our house. She willingly shared her own story and was most accepting and supportive of my concerns. She invited me to attend the next PFLAG meeting and emphasized the confidentiality that is honored by those attending meetings. She also suggested that I arrive early and meet with the *New Comers* group that precedes the regular meeting.

I cannot describe the apprehension I felt walking from the parking lot to the church for that first meeting. When I found the *New Comers* room, I walked in quietly and found a seat near the front. The facilitators were hospitable and it was easier to share with the group than I had imagined. The group was small and diverse, old and young, male and female, etc. Most unexpected was a college student who figured out who I was because of the story I told about Brian. I had not met this young man previously, but he was a friend of Brian's, and Brian had told the friend the same story I shared. Maybe it was from such connections with strangers that I gained hope and motivation to keep searching for more answers to my identity.

Events, people, and projects continued to support my growth. Meeting gay individuals and gay couples improved my understanding of homosexuality. Brian has helped immensely. He has introduced me to some of the most talented, most accepting individuals I know, both male and female, from all walks of life. Race, age, and economic status of those individuals are diverse. Many have sacrificed much for the welfare of others and have shared some of the most perplexing and saddest stories I have heard.

I believe having a gay son has helped me become a better person, albeit one who is still learning. I am proud of the person my son is and for his compassion for those less fortunate than he. He has exhibited much strength, faith, hope, and perseverance as he has discerned his own identity. Brian has the support of my husband and me, his brother, and of those family members who know he is gay. I believe God loves Brian and my faith in God sustains me as I am challenged by the obstacles that Brian and my family encounter.

My desire as a mother of a gay son is to become a spokesperson for homosexuals, so they can use their talents and abilities to enhance their lives and the lives of others. Homosexuals should not have to deplete their generous capabilities, skills, and energy struggling for rights that should be theirs without reservation. I want the "others" in society to recognize the positive contributions gays have to offer, to see gays as just people (no better, no worse than anyone else). All citizens should be aware that freedom and independence may only be a "gene" away, that there is no guarantee that heterosexual parents will bear heterosexual children, and that one of the most accurate ways of understanding others is to walk with them down the path to their heart, soul, and being.

I feel my story has no term limits. I will continue to change, question, and grow as my son changes and as society changes. I must accept myself for mistakes I have made in the past or may make in the future. I expect no less from myself than I expect from others. I will continue to work on my forgiveness of those who do not want to understand the gay individual's plight or those who harm (verbally, emotionally, spiritually, or physically) the gay individual. I will continually ask myself if there are groups in society that I, knowingly or unknowingly, discriminate against. Being a mother of a gay son does not free me from working for justice for other oppressed people. Being the mother of a gay son energizes me.

Pedagogical Reflection I:
Teaching Multicultural
Education through Autobiographies

Hongyu Wang

As I mention in the Introduction, teacher educators have been concerned with students' resistance to learning difficult knowledge about race, gender, class, and sexuality in teacher education for more than a decade. Since autobiography has great potential to depict the complex, lived reality of social differences and to move students out of their comfort zones, it offers a promise to address this resistance in a transformative way. However, my teaching experience reveals that such a transformative possibility cannot be fulfilled without careful pedagogical crafting. When autobiography is not read or written critically, it can reinforce the assimilating tendency and emotional stability against the need for social change. This reflection focuses on the pedagogical efforts to guide students through resistance by reading and writing autobiographies.

The term "unlearning" as a way of tearing away from the old, implies a sense of temporal and spatial pause in order to open up new awareness and new landscapes. This pause can loosen the "attachment to ignorance" (Pitt, 2003) and enable moments of awakening and opening to alternative paths. To deal with resistance, straightforward instruction and the imposition of knowledge from the external expectation usually reinforce rather than unlock the blocked site. Reading and writing autobiography may offer detours for students to travel back and forth between the self and the other. Good autobiography captures the complexity of a person's life in its narrations of experience through both personal and cultural history, full of multiplicity and ambiguity, which unsettles the fixation of identity and in turn encourages departure and movement. It can provide both intellectual and emotional experiences that are necessary for students to turn around and see things differently. Thus I have intentionally chosen literature that is related to students' lives one way or another in order to facilitate students' critical understanding.

However, the use of autobiography in teacher education is not a straightforward process. Being touched by the text does not guarantee being able to move towards cultural and personal critique. The complicated inner working of emotion and thought evoked by reading and writing autobiography may dissolve difficulties and bring revelations in a surprising way, but it also can produce further blocks, reinforcing a culturally sanctioned sense of self-identity and eluding the need for transformative restructuring of subjectivity. This process can be demonstrated well by the pedagogical effects of using two autobiographies.

I Know Why the Caged Bird Sings, written by Maya Angelou (1997/1969), is a highly acclaimed autobiography which portrays the childhood of a Black girl in a small, rural community in the segregated South and her journey into young womanhood when she became a mother in San Francisco. *Invisible Privilege: A Memoir about Race, Class, and Gender*, written by Paula Rothenberg (2000), reflects on a Jewish, upper-middle-class woman's journey—through understanding how privilege operates beneath the surface of our everyday lives—of becoming an anti-racist and anti-sexist educator. I asked students to read Angelou's book first and then Rothenberg's book. The intention was for the students to engage the"other's" life first before looking back on the life of the racial "self" since understanding others' lives is essential for re-thinking about one's own.

Many students celebrated Angelou's book: Angelou's vivid description, great sense of humor, and especially her depiction of the effects of racism through a little girl's eyes made a great impression on students. To my surprise, however, Rothenberg's book initially provoked strong resistance from students despite my assumption that they shared similar racial backgrounds to hers. Now I realize that Rothenberg's book confronts students directly with an uncomfortable truth that they seldom if ever think about. It can be a frustrating reading for students in multiple senses. First, many students in the classes cannot identify with the author and consequently cannot identify with her racial self-reflection. Having grown up in rural Oklahoma, they can hardly share her privileged upbringing. In other words, her wealth discredits her perspective on race. Second, Rothenberg's insistence that racism is prejudice plus power and therefore racism is a White problem in that Whites "have a special responsibility for undoing the damage" (p. 2) is utterly offensive to many students. It takes away a comfortable distance in which they can claim innocence: it is not *my* problem because *I* am not a racist. It also takes away the defensive comfort of claiming reverse racism to complain about minorities' biases. Third, Rothenberg's radical lens on race and her wealth discredits her perspective on gender. Even though her experience as a woman generates a great degree of sympathy from many female students, many refuse to empathize with her, as they see her demands for gender equity as unreasonable. With all these multiple registers of difficulty, no wonder students had a hard time with the book.

Reading a book by Angelou, who hardly had any privilege in a racist society but who won her battle in a pre–civil rights movement era without much complaint, followed by Rothenberg, who enjoyed the privilege of race and class, living through the civil rights and women's movement, but "whining"—as my students phrase it—about her underprivileged role as a woman, produces a dramatic disjuncture. Celebrating a minority person's success, especially at a distance of time and place, evokes students' empathetic response, which opens up their horizons. The devastating effects of racism are tangible in Angelou's book, and students are brought to experience that horror through Angelou's moving narrations. However, such a celebration, when not penetrating into one's own sense of the self, stays at the harbor and does not permeate one's inner world to shatter the old shell of the self. Truly opening to the other also means giving up part of one's own comfort for the purpose of alleviating others' suffering. It is on this site of one's own role in others' lives that Rothenberg calls for our attention. This call is difficult to hear at the beginning but gradually sinks in to influence students' inner landscape. As Mortensen's and Utley and Showalter's essays (and Julie Macomb's essay in Part III) show, privilege in its invisible forms is uncovered as they make efforts to think, see, and hear.

To cultivate students' receptiveness to "the surprise of the other" (Edgerton, 1996) and encourage their critical readings of the texts in an emotionally sustainable way, I try different strategies to open students to multiple perspectives. One of the activities I do in class is to perform the same event through different people's standpoints. I give students stories taken from the texts and ask them to take on each party's eyes and articulate what the person in the story is thinking and feeling in that particular event. Such an activity encourages the suspension of judgment so that students not only feel the outrage from the underprivileged positions but also think about the logic of racism in order to unravel and dismantle such logic. This effort further encourages students, when they make a connection between the multiplicity of perspectives and what happens in their own lives, to understand the pervasive structure of racism throughout our daily activities rather than simply equating it with overt racist languages and behaviors. Such kinds of activities can make the class come alive, full of imagination and performance.

Another activity I do in class is to put students in pairs to pick out a quotation from the text that reminds them of their own experience and share that story with the discussion partner. Particularly, I ask: "What emotions are provoked by the quote?" "What is your own story?" and "What do you think about the author's viewpoint after relating your own story?" After discussion among peers, I ask students to share their partner's story, emotion, and thought in class rather than their own. The connection between one's own life and the text is explicitly elicited but through the privileged site of emotions to suspend rational judgment. Moreover, in this activity, it is the understanding of others' emotions that needs to be shared rather than one's own. In this way, multiple layers of reality, including emotional reality, have opportunities to emerge. This strategy sometimes worked well with Rothenberg's book. The trouble with Rothenberg became more educative as the class progressed, and even though students could not identify with her, they learned from her book, especially from the notion of invisible privilege.

This strategy also helped some students to work through their initial resistance to reading Mary Aswell Doll's (1995) book, *To the Lighthouse and Back: Writings on Teaching and Living*. The book is a personal account of her life as daughter, wife, sister, mother, and teacher, clearly demonstrating the relationship between one's life and one's teaching. The split between the private and the public is still a deep-seated belief, so encountering Doll's intensely personal narratives was hardly comfortable for students. Dealing with such responses in an educative way often requires walking a delicate line. On the one hand, I encouraged students to make links with the text; on the other hand, I was cautious in combining pair, small group, and whole class discussions so that students could educate themselves through engagement with the book without feeling pressured to expose their own innermost thoughts and emotions. A combination of openness and boundary is necessary in this case. When students had finished reading the book, many of them appreciated the opportunities to engage the author's inner world in order to further understand their own inner worlds. This autobiography is unique among the collection of books, as it is not about a culturally celebratory figure or a historical trauma, but it is precisely the theme of an educator's everyday life that is particularly informative to students' daily teacher identity work. Rankin's poetic elaboration on the "non-word ground" flows well with the book's undercurrent for nurturing educational insights.

Reading autobiography is often accompanied by writing autobiography. In writing their responses to books, many students write in an autobiographical way even when writing autobiography is not required. Ward's moving story is an exemplar of how her writing is a direct result of making efforts to live a fuller life. In recent years I began to use a systematic method of autobiographical writing, *currere*, to encourage students' reflections on the meanings of diversity experiences. *Currere* (Pinar & Grumet, 1976; Pinar, 1994) is designed for pre-service or in-service teachers to reflect on their educational experiences, following the sequence of regressive, progressive, analytic, and synthetic steps. I shifted the focus of *currere* to multicultural and diversity issues, and asked students to follow its four steps during the semester, roughly devoting one month to each step and writing at least an hour each week. From Yang's and Muse's essays, we can see the impact of this writing project. The inner working of temporality, the interaction between personal reflections and textual readings, and the dialogues between the instructor and students all contribute to the shift of students' perspectives in this semester-long writing project (Wang, in press). During the process, both a dramatic release from the past and a gradual process of awareness occur. Transformative change is enabled by memory and vision work in autobiographical writings. Some of the challenges that emerged from working with students to engage in the *currere* project are similar to the challenges I have faced in encouraging students' critical readings of autobiographical books. The key issue is to enable movement out of the taken-for-granted world and to let the past and the future meet in the movement to transform the present.

It has become clear to me that reading and writing autobiographies can create multicultural educational experiences in the classroom, but the transformation of students' subjectivity does not happen linearly. My own pedagogical desire to make students meet texts often fails, but even in students' refusal to meet the texts, they still learn when the teacher encourages them to follow their own paths. Perhaps precisely in this non-meeting lies the necessity of learning difficult truths through gaps and cracks, rather than in the smooth transition of multicultural knowledge. Perhaps what is more important is not whether the texts match students' experiences as I initially assumed, because there are always gaps between the teacher educator's pedagogical intentions and the students' expectation of what they want to learn. Rather, it is whether we engage the variety of texts in such a way that students are encouraged to reach new awareness, new insights, and new interconnectedness. In this sense, resistance becomes an invitation for dialogical encounter, and the pedagogical gaps allow the light to come in and sustain an ongoing process of unlearning and learning, both for students and for teacher educators. Such pedagogical efforts demonstrate the power of multicultural teaching and learning in a third space where difference is a productive site for intercultural dynamics.

Finally, understanding the institutional, structural, and social formation of inequality and inequity presents a challenge to reading and writing autobiography in the classroom. Political and cultural critiques, while they can be embedded in the discussions of stories and life histories, also need theoretical analysis tools. Therefore, teaching through autobiography must be coupled with teaching multicultural theory so that both the overlapping *and* the clash between life and thought can work *with* and *against* each other for producing multiple layers of understanding and experiencing. The multicultural theories and comprehensive textbooks (see Anzaldúa, 1999; Banks, 2008; Derrida, 1992; Edgerton, 1996; Freire, 2005/1970; Grande, 2004; Howard, 2006; Loewen, 1995; McCarthy, Crichlow, Dimitriadis, & Dolby, 2005; Nieto, 2004; Steinberg, 2001; Trifonas,

2003; Weiler, 2000) provide a solid theoretical foundation for students to engage in critical analysis of literature. Students' reading and responding to multicultural autobiography in dialogue with self, often supported by writing autobiography themselves, and in dialogue with multicultural theory, can reach awareness in a richness and depth that only encountering theory or story cannot inspire. In this way, autobiography becomes an effective site for understanding and *experiencing* the complicated interaction between social structure and personal identity and for addressing students' resistance to learn difficult knowledge, in order to promote democratization of both self and culture.

Part II

What Happened in My Backyard?

7. The Tulsa Race Riot of 1921: An Account

Bonita S. Johnson and Steve Hahn

The Tulsa Race Riot of 1921 was a major tragedy in Tulsa as well as the Untied States. It affected many people economically, socially, and psychologically at the beginning of the 20th century. Greenwood Avenue was known as the home of the "Black Wall Street" and Blacks were prosperous on numerous levels during a time full of racism, discrimination, and oppression. This essay provides a brief account of what happened before, during, and after the Riot. Because of the historical cover-up and the conflicting reports from different resources, this essay only serves as one account, providing background information for further reflection.

Tulsa became a prosperous city from the oil boom. Although Jim Crow laws and White racism segregated Tulsa into two cities, Black Tulsa in the Greenwood District, just northeast of Downtown Tulsa, also became a flourishing beacon of progress for the African American community locally and nationally. By 1921, the Black population had grown to almost 11,000, and Black Tulsa had many businesses such as grocery stores, shops, restaurants, theaters, hotels, and professional offices. Black churches, schools, a library, a hospital, and newspapers, along with Black professionals such as lawyers, physicians, and dentists, made this community a society of its own (Ellsworth, 1982). All these successes were unsettling to Tulsa's White population.

During the years prior to the race riot, though there had been a number of racial encounters in Tulsa, there had never been a lynching of an African American before 1920 (Estes, 1942, p. 131). Most people believed that the first major incident, which occurred in the summer of 1920, was the precursor to the race riot the next year. According to *Tulsa World,* August 22, 1920, a White cab driver was robbed and shot by two Black men and a woman. A Black man, Roy Belton, was arrested in connection with the case. The *Tulsa Tribune* of August 23, 1920 reports that Whites heard the news through the newspaper the next day and they went to the jail to get Belton so they could lynch him. The police didn't make any effort to stop the angry mob. The sheriff told the police not to intervene, as though justice would be served due to Belton's partial confession. They took Belton to Jenks, Oklahoma, and lynched him while the police watched. This incident aroused anger within the Black community, but it definitely would not be the last injustice to happen in Oklahoma. (See Ellsworth, 1982, Chapter 2.)

On May 30, 1921, nine months after the lynching of Belton, a young Black man named Dick Rowland was accused of violating a White woman, Sarah Page, in an elevator. What really happened in the elevator may never be accurately uncovered, but the common description was that Rowland stepped on Page's foot and in order to keep her from falling, he grabbed her arm (Ellsworth, 1982). But White Tulsa was ready to believe that he attacked her. Rowland was arrested the next day and an investigation began. The *Tulsa Tribune* headlined the story, as many remembered, with "To Lynch Negro Tonight." Interestingly, this editorial was mysteriously lost and permanently cut out of the microfiche of the newspaper. Obviously there was an effort to cover it up (Wilkerson, 2000).

With such an inflammatory announcement, the racial tension in Tulsa was immediately tangible. Whites wanted Roland to be lynched, and Blacks wanted Roland to be protected from the mob killing. With the memory of Belton's horrible death still fresh, Blacks wanted to rescue Rowland. In the late afternoon of May 31, a crowd of Whites began to gather outside of the courthouse and soon grew to hundreds. As a response, twenty to thirty armed Blacks went to the courthouse to offer the sheriff help for defending the jail. Assured that the authorities would handle the situation, they left. However the White crowd continued to grow into thousands and groups appeared, making efforts to force their way into the courthouse. The Black group returned in a bigger number. In the middle of the tension, a shot was fired. Gunfire between Whites and Blacks broke into the night, and quickly the fight moved away from the courthouse to the Greenwood District, where the Black community lived. The race war broke out (Ellsworth, 1982).

The Black community was invaded while many were asleep. Within several hours after midnight and before dawn on June 1, the Greenwood community was set ablaze. Black men, women and children were awakened when the mob kicked in doors and dragged them out into the streets, where some of them were shot and killed. The homes were looted and then set on fire, block by block. People ran from their homes in fear for their lives. Mount Zion Baptist Church, newly built and a symbol of Black prosperity, was burned to the ground. Arguably, even airplanes were used to attack the Black district. The National Guard from Oklahoma City arrived at 9AM and martial law was declared at 11:30AM on June 1. Within a day's time the community known as the "Black Wall Street" was turned into ashes. Millions of dollars worth of property was lost and thousands of homes were destroyed. According to the report in 2001 by the Oklahoma Commission to Study the Tulsa Race Riot of 1921, "in less than twenty-four hours, nearly all of Tulsa's African American residential district—some forty-square-blocks in all—had been laid to waste, leaving nearly nine-thousand people homeless" (Franklin & Ellsworth, 2001, p. 22). There are still some debates as to how many people were killed. The newspaper at that time reported 36 deaths. Today, it is believed by many that at least 300 or more were killed. The number will never be known because Whites burned bodies, buried bodies in mass graves, and dumped bodies in the Arkansas River to cover up the deaths (Wilkerson, 2000).

Most events of that day have been preserved through oral history. With the official cover-up there was little left in records, but much controversy has remained about what really happened. Survivors' testimonies became a reliable source for historical remembering. In 2003 there were still 39 survivors who were not afraid to share their memories as well as feelings about the riot (Gates, 2003). Some of these stories are included in *The 1921 Tulsa Race Riot Remembrance* at the Greenwood Cultural Center. J. B. Bates, who was five years old at that time, recalls the militia taking all the Black men from their homes to detention to be tortured or murdered. Kinny L. Booker remembers being awakened by her father and sent to the attic with her mother. They could hear Whites ordering her father to come with them. Later the father escaped from the White men in order to rescue his family from the house before it was set on fire. Otis G. Clark said he was caught in the middle of the riot and stood close enough to witness people being shot by machine guns. He managed to get away, although he was covered in another man's blood. He wishes he knew where his father was buried. Ernestine B. Gibbs recalls that during the fleeing frenzy, she made it to Golden Gate Park near 36th Street North and saw Whites shooting Blacks from airplanes. The families of some survivors had moved to Tulsa because of its Black community's prosperity, but this prosperity ended quickly.

The aftermath of the riot was equally appalling. As victims of the riots, Blacks were put into an internment camp and could be released only if a White person came to vouch for them. According to the Tulsa Historical Society website (see http://www.tulsahistory.org/learn/riot.htm), as many as 6,000 Blacks were detained for 8 days. On the street, Blacks were forced to wear a green card saying "Police Protection"; otherwise, they would be subject to arrest. Obviously, the National Guard had come in to protect White perpetrators rather than help Black victims. The city also imposed all kinds of restrictions upon Black Tulsans, including prohibition against funerals, restrictions on building new houses, interned Blacks had to perform forced labor, and the city even planned to sell the Greenwood area as a public land (Wilkerson, 2000). No Whites have ever been in prison for the killing, looting, and burning, and no Blacks have ever recieved a dime from an insurance company for their loss. The blame was set on Blacks and Black leaders. Law and order in the Tulsa of 1921 was stamped by White hegemony.

Some survivors left Tulsa and moved to other parts of the country to start a new life. Losing everything in one day can diminish all hopes and dreams. Many Black Tulsans, however, persevered, and by 1922 began to rebuild their lost community in Greenwood. They had to start over from scratch, an important reason that survivors and their families believe they deserve reparations now. Over the next 10 years, Greenwood was rebuilt to a certain degree, but in the 1940s and 1950s Greenwood declined and never regained its former success (Ellsworth, 1982). On May 31 and June 1, 1921, Whites sent a loud and clear message that Blacks were inferior and unwelcome. The acts committed would, we believe, be more accurately described as a massacre or genocide rather than a riot.

However, what is more tragic about this historical trauma is that the riot was covered up. According to historians John Hope Franklin and Scott Ellsworth (2001), "For decades afterwards, Oklahoma newspapers rarely mentioned the riot, the state's historical establishment essentially ignored it, and entire generations of Oklahoma school children were taught little or nothing about what happened" (p. 24). Only in the past decade has this tragedy been brought into the public light locally and nationally. Not until 1996, the 75th anniversary of the riot, was the first official apology issued by an African American state representative, Don Ross. The Greenwood Cultural Center was established in 1995 and in 1996 The Black Wall Street Monument was erected in front of the center in memory of those who had lost their lives in the race riot. A permanent photographic exhibition titled *Greenwood: From Ruins to Renaissance* has been installed at the center. In 1997, Oklahoma passed legislation sponsored by State Representative Ross and Senator Maxine Horne to create the Oklahoma Commission to Study the 1921 Race Riot. A report was released on February 28, 2001, by the Commission, but its request for reparations did not get through the state legislature and was later dismissed by the federal court. Currently, however, the Oklahoma Department of Education includes the Tulsa Race Riot in the Priority Academic Students Skills (PASS) secondary school curriculum (Ross, 2003, p. 37).

Bonita's Reflection

The Tulsa Race War of 1921 was not alone in the history of the United States. Growing up in Detroit, I recall the Detroit Race Riot of 1967. I remember waking up to a sound I had not heard before. I went to the living room window to see what was making the noise. I could not believe my eyes: soldiers and tanks were coming down the street! I could hear one of the soldiers shouting, "Get away from the windows, turn out the lights, and go back to bed or we will open fire! We have orders to shoot! To kill!" We did not live on the side of the city where the riot was taking place, but the soldiers were here to use the junior high school for a staging area, as I was told later. And then it hit me. They would rather kill us than give us our constitutional rights! My social studies teacher would have been proud of me for making that connection. This 1967 riot is known as another one of the worst riots in history. In this case, it was the police who initiated the altercation. Whites were not the only ones rioting and Blacks were rioting as well. Those who wouldn't participate on either side were punished by physical violence or loss of home or business. The causes of this riot were a multitude of political, economic, and social factors. The madness continued for seven days.

These devastating moments in history should never be forgotten because of the impact they have passed on. Racism continues to be a social concern because of its harmful effects. The Tulsa Race Riot of 1921 was a painful experience but we must remember it in order to open doors to social change. Racism may not be a thing of the past, but as a result of our collective struggles against it, racism is not as bold and malicious as it used to be. The purpose of the Greenwood Cultural Center, which houses a major display of the Tulsa Race Riot of 1921, is for all of us, Blacks and Whites, to remember and understand the history of racism so that we can work against the grain for a more equal and equitable life together. The role of education in witnessing historical memory cannot be overemphasized.

Steve Hahn's Reflection

I do not recall studying the Tulsa Race Riot in Oklahoma History at school. I did not study the riot at Oral Roberts University in Tulsa as an undergraduate student. However, I do remember catching a tidbit of information about it when surviving African Americans sought out reparations from the City of Tulsa in 2001. Local media covered the storyline and the responses from the White community were not in favor of paying debts for the past wrongs. Only when I was in graduate school did I begin to study what happened more than eighty years ago in Tulsa. In my multicultural education class, we read James W. Loewen's (1995) *Lies My Teacher Told Me.* I was shocked to read his comments that possibly bombs were dropped from airplanes to attack the African American community in the Tulsa Race Riot in 1921. How could I know nothing about it? I began to seek information and made a presentation on the topic in that class.

Today, the Greenwood District is only a shadow of its past. Interstate 244 runs right through the center of the Greenwood District. There remains a distinct line of segregation in Tulsa. North Tulsa contains a majority of Tulsa's African American population; the farther north a person goes in Tulsa the denser the African American population. Likewise, the farther south a person goes, the whiter the population becomes. For example, according to Tulsa Public School's website (http://www.tulsaschools.org/profiles/page1.shtm), as of October 4, 2007, Alcott elementary, a school in the far north and situated in tremendous economic poverty, has 96.6 percent African American, 2.0 percent American Indian, 1.0 percent Caucasian, and 0.3 percent Hispanic. Alcott is a Title I school where, of its 322 students, 301 students received free lunches and 14 received reduced-price lunches during the 2005–2006 school year (National Center for Educational Statistics). Alcott has not made adequate yearly progress. Grissom elementary, a TPS school, is located farther south in Tulsa. It has 69.9 percent Caucasian, 10.9 percent African American, 8.5 percent American Indian, and 7.1 percent Hispanic students. Grissom is not a Title I school: only 22.3 percent of students received free lunches in 2007–2008. The dividing line of race in Tulsa is present today, even though officially "segregation" is a thing of the past. Understanding Tulsa's past helps us better understand its present.

Today, in Tulsa the south is White, the north is Black, and due to a rise in the Hispanic population over the past two decades, the East side of town is becoming Hispanic. The economic disparity among different areas is evident. Along with the change of demography, we are witnessing another form of racial tension emerge in Tulsa (and nationally) that challenges not only Whites but also Blacks to confront racial issues yet again in a new picture. Learning from the lessons of the 1921 Tulsa Race Riot, we as educators always need to attend to those silenced voices, whether of African American students or of Hispanic students, so that education opens up possibilities for all students. We especially must confront new forms of racism in its explicit ways to new groups and implicit ways to historically marginalized groups. We have a lot of work to do.

8. Behind the Rowland Incident: What Was the Real Motive?

Felly Chiteng Kot

The history of humankind is paved with violent episodes involving antagonistic relationships between dominant and dominated groups. Racial motivations have often been at the heart of this antagonism. Some of the best illustrations are provided by historical events around the world, as has been the case with South Africa, the Democratic Republic of Congo, and the United States. A careful examination of such events often leads to the identification of similar patterns in spite of the distance that separates these societies. As I visited Tulsa's Greenwood Cultural Center, watched the video about the Tulsa Race Riot of 1921, engaged in discussions about this violent episode, and explored historical documents that narrate what happened in 1921, I could not help but see a link between this dramatic event and similar events in such African countries as the Democratic Republic of Congo (ex-Belgian Congo) and South Africa in the second half of the twentieth century. The focus of this paper is not to examine events that happened in the Congo and South Africa, but due to the similar racial nature of these historical tragedies, I briefly describe some African experiences to contextualize the Tulsa Race Riot and my critical analysis of the real motive behind it.

The colonial period in the Congo and the Apartheid regime in South Africa were both based on a system in which a dominated group (Black) worked for the social and economic welfare of a dominant group (White). This relationship was clearly similar to the one between a slave and a master, with the slave being not only systematically denied the opportunity to advance politically and economically but also condemned to an inferior social status. Such a situation can be understood through what Patrice Lumumba, a Congolese revolutionary leader, said in his speech delivered on the day when the Congo gained its independence from Belgium:

> We have seen that in the towns there were magnificent houses for the whites and crumbling shanties for the blacks, that a black was not admitted in the motion-picture houses, in restaurants, in the stores of the Europeans; that a black traveled in the holds, at the feet of the whites in their luxury cabins. (Quoted in Kanza, 1979, p. 162)

Nelson Mandela, a South African revolutionary leader, also expressed a similar concern when he said:

> Whites enjoy what may well be the highest standard of living in the world....The complaint of Africans, however, is not only that they are poor and the Whites are rich, but the laws which are made by the Whites are designed to preserve this situation. (as cited in Meer, 1990, pp. 255–256)

Both countries went through dramatic experiences in which the dominant and ruling group sought to subdue the dominated group by violent means. For instance, in January 1959, the Congo experienced a riot in which dozens of Congolese people were killed and hundreds more were wounded by colonial forces.[1] Similarly, the Soweto riot of 1976 in South Africa resulted in the shooting and killing of more than 360 Black people, most of whom were secondary school students.[2]

These two events bear a lot of similarities with the Tulsa Race Riot of 1921, and in fact, only one major difference seems to emerge. In the Congo and in South Africa, Black people were slaughtered because they had dared to peacefully protest against laws established by the dominant group and to express their desire to "emerge" to human dignity. In Tulsa, by contrast, the Black community was destroyed because its members had emerged to human dignity. One could therefore argue that the destruction of Greenwood and the massacre of Black people in 1921 had a hidden motive. My purpose in this paper is to examine and analyze this hidden motive.

As I explored historical documents that retrace the Tulsa Race Riot of 1921, I was struck, and somehow disappointed, by the gap in the information they provided. Nearly all the documents attempted only to present historical facts about the riot, and most of them fully described and also celebrated Black people's prosperity during that period. These sources traced the trigger of the tragedy to the Rowland incident but seldom really dug to the bottom of the matter in order to disclose the real motives behind the riot, or more accurately, the massacre.

To study such a historical tragedy, it is important to make a clear distinction between *incident*, understood here as occasion or apparent cause, and *real motive* or *actual cause*. "Incident" could be perceived as the immediate occurrence that melded into the event itself. This one (event), as it clearly appears, is the destruction of the Black community. Hence, whatever happened between Dick Rowland, the Black youth, and Sarah Page, the White girl, as described by many historical sources, such as Ellsworth (1982) and Hirsch (2002), could simply be an incident that led to the destruction of Greenwood. However, this incident seems to have only served as an occasion to carry out a preconceived plan that had a deeper motive at its core. To understand this point, it is important to briefly examine the situation within the Black community on one hand and the White community on the other.

It is well known and documented that Black people had been crushed by centuries of slavery in every aspect of life: social, economic, and political. Slavery, as an institution, had long served as a powerful instrument that allowed White people to achieve social, economic and political prosperity at the expense of Black people. Black people thus lagged behind in every aspect. However, the abolition of slavery in the nineteenth century opened up a new horizon of hope for Black people. The former slaves and their descendants had one main dream: catching up at least socially and economically and rising to human dignity. Such a dream is exemplified by the ingenuity with which they built *Greenwood*, also called *Black Wall Street*, in Tulsa, Oklahoma. Although segregated from Whites, Blacks were able to create their own community. Many stories highlight Black people's success, one of which features John Williams and his wife Lalou (Ellsworth, 1982). Having started from a modest background, as a worker in an ice cream company, John utilized his knowledge of mechanics to open a garage. This business turned out to be a flourishing financial resource. Together with his wife, they constructed buildings and opened a confectionary and a theater. The Williams' story is only one among many other stories of Black people who had succeeded in Tulsa. Greenwood offers a powerful and moving story about the building of a socially and economically strong community by Black people who had started from scratch. This kind of story should be taught and learned and should be a source of inspiration for many generations. In short, the Black community was engaged in a transformative process that was characterized by ingenuity, hard work, prosperity, and the reconstruction of the self (after the wounds of slavery).

A look at the White community reveals a different process. The former masters were observing their former slaves' prosperity and progress. They saw how Blacks were building houses, schools, hospitals, hotels, and churches as beautiful as their own, and in some cases even more beautiful. They realized that Blacks were progressively building a socially, economically, and culturally wealthy community. They noticed that, unlike during the old days of slavery, those people they referred to as "niggers" started driving cars, sending their children to school, opening bank accounts, and successfully managing prosperous businesses. In short, they watched the swift and ingenious transformation that Black people achieved within a relatively short time frame, mostly between 1905 and 1920.

The history of humankind in general, and the Tulsa Race Riot in particular, has taught us that the dominant group rarely (if ever) allows or tolerates the emergence of the dominated group. In South Africa and the Congo, this lack of tolerance was demonstrated by the promulgation of various policies with various aims including: forbidding public meetings by Black South Africans or Congolese, institutionalizing racial segregation, and inflicting punishment for violating rules. When slavery was abolished in the United States, racism in other forms intensified. Yet, in a racist system in which the key to success mainly resided within the dominant group, Black people had managed to achieve what was unthinkable at that time. As many stories of success illustrate, the community that the former slaves succeeded in building in Tulsa somehow reduced the gap between Blacks and Whites, a gap that had been maintained by a long period of slavery.

One could therefore easily understand that members of the White community perceived the Black peoples' achievement as a threat that needed to be removed. Mayor Evans's statement after the 1921 massacre is telling: "It was good generalship to let the destruction come to that section where the trouble was hatched up…that this menace has been fully conquered and that we are going on in a normal way" (in Ross, 2003, p. 19). Thus, the destruction of the Black community could be perceived as an *intentional* attempt by some members of the White community to use everything in their power to stop the Black community from rising higher and from achieving further progress. But why did they have to destroy the whole Black community? It is possible that the White mob considered the destruction as the swiftest and most ultimate means for achieving the intended goal. Merely reinforcing pro-racist and segregation laws would not have been sufficient, as Black people had managed to do well even within the racist system. Thus, the destruction of Greenwood was to not only affect Black people materially but also break down their social unity and cohesion, thus blocking any future progress.

Finally, looking at the other facets of the Rowland incident can raise a number of critical questions. No one has ever been able to accurately describe what actually happened between Rowland and Page. If we consider this incident as the real motive behind the massacre and destruction, how do we explain the scale of manslaughter and looting of the bank, post office, businesses, schools, hospital, theaters, restaurants, churches, and many other infrastructures? How do we explain the fatal role that the *Tulsa Tribune* played with its headline "Nab Negro for Attacking Girl in Elevator" (Ellsworth, 1982, p. 48) and its racist editorial that called for a lynching (Patrick, 1999)? In the same way, how do we explain the inefficiency and reported complicity of the police and the National Guard, or the use of airplanes to bomb Greenwood (Ross, 2003)? Finally, how do we explain White officials' resistance through various means against Black people's efforts to rebuild their destroyed community?

These issues tell us that the Rowland incident was merely the excuse White racists used to carry out an intentional plan for racial massacre. The plan consisted of stopping the social and economic progress of former slaves. Preventing and blocking the Black community's growth through violent destruction was certainly a means to ensure that Black people remained in the inferior condition to which they had been condemned by centuries of slavery.

To close this discussion, it is important to emphasize that the building of Greenwood by the former slaves and its violent destruction by White racists ought to be a learning experience for today's youth. Unfortunately, American history textbooks do not give enough space to this dramatic event. Chomsky (1987) calls intellectuals to take the responsibility to speak the truth, examine events in their historical development, and analyze actions according to their causes, motives, and hidden intentions. Such a responsibility is also an educator's task. In particular, the real motive for destroying Greenwood must be exposed in order to deal with the root problem of racism. Exposure to both the event and its motive can lead students to uncover and understand not only mechanisms through which social injustice and domination operated in the past but also the sophisticated ways in which they operate in the present. By drawing connections between past and present, students could work toward a better future, a future based on justice, mutual understanding, and social integration.

Notes

1. Historical accounts are not consistent on the number of Congolese people who were killed. The number generally varies from fifty (See Robert Craig Johnson's article at http://worldatwar.net/chandelle/v2/v2n3/congo.html) to 300 (from a Congolese source at http://www.deboutcongolais.info/lumumba-independence-hist.html).
2. See Matt McAulay's article, "The Soweto riots" at http://www.ccds.charlotte.nc.us/History/Africa/save/mcaulay/maculay.htm

9. Stopping "Willful Amnesia"

Julie K. Nethon

"We will never forget." Those are powerful words in American history. All across the nation, cities and towns echo this sentiment. Americans have come together to try to ease the pain from the horrible trauma inflicted by the September 11 attack in New York City in 2001. American children growing up in this era witness a sense of camaraderie and a vow of determination to *never forget*. However, many of these children will never know the lost stories of those who lived in a different time. A time in which there was an *effort to forget*. A time in which some American citizens were despised and harmed by fellow Americans, based on the simple factor of race. There was such an era in American history, and how quickly we as a society can willingly and knowingly "forget."

Tulsa, Oklahoma, summer of 1921. During this time, Tulsa, a booming oil town on the rise, enforced Jim Crow laws, and the city was segregated. But both sides of town were growing rapidly. The African American side of town was on the north, known as Black Wall Street. At the time, Black Wall Street was the Nation's most prosperous all-Black community. It was a significant phenomenon in Black history, but what became of it? What contributed to its downfall?

I first learned about Tulsa's Black Wall Street in high school. I vaguely remember my Oklahoma history textbooks spoke of the illustriousness of the city. Not born yet during the era, the only information I had was what I had gathered from my textbooks and teachers at the time. But what happened to the Black Wall Street? Having been born and raised in Oklahoma, how did I not know? Had I fallen asleep in class during that discussion? Had I somehow missed reading that chapter in my homework? No, I hadn't. The harsh reality is that my textbooks had purposely left out an important moment in American history. They left out a deep dark secret that the city of Tulsa, and Oklahoma as a whole, seems to have wanted to forget.

Black Wall Street did not disappear: It was burned to the ground. The destruction of that area, also known as Greenwood, was horrific. It continues to amaze me that very little has been done to make amends for the wrong doings during that time. Many Tulsans still know little about it today. As an African American, I am really disturbed by the way the Riot has been recorded in history and the way that it is *not* memorialized.

Charles Ogeltree (2005) points out that, "Tragedy sometimes has to remain in our national memory in order to provide meaning" (p. A4). How can we make sense of the Tulsa Race Riot of 1921 if it is forgotten? Its absence in history books and in classrooms speaks volumes, but what is the intended message? "Willful amnesia" is a term Adam Nossiter (2001) uses in discussing the Tulsa Race Riot of 1921. The phrase refers to a conscious effort to forget. It is that level of awareness and effort to forget that makes the concept so significant. Just the thought of a society being so strongly invested in willful amnesia sends chills through me. The Tulsa Race Riot of 1921 has been pushed aside and kept secret for many years. "Willful amnesia" seems to represent the overall mindset of many Tulsa citizens towards the devastating incident that occurred, not that long ago, in our American history.

The phrase, "willful amnesia," continued to echo clearly and loudly in my mind as I examined various artifacts about the Tulsa Race Riot. I had to fight back the anger, the anger that such a horrific injustice had taken place, not in some distant land but right here in my own backyard. I felt shame, shame for the fact that I was so ignorant about the events, and shame for the realization that I was commuting to that "hallowed" ground every week, attending classes without knowing the homage that was due. How could a society hide such important facts from its citizens? How could the information about the event be so misconstrued? The property damage is listed between $1.5 and $4 million dollars in 1921 dollars. Within 24 hours an entire community was leveled. There were mass graves where bodies were discarded. As many as 300 died, including women and children. The 1997 Tulsa Race Riot Commission reported in 2001 that, "The Oklahoma National Guard and the Tulsa Police Department aided a white mob—many of whom were deputized and armed by local law enforcement—in burning nearly every square inch of Greenwood" (Quoted in Ogeltree, 2005, p. A4). When government officials are involved in this way, the intensity of the willful amnesia is hardly surprising.

How can a city or a nation ever truly change and grow if it never sees its mistakes? How can a society change for the better if it lacks the skill or the effort to correct past wrongs? "A society so deeply unreflective is capable of just about anything" (Nossiter, 2001, p. 33). As a child I was taught that we all make mistakes but we need to learn from our mistakes. How can one learn from a mistake if the mistake is never acknowledged? Growth comes from reflection. It comes in those moments when one looks back and contemplates the steps that were taken. Sometimes the steps were good, and led to great things. Sometimes the steps were misguided, and led to mistakes. I believe notes should be taken on both ways so that we can make a wise choice later. As a society, we pride ourselves on self-knowledge and achievement. There should be pride in confronting our own failures as well.

Charles Ogeltree (2005) compared the public responses to two major tragedies in Oklahoma: the Oklahoma City Bombing in 1995 and the Tulsa Race Riot of 1921. His findings suggest vast differences in the public's response to the two events. He points out: "The victims of the bombing have rightfully been exalted as heroes, and their lives are commemorated with an elaborate memorial that is the crown jewel of downtown Oklahoma City" (p. A4). There have been convictions and compensations to some of the Oklahoma city victims. After the OKC Bombing the OKC National Memorial Institute for the Prevention of Terrorism (MIPT) was set up by Congress (Brune, 2002), receiving $15 million from the federal government in 2000, another $14 million in 2001, and it now runs on a budget of $4 million a year. In contrast, the Tulsa Riot victims have yet to see a single conviction and have received no reparations. Sadly, I do not find the clear-cut disparities surprising.

Ogeltree (2005) also considered the differences in eras between the events, as one event occurred in 1921 and the other in 1995. In 1921, the media and delivery of news was a lot slower and not worldwide. Yet, I do not regard the dramatic difference to be a good justification for the lack of public response to the Tulsa Race Riot. It is inexcusable for a tragedy of this magnitude to continue to be swept under the rug. No excuse at all. It is a travesty for Oklahoma's and our nation's textbooks to skip over or only briefly mention this event. Who decides which historical events or tragedies are worthy of never being forgotten? Who decides which events like that should be mentioned in text books? The Race Riot of 1921 is not an event that any city would necessarily be proud of, but historical traumas have to be acknowledged.

"Greenwood was eventually rebuilt, but things were never quite the same" (Brune, 2002 p. 13). The spirit of the Greenwood community was not only crushed but demolished, and never recaptured in quite the same way. It is as if some people believe that since Greenwood has been rebuilt, all is fine and nothing more should be said about the subject. I find this to be so disturbing! This type of mindset just allows people to wash their hands of things and say, "Well, it wasn't me who did it, so why should I have to pay?" Who said that reparations should only be monetary? According to Brune (2002), "Only 26 percent of Oklahomans favored reparations even if no tax dollars were used, while 57 percent were against reparations regardless of funding" (p. 12). Regardless of funding, things always seem to have a way of boiling down to "money." But reparations are not all about money. It is about the basic human right of being treated fairly. If you do something wrong, you should have to correct it. No matter what the "cost." I believe that a nation cannot say "I will not make amends," yet that is what is said about the Tulsa Race Riot of 1921.

Many people in the United States, or even in Tulsa, do not seem to care much about the Tulsa Race Riot, nor do they even really know much if anything about it. I think their lack of knowledge about the subject is detrimental to our society as a whole given the understanding and growth that could come from discussing the matter. The information about the Riot should not have been kept hidden for so long. It is easy to forget something when its information is no longer readily available. Because of gaps that were themselves produced by historical willful forgetting, there are various versions of the actual events and this "confusion" has been used as an excuse to undermine the actual tragedy. It works to the advantage of those who want the events of that fateful day to disappear. But those who experienced it and those who lived through the disastrous impact will never forget.

Some victims from the 1921 Riot are still alive, but not very many. My wish is that their memory never dies. They are the unsung heroes who endured such injustice and lived on to rebuild the Greenwood area. They are the innocent victims who held their heads high and carried on with their lives often with silent pain in their hearts from the injustice they endured. The 1921 Tulsa Race Riot victims are a generation of African Americans who had no choice but to go on. That is their legacy. They endured a horrible injustice brought on them yet they persevered. It is sad that many of the victims were never able to witness a single conviction or receive any compensation. Many died with no real sense of "closure." Even after the findings of the Tulsa Race Riot Commission in 2001, no reparation has been paid to victims or their families. Governor Frank Keating in October 2001 addressed the commission in a statement saying, "A state law prohibits Oklahoma from making reparations for any past mass crime committed by its officials or on the state's behalf" (Quoted in Brune, 2002, p. 11). What sense of closure could such a statement bring to victims and their families? What comfort can they take from it? Only recently has there been some type of memorial to commemorate what took place in Greenwood. In 1995 the Greenwood Cultural Center was dedicated and then a marble monument was erected in front of the center. There is at least that.

So much more should be done to pay homage to the many who lost their lives, and not just in the state of Oklahoma. I find it ironic that the only memorial to the tragedy is in a small corner on the back side of a campus in a small building. It should not be that way. The event should be taught and talked about so that the same brutality does not continue to happen. The Tulsa Race Riot will never disappear despite the nation's continued willful amnesia. The event happened many years ago, but lives on in the hearts of many African Americans today. It will never be forgotten, nor should it ever be. The lives that were lost should stand for something. They meant something, and no amount of amnesia will keep the truth hidden. The *willful amnesia* towards racial injustice in this country must stop.

10. Studying the Tulsa Race Riot for Social Renewal

David Chadwick

Tulsa, known historically for its prosperity, gained this reputation originally from the discovery of large oil deposits during the early 1900s. In recognition of Tulsa's entrepreneurial spirit and business successes, Tulsans have dubbed their city with various spirited and glamorous titles through the years (Goble, 1997): "The Magic City" in its early, oil discovery years, "Oil Capital of the World" after the First World War, when Tulsa's vast oil supplies entered the international market; "America's Most Beautiful City" after the oil-boom days, and as the twentieth century passed, the "All-American City." In many ways, these titles have all been appropriate. However, Tulsa has another title, one that has not been officially recognized or publicized, and may never be: the "City of America's Worst Race Riot."

This scandalous title, really more a historical stigma than a title, represents the gross escalation of racial tensions in Tulsa during the late spring of 1921. The term "riot" in this context is a clear understatement; it was, in fact, a catastrophic event during which, a large number of White Tulsans took life and liberty away from thousands of African American Tulsans. This blemish on Tulsa's history is an extreme example of the destructive power of racism. Moreover, the history of the riot can serve as a reminder to Tulsans today and in the future how a boiling racism can be hidden underneath the glamorous exterior of prosperity, and so it remains a historical lesson with numerous ethical and moral implications. But how can the accounts of the Tulsa Race Riot help Tulsa to avoid racism and racial violence today? *Used as a historical case study, the accounts can help Tulsans recognize the factors of social power that can underlie racial prejudice and unjust ideology, in the hope that events like the Tulsa Race Riot may not happen again.*

To avoid racism and its violent outcomes, Tulsans should learn to recognize confluent factors of social power that can contribute to racial prejudice and oppression. One of these factors is an unequal power relationship between groups of people that leads to the violation of the human rights of a minority group. In 1921, White Tulsans held significant power over their fellow African

American Tulsans, not only because they outnumbered Africa-Americans, but also because they occupied places of authority (Ellsworth, 1982). The fact that White Tulsans had such social power was not, in itself, the direct cause of the race riot, but it provided a social context that allowed for the coalescence and escalation of racial tensions. The asymmetry in social power left African American Tulsans alone to work out the complex psychological and economic consequences of the racist acts committed against them, consequences that affected their lives, their children's lives, and the lives of their children's children.

Tulsa, prior to the race riot, was a segregated community. White Tulsans lived mostly on the south side of downtown, and African American Tulsans lived primarily on the north side of downtown, in the Greenwood district. Through city ordinances, White Tulsans made sure that Black Tulsans stayed in Greenwood (Goble, 1997).

The dominant social and political power of White Tulsans was legitimized by racist ideology. Much of this ideology reflected the view that anyone other than a W.A.S.P. (White Anglo-Saxon Protestant) was not really welcome to put down roots into Tulsa's socio-economic infrastructure, especially African Americans who had migrated in droves from Southern states to Tulsa, and were thriving in the northern Greenwood district. Many White Tulsans saw the existence of Greenwood as merely a tenuous claim by African Americans upon the prosperity existing in the Tulsa community.

One major source of racist ideology in Tulsa came from the popular film called *The Birth of a Nation*, widely released across the U.S. in 1915 and playing to large audiences. Its message was overtly pro-Ku Klux Klan and anti-Black (Chalmers, 1981). Many Tulsans saw this popular film at local movie theaters and were likely influenced by it for several years prior to the riot of 1921. The film and the growing presence of the Ku Klux Klan in Oklahoma promoted a militant edge to the White supremacist ideology in Tulsa. The organization's influence pervaded various levels of the community, even infiltrating pews and pulpits of some White churches and positions of governmental authority (Chalmers, 1981; Ellsworth, 1982). These factors may be why several thousand White Tulsans eagerly gathered in front of the courthouse on May 31, 1921, a short time before they commenced their assault on the Greenwood district (Ross, 2003).

Another major source of racist ideology, and one that was perhaps a vital link in causing the riot was the *Tulsa Tribune,* one of the city's newspapers. The *Tribune* printed racially charged articles, often in supposed connection to criminal elements in Tulsa. The *Tribune* quickly informed many White Tulsans about a mishap in a downtown elevator between a young African American Tulsa man, Dick Rowland, and a young White Tulsa girl, Sarah Page (Goble, 1997). Apparently, many White Tulsans in the area believed what they read: "It is clear that the single most important precipitating ingredient in the Tulsa race riot was the manner in which the Tulsa *Tribune* 'covered' the Rowland-Page incident" (Ellsworth, 1982, p. 101). The role of the *Tulsa Tribune* in the riot illustrates the relationship between human perception and printed media, and how one can affect the other.

The dominant social power held by White Tulsans was further augmented by law enforcers' biased and uneven approach to securing Tulsa's districts. This factor, perhaps more than others, contributed to the escalation of White, racist tensions. Ellsworth (1982) elaborates:

> The Tulsa police force could not be depended upon to protect [African Americans]. This fact, joined with the rising number of lynchings in Oklahoma, pointed to the involvement of the city police force in a more generalized civic ethos of anti-black, anti-radical militance…The predominately white police force must also share heavily in the blame for the destruction of black Tulsa. Had their efforts, and those of the other law enforcement bodies, including the National Guard, been geared toward disarming and dispersing the white rioters, rather than disarming and interning blacks, much of the black district might have been saved. The mass deputizing of whites from the lynch mob by the police only encouraged the devastation. (pp. 100–102)

As can be seen above, the Tulsa Race Riot was the culmination of several interacting social forces. These factors alone do not completely explain why Tulsa's Greenwood district was destroyed; however, they do serve as a starting point to sensitize Tulsans to the causes and effects of racism and racial violence.

Some White Tulsans may think that the lessons of the past hold little relevance or application today and that they themselves are free from any social critique that may come out of the study of the Tulsa Race Riot. Although it is true that today's White Tulsans did not directly cause the pain and suffering experienced in the riot, they may still unintentionally and indirectly perpetuate the divisions between various ethnic groups in Tulsa by ignoring the ethical lessons of the 1921 riot. A comment by multicultural educator, Sonia Nieto (2004), echoes this concern:

> Although not everyone is directly guilty of racism and discrimination, we are all responsible for it. What does this mean? Primarily, it means that working actively for social justice is everyone's business. Yet it is often the victims of racism and other kinds of discrimination who are left to act on their own. (p. 350)

While Tulsans today are not directly responsible for the 1921 Tulsa Riot, we are all responsible for ameliorating the after-effects that are still felt by the relatives of the original victims, survivors, and perpetrators. And why are we responsible for this? First, some of the same social dynamics that were present in 1921 are still present today. Despite the fact that sensitivity to multicultural issues is growing, Tulsa is still mostly segregated, and the increasing rate at which non-European immigrants are settling in Tulsa creates a potential for racial animosity. Secondly, and more importantly, we must learn that we all contribute to the organization of our community in Tulsa. Inaction on our part contributes to our community's social formation just as much as our actions do. If we want a society where each individual can play a respected and significant role and compassion is the force that bonds diverse people in our community, each of us needs to be active in promoting such a society. The insights from the critical study of an event like the Tulsa Race Riot can help each generation continue to learn how to build a more caring Tulsa, where the remnants of racism fade away.

To enhance the democratic values of mutual respect, tolerance, and compassion in Tulsa, the study of the race riot should have a place in the curriculum of all Tulsa public schools; all educators should understand the social significance embedded in the accounts of the riot. Every Tulsa student should learn about the riot and its social implications so that each student develops respect for other cultural identities, as well as becomes aware of how his or her social actions contribute to social justice or injustice. A Curriculum and Study Guide promoted by the Greenwood Cultural Center (2003) states,

> The goal is not only to teach about the 1921 Tulsa Race Riot as an historic event, but to aid in developing critical thinking skills, compassion and awareness of the capacity for humans to live in peace or war, depending upon the level of self knowledge, self reflection, personal courage and understanding of the history of man's inhumanity to other humans. (Quoted in Ross, p. 38)

The development of social skills contributing to ongoing improvements in race relations in Tulsa is important simply because our city has experienced the effects of racism. Some Tulsans may relegate the riot to a past that seems no longer relevant, but as Tulsa's community becomes more diverse, with the growth of Tulsa's Hispanic community and the gradual movement of African American Tulsans into what have been predominantly White neighborhoods, the social values of empathy and multicultural understanding among Tulsans become even more vital.

11. Learning Together: An Instructor's and Pre-Service Teachers' Journey to Understanding a City's Past

Elizabeth Elias

A riot is the language of the unheard.

—Dr. Martin Luther King, Jr., 2004, p. 25

Being a native Tulsan and having lived in Tulsa all but two years of my life, I was shocked the first time I heard about the 1921 Tulsa Race Riot. It was my freshman year in college and I remember being in my American History class. Normally that class was boring and I did not care for my pompous professor, but on that particular day he had my full attention. I looked twice at him to see if he was serious, because I honestly could not believe what I was hearing.

When he first told us about the riot, I felt betrayed and misled by my family, my teachers, and other adults in my life, all of whom should have told me about this horrific event. My professor proceeded to show us a film, a documentary about the riot, and I remember putting my head down and crying in class. It was all so surreal to me. I had lived in Tulsa my whole life and in an instant my birthplace became foreign and repulsive to me.

Tulsa was my home. I knew it must have been some kind of mistake and that someone had just forgotten to tell me about this holocaust. It felt like some deep, dark secret that no one dares to mention. One of my reactions was, "How could this have happened here, where I live and where my family has lived for three generations, without me ever knowing about something so catastrophic, dehumanizing, and unimaginable?"

A few days later I decided to ask my grandma about the riot. She had been born only five years after the event, so I thought she must know something. Both sides of my family had been residents of Oklahoma since statehood in 1907. I knew I was treading dangerous waters with my grandma and might not really want to know what she had to say, but I pressed on. My grandma's response was very matter-of-fact and curt: "Yes, my mother was upset that her

[African American] housemaids couldn't come to work because of the riot. Something about their houses burning down." There was no emotion in her voice. That was that, the end of the conversation, and I never asked about the riot again.

That happened back in the early 1990s and it was not until the fall of 2006, during my doctoral class, *Diversity and Equity*, that I finally read Freire's *Pedagogy of the Oppressed* (1970). It was then that I realized I had been raised in what Freire referred to as the "Culture of Silence." His term related to the dominating class of oppressors who alienated other people and kept them silent by not acknowledging their oppression. Dominant members of society do not allow the words of the oppressed to be heard and control the oppressed by imposing silence. Oppressed people become more disempowered and might internalize negative self-image, further perpetuating their own oppression by the dominating members (Freire, 1970). As I learned about this culture of silence, I began to understand more about the culture in which I was raised and the people whom I considered to be my family and community. Many of us had done a good job of turning a blind eye to the social injustices of past and present. In doing so, we perpetuated these injustices.

As I read the syllabus for my *Diversity and Equity* class in the fall of 2006, thoughts about the Tulsa Race Riot began to surface and haunt me. For our final project we were given the opportunity to research a culture near us, to make a presentation to our class, and then write a paper regarding our experiences. One suggestion was to visit the Greenwood Cultural Center near the Oklahoma State University-Tulsa campus, which housed materials about the Tulsa Race Riot. I remember having a twinge of guilt as I read that part of the syllabus, because I knew I had driven by the Greenwood Cultural Center many times over the previous six years, as I met for my graduate classes. I never knew the Center housed a museum. I was also afraid that I would not be welcomed at the Center because I was White. Nervous energy ran through my body as I realized that this was an invitation, an opportunity calling me to learn more about the history of my city and the many people who lived through and died during the riot. I had been too scared to deal with the subject of racism and murder until now. I welcomed this chance to face this skeleton in my closet. Little did I know then how this would also affect the students I was teaching that semester.

Pre-Service Teachers' Encounters with the Unknown

Our lives begin to end the day we become silent about things that matter.
—Dr. Martin Luther King, Jr., 2004, p. 18

At that time, the fall of 2006, I was also teaching two undergraduate classes of pre-service teachers at a regional university. The course title was "Literacy in the Content Areas." I thought about my own experience as a freshman in college and wanted to see whether my pre-service teachers knew anything about the Tulsa Race Riot. I saw this as an opportunity for all of us to learn about the riot through an inquiry-based approach to teaching literacy.

The next week I asked my students about the Tulsa Race Riot. I thought, more like hoped, things had surely changed since I was a freshman in college. I believed that my students would know about the riot and that they would have been taught about it in their history classes in high school. However, only two of my forty students had heard of the riot. Both of those students were not from Oklahoma, had been educated outside of the state, and had learned about the riot in high school. As I looked at the students in my classes, I saw my own initial shock, disbelief, confusion, and betrayal on their faces. They asked: "Race Riot?" "What are you talking about?" "Here in Tulsa, Oklahoma?" I assured them I was not making the riot up and approached them about using the semester as a chance to learn more about our city's history, a place many of us had called home our entire lives.

We began our journey by thinking about how students learn best and how literacy development is a part of that. Students rattled off that they Googled information on the Internet, asked people or experts questions, read books, visited museums, took field trips, journaled, wrote poetry, watched documentaries, among other things. We decided these kinds of literacy activities were how we were going to learn about the Tulsa Race Riot. All students agreed to keep a journal during the semester in order to write down their feelings, thoughts, and questions. Shortly thereafter students began bringing to the class books, videos, and other resources related to the riot and we listened to each other and engaged in all kinds of conversation. We talked about how and why we and our future students needed to become critical readers.

Critical Literacy

Freedom is never voluntarily given by the oppressor; it must be demanded by the oppressed.

—Dr. Martin Luther King, Jr., 2004, p. 23

Critical literacy views readers as active participants in the reading process, in which they question and examine the author's purpose and point of view (Freire, 2005/1970). During critical literacy instruction, teachers and students look for relationships of power between the author and the readers in the text and in the context of what is written. By recognizing these relationships of power, the students are able to reflect, transform, and act on their world. They begin to ask questions like, "Why did the author include this information, but not other? Why was the Tulsa Race Riot only given one page in the history textbook? Was it not significant?" Readers use reading and writing as ways of liberating themselves from the oppressive powers in their world.

My students became intrigued with the idea of critical literacy. As we began discussing how textbooks and curricula are written, who writes them, and for what audiences, my students made efforts to become critical readers and thinkers. One student brought in her daughter's fourth grade social studies curriculum. In the copies that she shared with us, we found mistakes based on our own research of the Tulsa Race Riot. Dates and names of people were incorrect; we felt that the information was not written in a powerful way, conveying the true disaster that occurred. We discussed that had we been fourth graders reading about the riot in this textbook, we might not have been too concerned about it based on the information given in this particular text. Was that the intent of the author? Why downplay the tragedy and the horror? Was the riot not that important? Our emotions were fired. How could our curriculum not convey the darkness of what happened in our city? There was no mention of businesses completely destroyed, lynchings of African Americans, motherless children, people living in shanties for months and years after the riot, funerals being outlawed, mass graves, and a town who turned its back on North Tulsa, a place destroyed by angry White mobs. We talked about how such a horrific event could be diminished to just one page in a history book. Our reflections and discussions continued.

Guest Speakers

As my students' research continued, I contacted Ava Myers (2004), the author of *Tulsa Burning*, an adolescent historical novel. She agreed to come and meet my pre-service teachers free of charge. I was amazed at how gracious she was. Before she came, my students read her book and discussed it in literature circles. When she came to our class, my students asked her many questions. Ava admitted that she was nervous about writing this particular book because she was a White woman and did not know if her work would be taken seriously. This, she explained, accounted for why she wrote the story from a White adolescent boy's perspective.

Another student contacted Eddie Faye Gates, an educator, author, and speaker about civil rights, and she also agreed to come to our class. She talked about her part in the city's council on the reparations for survivors of the Tulsa Race Riot. My students asked her what she thought was the reason for so many people not knowing about the riot. She said, "It is just too painful for many. It was horrible and the destruction was almost unfathomable." She told us about how important it was for us as educators to look for social injustice in education and to talk about it, to advocate for our students, and to keep pressing until fairness and equity comes about. I could tell that my students walked out of our classroom different people that day. They saw the value in being teachers and they knew their jobs were much more important than merely teaching reading, writing, and arithmetic. Teaching is a calling.

Greenwood Cultural Center

My students continued researching and sharing their work with great passion. They began bringing in more newspaper clippings, poems they had written, and reflections. They read passages from their journals and asked each other questions about current social injustices in our schools. We also visited the Greenwood Cultural Center together on a field trip.

When I first went to the Greenwood Cultural Center to plan my field trips for my two classes, I did not know what to expect. I did not know whether I would be welcomed in a place where the survivors and victims of the riot were memorialized. I felt guilty and ashamed for what my great-grandparents and their community had done in North Tulsa. I knew that my family members did not personally partake in the destruction of Greenwood, but they were a part of the community that did destroy it. I was warmly greeted, however, and introduced to Cindy Driver, the Education Director. I stayed and spoke with her for two hours. She gave me a history lesson and encouraged me to ask questions. She told me that she normally does not guide tours but wanted to have this opportunity to be with my pre-service teachers. I felt more relaxed but still uncomfortable about being in a center where I was the minority. Being a minority is not something I usually paid attention to. But at the Center I felt it.

As my students met at the Center for our field trip, I was surprised when a few people from each class brought daughters, sons, husbands, and sisters. I never encouraged anyone to bring others, but somehow they wanted to. When I introduced myself to the visitors, more than one student told me, "I just wanted to share this experience because we need to know about the riot." I was glad they were sharing this with others. They were right: We needed to know.

At the Center we watched a documentary, examined photographs and artifacts, and visited a house similar to the ones burnt down during the riot. We continued to learn and grow together, but it was not easy. Some pictures, such as the premature baby that was born during the riot and died only a few days later, made a group of my students hold each other and cry. One of my students, who was eight months pregnant at the time, kept saying, "How could we do this?" I knew what she meant. This place made me feel ashamed and guilty.

I understood where my students were coming from. I could tell by our class discussions and what I read in their journals that this issue of racism was hard for many of us to deal with. It was as if we had been taught not to examine our feelings about injustice and not to question parts of our world that make us uncomfortable. We became silent. We needed more time, more discussion, and more guidance in dealing with all these emotions. Personally, I believe I had only begun to scratch the surface of my own inward journey and questioning. How can we work through the feelings of defensiveness, guilt, and shame in order to take on social responsibility with light packs? It is a question that stays with me.

Journal Entries

As I read students' journal entries, I realized how profoundly some of my students were affected. Reading their words gave me a deeper glimpse into the kind of learning that was taking place. This was not supposed to be a class on issues of diversity and equity, but somehow it was closely tied to what we all were learning about critical literacy instruction that semester. Many wrote about how difficult race and prejudice are to talk about, but how they wanted to talk about these issues because the issues are real. Some described how North Tulsa is still affected by the riot of 1921 and how schools in North Tulsa are different from other schools in Tulsa. In class, we delved into the topic of schools in poverty, how these schools are plagued with higher teacher attrition rates, more inexperienced teachers working in these schools, lack of monetary resources, student mobility, and higher drop-out rates.

In other journal entries students discussed how Tulsa was still very segregated and that some of them had never been "to that side of town" until we took our field trip to the Center. Other students discussed how the kinds of opportunities and educational experiences students are afforded are strongly tied to the amount of money a community has. An African American student, who lived in North Tulsa, commented on how there are not as many parks, stores, and resources on the north side of town. In class we talked about how not having resources affects the kinds of educational experiences our children have. My students agreed that if students are not given experiences and opportunities they fall further behind those who are given more. Many times our discussions came to the message that money and opportunities are not equally dispersed, that poverty is constantly being perpetuated, and that education is directly affected by and tied to all of this.

My Own Lesson

While preparing my final presentation for my *Diversity and Equity* doctoral class, I created a slide show of my students' poetry, history, and pictures of the riot I had gathered during my own research activities that semester. My sister-in-law, a photographer, was helping me put the photographs into my Power Point presentation when my 9-year-old niece came into her office where we were working. I had looked at so many of the pictures of burnt victims of the riot that I had forgotten my own initial shock and devastation until I looked at my little niece's face. Immediately she asked, "What is that a picture of? Is that a man?" I responded sadly and told her that it was a picture of a man who had been burnt to death because he had brown skin instead of white skin. She looked shaken. My sister-in-law was not happy with my response and countered, "You don't need to worry. That is not a real picture. It is nothing." *It is nothing* churned in my mind for some time after that. That is how history repeats itself, by ignoring history and forgetting mistakes like they never happened. This was my own history lesson. I saw how we continued and grew our "Culture of Silence." We perpetuate it and teach our children to turn a blind eye to what we find uncomfortable. That *It is nothing* was not true. It was a man, most likely a father, someone's child, a brother. It was a man, burnt to death, someone who died possibly defending his home and his family. My sister-in-law had instantly dismissed it like it had not happened, like it did not happen. I told my niece that the Tulsa Race Riot was real.

Conclusion

We continued to grow, question, and learn with each other. Many of us, for the first time, were uncovering truths about an event that we had known nothing about. This experience changed us forever. Some students discovered a side of town that was very foreign to them, yet only 10 miles from where they lived. We considered how our past history continues to affect and shape our present and the kinds of education, experiences, and opportunities our children are given. We better understood the role critical literacy needed to play in our future classrooms. We needed to challenge our students and teach them to question their textbooks, teachers, communities, and each other. I felt how close we grew that fall and believed that maybe we could transform our world by acting on it. By teaching. I still receive emails from students informing me of our city's latest court decisions regarding the Tulsa Race Riot, or about how much our class meant to them because they began to look at teaching differently. I miss them, but know we became a part of each other because we had the courage to talk about prejudice and social injustice—topics that many of us still find uncomfortable. I end this chapter with a quote I found in one of my students' journals. I believe she touched on what many of us learned in the fall of 2006:

> In order to understand one's own history and culture, an individual must have a basic understanding of the significance of history and culture of all mankind [*sic*]. An understanding of man's curiosity, of his deep-seated need to share his own culture and history with others, and the ability to adapt to and accommodate other cultures (and to learn vital lessons from all of these experiences) will help one better understand all cultures, all history. (Gates, 2003, p. xii)

Pedagogical Reflection II: Historical Memory and Pedagogical Encounter

Hongyu Wang

> For only by looking to the past can we see not only who we are, but also where we are going. And as the first one-hundred years of Oklahoma statehood draws to a close, and a new century begins, we can best honor that past not by burying it, but by facing it squarely, honestly, and above all, openly.
>
> —John Hope Franklin and Scott Ellsworth, 2001, p. 32

When I first started to teach at OSU in 2001, a colleague gave me the video, *The Tulsa Lynching of 1921: A Hidden Story* (Wilkerson, 2000). It is a documentary film describing one of the worst race riots in the nation, the Tulsa Race Riot of 1921. The film covers what happened before, during, and after the riot when the African American community in Tulsa was destroyed by White mobs. Even though I was a newcomer to Oklahoma and neither White nor Black, watching it provoked many strong emotions in me. Since this happened here in Oklahoma—the campus of OSU-Tulsa is located on the ruined site of the Black Wall Street—I reasoned that students should confront such a historical trauma. I selected a part of the film and prepared to show it to my class. Right before the scheduled class time for showing the film, the September 11 attack happened. I immediately faced the issue of whether I would be insensitive to my students' feelings if I still chose to show the film. After some internal debate, I decided to show it. I did not ask for students' comments, though, and only asked for a moment of silence to pay tribute to tragedy in all forms.

In the next couple of years, I did not teach about the 1921 Tulsa Race Riot in class. The post-September 11 era does not have a hospitable atmosphere for a Chinese professor to teach sensitive issues too provocatively. I was also not fully confident in my own pedagogical craft in leading students through such a historical memory. It was one of my students, Steve Hahn, who first brought his classmates' attention to the riot. When reading *Lies My Teacher Told Me* (Loewen, 1995) he "discovered" the riot. Since he knew nothing about it, he began to study it and then presented his astonishing findings to the class. They came as a big surprise to the whole class, as few students knew about it in much detail. As I listened to students and watched how they reacted to Steve's presentation, I realized that this was an education long overdue. (See Bonita Johnson's and Steve Hahn's description of the riot for details—a description co-written by a Black American and a White American, respectively.)

After that class, I began to incorporate the study of the 1921 Tulsa Race Riot into all my multicultural education classes. Typically, I require students to make a field trip to the Greenwood Cultural Center, which houses materials about the riot, and ask them to feel the place at the site of the historical ruin. I then show *The Tulsa Lynching of 1921: A Hidden Story* in class and students discuss the documentary film based upon their experiences at the center and their own studies. Students also write a response paper as a summary of this study. Students have reacted to this task differently, some of them with fear and resistance, but more with courage and willingness to learn. A couple of students also took the initiative to interview the riot survivors and Steve Waldvogel made a DVD of his interview with Otis Clark who is already more than 100 years old. Such a study has left a long-lasting influence on students. They discuss it on other occasions long after the class is over, bring it to their families' and co-workers' attention, or teach their own students about it. Such a rippling impact has been profoundly moving to me. It is students' courage to unlearn and learn that has sustained my courage to teach against the grain.

But the courage to teach it is only the first step. The bigger challenge is to make an educational use of it. The most difficult issue for me is how to enable students to experience and express their intense emotions and then work through those emotions in order to emerge from their studies with a new sense of multicultural awareness and social responsibility. For those who know little about the riot, watching the film itself can be an ordeal. Anger, shame, guilt, shock, fear, or sadness can be written on their faces. Sometimes when I see students react to it intensely, I ask students to write anonymous responses in class to express their feelings and thoughts without having to speak about them in public. Then I collect their written responses and read them in class one by one to open up discussions so that students can feel relatively safe to respond.

Students' encounters with the historical trauma happening in their backyard and the instructor's pedagogical mediations are both laden with emotions. Moral anger (see Julie Nethon's powerful call to stop willful amnesia), shame, and guilt (See Elizabeth Elias's thoughtful reflection) in the classroom co-exist. In many multicultural education textbooks, the role of empathy is addressed, but many other important emotions are not fully discussed. However, a truly democratic classroom is where "conflicts and anger, tears and pain" (Kohli, 1991, p. 45) can be shared. Minority students and White students have different emotional relationships with the trauma, and understanding cannot be reached without addressing these difficult feelings.

Here I highlight the significance of one emotion—guilt—common especially among White students in encountering historical racial traumas and its role in pedagogical interactions. Sharon Todd (2003) points out that the role of guilt is usually dismissed in privileging social and political action in social justice education. She argues that "guilt has the potential to incite moral action" because guilt is essential to forming social and moral relationships with others and because "we feel love and cause pain simultaneously that we experience guilt" (p. 104). In other words, reparation and love do not happen if we witness (directly and indirectly) others' suffering without feeling guilty. William Pinar (1993) also suggests that, in understanding curriculum as a racial text, the denial of guilt is more damaging and paralyzing than the guilt itself. Guilt begs the question: How do I respond?

We usually say that we learn history so that the same mistakes are not repeated, but history repeats in various forms despite our intentions. I argue that the more important purpose of pedagogical encounters with historical memories is to evoke social responsibility so that we can respond responsibly in the midst of societal wrongs, even when individual action cannot prevent the wrongdoings of a group, or even when history does repeat itself. If the formation of social relationships is related to guilt, then the intention of protecting students from guilt potentially protects students *only* from true education. As the instructor, there are times when I find myself feeling guilty for putting students through all these difficult issues and feel the need to protect them from the pain of unlearning. In a sense, teacher educators have to work through guilt in a double sense: guilt for social sufferings and guilt for making students confront such sufferings. But if guilt is better acknowledged, rather than denied, for the public good and personal growth, as a multicultural educator I must meet such a challenge and live through what I ask students to live through, because teacher educators' professional commitment is also doubled—we are educating students who are or will become teachers. Transforming guilt into social responsibility is an educational work in which teacher and student must both engage. As James W. Lowen (1995) claims:

> If we look Indian history squarely in the eye, we are going to get red eyes. This is our past, however, and we must acknowledge it. It is time for textbooks to send white children home, if not with red eyes, at least with thought-provoking questions. (p. 92)

I would add that teachers also need to go home with red eyes.

In my teaching, I used to hope that students could work through guilt and then take on educational responsibility without feeling guilty, as Gary Howard (2006) lists "responsibility without guilt" as a characteristic of a transformational educator. But I've found that guilt is quite pervasive and very difficult to

evade. Even students' strongest refusal to feel guilty is implicated in the awareness that something wrong *already* happened. Quite recently I have begun to
question my own desire for students to relinquish guilt after experiencing it.
Perhaps what is more important is to accept guilt and let this acceptance dissolve the difficulty where one might be stuck and then move on with new
insights. When guilt is expressed in the classroom, teacher educators need to be
open, nonjudgmental, and receptive rather than trying to push it away. Ultimately, this also means that educators accept the pedagogical guilt of engaging
students with unlearning difficult knowledge through historical memory work.

However, there are alternative paths. Historical trauma requires an organic
healing which allows the network to work its magic. In the art of Chinese
acupuncture, needles are not necessarily put into the area where hurts happen in
order to cure the pain. Needles can be put into another part of the body to
relieve the symptoms for long-term effects. This principle is based upon the
inner connectedness of the body (as well as connections between the body and
the external environment) and the circulation of *qi* through the whole body. For
pedagogical considerations, students' angry resistance against difficult knowledge is understandable if the needle is put directly into the area of hurt (even
though such an insertion can be effective sometimes), but if we situate the issue
in the larger context, students might be less defensive and more receptive to
learning from historical encounters for social renewal (see David Chadwick's
analysis). In other words, while I agree with Todd that guilt might be essential
to the formation of relationship and responsibility, I also think that the organic
interconnectedness already in life is prior to individual experiencing of guilt. On
the one hand, as pedagogy may induce guilt and pain, we should not avoid it.
On the other hand, we need to be attentive to create more receptive learning
environments so that pain can be lessened rather than reinforced.

As Felly Chiteng Kot's analysis clearly shows, the motive behind the Tulsa
Race Riot of 1921 was not separate from the international context of coloniza-
tion and racism. At the time when I write this reflection, I am trying another
pedagogical path. Students read *There Is No Future without Forgiveness*, written by
Desmond Tutu (1999) before their studies of the Tulsa Race Riot. The book
describes the extraordinary and unprecedented efforts made by South Africa's
Truth and Reconciliation Commission to reconcile the terrible trauma inflicted
by the apartheid regime. Refusing the route of either national amnesia or re-
tributive justice, South Africa searches her soul by following a third way to
promote restorative justice in the spirit of *ubuntu* for the possibility of amnesty,
reparation, forgiveness, and hope. My purpose in using this book before the
students' direct encounter with the Tulsa Race Riot is not for diverting students'
attention from racial injustice within the nation, but for situating the problem in
the global context so that they become more aware and are more willing to take

on individual responsibility for dealing with racism in its various forms and at different levels. To use the acupuncture art as a metaphor, this pedagogical arrangement is a way to heal the pain through the circulation of spirit in a network rather than paying attention only to the isolated area that hurts. Students have been profoundly moved by Tutu's book, and my hope is that it will help them achieve a healthy distance from our own racial scar in order to respond to it with compassion, courage, and the capacity to move forward.

Every place has its own history. Many lessons can be learned when we open up geographical, social, and subjective spaces for education. Teacher educators can venture with their students onto many pathways. Pedagogical encounters of historical memories can take us to alterative landscapes—both external and internal landscapes of unlearning and learning.

Part III

Reclaiming Roots

12. Growing Up Native American in a White Society: My Educational Journey

Deidre Prevett

There is not one Indian in the whole of this country who does not cringe in anguish and frustration because of these textbooks. There is not one Indian child who has not come home in shame and tears.

—Rupert Costo, 1974, pp. 192–193

At an early age I sat at my grandmother's feet listening to her stories of growing up in the Indian Territory. She told me about the times her family spent with her grandfather, Moty Tiger, who was Chief of the Creek Nation. He only conversed with her in Creek, even though English was the dominant language in their community of Tiger Flats. Perhaps her grandfather wanted to help her maintain her bilingualism. She even taught me to speak a little Creek, but that was a long time ago and I can only remember one phrase now: *Gaga nehe aou hustay.* It means: "Who is your sweet daddy?"

My grandmother's family went through a lot of struggles after the death of her father, George Tiger, when she was just a young girl. If not for the small oil royalties my grandmother received from oil production on her land allotment and for the help of Oklahoma's first female legislator and family friend, Alice Roberts, the family would have been removed from their farm and the children sent off to government-controlled orphanages. My great-grandmother had been raised in such an orphanage and she did not want her children going there. My grandmother was very proud of her Native American heritage. Even though she had little contact with Moty Tiger after the death of her father, my grandmother was still proud to call him her grandfather.

Of eight grandchildren, I am the only one who resembles a Native American. I have dark-olive skin tones, dark brown eyes, and long, straight, jet-black hair. Grandma always called me her little Indian princess. She made sure that I always had a pair of moccasins to wear and some sort of Native American book to read. She wanted me to be as proud of my Indian heritage as she was. While sitting at my grandmother's feet, listening to her stories about her childhood, I could vividly see the pride that she felt for her ancestors. Her tired, old eyes sparkled and her face glowed as if she had been transported back in time to an era that she held dear to her heart. Whoever listened to these stories could not help but be drawn in. As I listened to her stories over and over throughout my childhood, Grandma helped me to develop a sense of pride in who I was.

I was proud to be called a Native American until I went to elementary school. In first grade, I began to realize that being a Native American was not such a good thing. At the beginning of November, my class started to study about Thanksgiving and the reasons we celebrate this American holiday. At first I was excited because we were finally going to learn about Native Americans. I brought my Indian drum to school and proudly showed it off to my classmates. I even brought in my moccasins and let everyone try them on. But it was not long before my pride turned to shame. We read stories of the first Thanksgiving, and it was in those stories that I first heard the word "savage" associated with Native Americans. I really didn't know what to think, because the Native American people I knew were very nice and loving people, but the ones portrayed in the stories were vicious, murderous, scalping savages.

At recess time all the school kids wanted to play Cowboys and Indians. I was always chosen as the Indian, which wasn't very pleasant, because everyone started chasing me and shooting at me with their "pretend" guns. I was expected to fall down and play dead so they could pretend to scalp me. I must have been a bad shot, because my "pretend" arrows never hit the cowboys I was aiming for; at least they never fell to the ground, pretending to be dead. I grew to hate this game and to hate the physical features that signified my obviously Native American bloodline. It was not fun being chased all the time and being called "Injun," "squaw," and "savage." The day before Thanksgiving break was the annual school feast. A turkey lunch was served and parents and community members came to partake in the school's Thanksgiving lunch. All the students had to dress in either a black, construction-paper, Pilgrim hat or a brown, Native American, paper-bag vest decorated with stereotypical Native American symbols. I crossed my fingers and hoped that I would get a Pilgrim hat, because I was tired of being chased and called names. But I was out of luck. I had to wear a Native American vest. I was finally ashamed to be a Native American.

The library books and textbooks we read in class were often one sided. They told of the massacres committed by Native Americans against White pioneers. I couldn't believe that the same people my grandmother spoke of with such reverence were also the White man's greatest adversary. That was not the message conveyed to me in the stories my grandmother told me of honorable and caring Native American people who thrived on peace, preserved Mother Earth, and maintained great restraint when treated poorly. I was torn between my grandmother's Native American legends and the stories I read in school textbooks. The Native Americans were usually portrayed as dark, angry, scowling men holding tomahawks and chasing after peaceful, White, terrified settlers; the settlers were usually White women carrying babies. To the best of my recollection, very seldom were White men depicted in the "chase scene" illustrations. I was very relieved when the Thanksgiving holiday was over. That meant that our Thanksgiving unit had ended and we would no longer read books in class about peace-loving White settlers and murderous Native Americans. Christmas soon captivated the thoughts of the other children and they quickly forgot about Native Americans and instead focused on Santa Claus and the countdown to the holiday break.

But, the damage was done and I no longer wanted to be seen as Native American. I stopped talking about my native heritage and put my Native American drum and moccasins away in a box and placed it in the very back of my closet. I was embarrassed by my heritage. It did not take long for the pride that my grandmother had fostered in me over the years to be torn down. I just wanted to be like all the other kids in my class. I convinced my mother to let me get my long hair cut short. My hair had always been a source of pride, but I no longer wanted to wear braids, and without them, my hair was a mess. After Christmas break, when I came back to school with short hair, I was beginning to look like all the rest of the kids in my classroom. This was the first stage of my assimilation into the White culture.

As much as I tried to avoid my heritage, there were still reminders of my people everywhere I turned. I remember purchasing a "Big Chief" writing tablet that was required for handwriting. The cover of the tablet had the head of a solemn, Native American Chief wearing a ceremonial headdress. Every time I was instructed to take out this tablet, I looked at the chief and thought of the stories my Grandmother told me about my Great-Great Grandfather, Moty Tiger. My excitement for school had been replaced with dread before my first-grade year ended. My grades reflected my lack of enthusiasm and I began to struggle with all subjects, especially math. I was cautious of sharing my native background with anyone.

As I grew older, I realized that there was a separation between Whites and Native Americans in terms of social classification. There were Native Americans in my school who were from poor families. Many lived in rural areas. These people were trapped by their way of life and probably saw no way out. The families could not afford to pick up and move to find better jobs, so they stayed where they were. They became dependent on the federally funded Native American programs that were in place at the time. I remember hearing White people talk about how the Native Americans were always taking advantage of free, Indian health clinics and Native American food programs. Native Americans were stereotyped as poor, stupid, lazy drunks who would rather wait in a line all day to get free stuff than get out and find a job. This was the way that most of the people in my community, including myself, looked at Native Americans. I was so thankful that my family was not able to take advantage of the US government's food commodity program for Native Americans because my parents' income was above the allowable limit. That would have been a great embarrassment to me. We did, however, and to my dismay, utilize the free, Native American medical services. Knowing how people stereotyped Native Americans, I resented having to wait all day to see a doctor in a smelly waiting room surrounded by overweight Native Americans reeking of body odor, dirty children smelling of urine and, in some instances, Native Americans who were obviously intoxicated. It was a frightening experience because I felt as if I had been reduced to a needy child with my hand out, begging for help. I was not like them, and I despised sitting among them waiting for my name to be called, because I did not want to be associated with this class of "social degenerates." In my mind, this experience further solidified the White society's stereotypes about Native Americans.

The Native American heritage was not a subject of interest to me for some time, until I reached junior high school. Because the school district where I received my education was 42% Native American, the district was encouraged by local parents to add Native American education classes for students in junior high through high school. After applying for grants under Title IV, which has since been changed, the school district received several small, federally funded grants. By pooling all the grant money together, the school district was able to add Indian Arts and Crafts classes, as well as to provide counselors for Native American students. It was the Native American counselor's responsibility to help Native American students by monitoring their academic progress. The counselor also worked to expose the student body at large to Native American cultures. At the beginning of my seventh-grade year, while I was in the hallway changing classes, the school's Native American counselor handed me a note encouraging me to join the school's new Native American Club. At first, I would not even consider joining a club that would draw attention to my heritage. However, after much persuasion, I succumbed to the counselor's determination and joined the group.

It did not take long for me to begin enjoying my membership in the club, and I looked forward to club meetings. We learned about the cultural differences among Native American tribes, and participated in fieldtrips to Native American museums and events. During these engaging fieldtrips, my pride in my culture began to slowly return. Our sponsor taught us the Round Dance so we could go to the elementary schools and teach the kids how to dance. The Round Dance is a simple dance where everyone faces each other in a circle and each dancer extends a hand in friendship to the dancer on the left and on the right. The circle moves clockwise to the beat of the drum. The Round Dance is one of the few dances where non-natives are invited to participate. Being a part of this club enabled me to get to know other Native American students, whom I never would have tried to get to know on my own. Having a school guidance counselor who was proud of her own Native American heritage and who encouraged her students not only to learn about their culture, but to experience it first-hand, helped to erode my embarrassment and shame in being a minority. She helped to restore the pride my grandmother had instilled in me so long ago. My adoration for teaching began with the Native American Club, as I taught the Round Dance to inquisitive elementary school children who looked up to me.

My educational journey first took me away from my culture, yet later brought me back full circle. My story is one of disconnecting from my own rich, Native American roots and assimilating into White culture. At one time, I viewed the world as White: I was taught as a White, by White teachers, within White walls, and among White students. Then, one day I looked in the mirror and saw what others saw: I was a Native American girl with straight, black hair and dark skin. Once again I have embraced my Native American heritage. I will never again allow anyone to rob me of my Native American pride.

I often have flashbacks of my journey as a minority, living among a majority that sees little value in the history of my culture. As Howard (1999) concluded, White teachers cannot teach what they have not learned. My White, first-grade teacher obviously did not know about Native American history; otherwise, she would not have subjected me to the cruel myths constructed by Whites to portray Native Americans as savages. Her ignorance helped to erase my pride and, unwittingly, to force my assimilation into the White culture. Teachers often teach the way they were taught, and this pattern often alienates diverse populations and promotes the assimilation of minority students into the White culture. In order to stop the alienation and assimilation of minority students, Swisher and Schoorman (2001) suggest, "It is vital that educators become more familiar with the cultural backgrounds of their students and understand its potential impact on their learning" (p. 62). When I chose to become a teacher, I vowed to never be like some of the teachers I had in school.

There is more to our American society than just the White culture. Many different cultures are represented in our schools, and I want to know more about them so I can better connect with my students. I make home visits to meet family members and learn about their culture and beliefs. By doing so, I create a community in my classroom. It is my goal to teach more than basic subjects. I want to teach appreciation for differences by showcasing students and celebrating their diversity by having them bring artifacts from home for show-and-tell activities. I also invite family and friends to talk to students about their heritages.

I make it a point to learn all I can about the different cultures and beliefs of my students. I have personally experienced the benefits of getting to know my students and their family members through asking questions and allowing time for sharing through rich conversations about their family histories. As I have matured in my appreciation for my own culture, I have gained insight and appreciation for other cultures. This is a process that can only be developed through years of teaching experiences with minority students and families. Two cultures that I have had direct experiences with in my classroom are African Americans and Hispanics. Like Native Americans, these cultures also must deal with the marginalization of their people by a predominantly White society.

Drawing upon personal experiences and research, I can begin to help in bringing changes to students' lives. I can use my own experiences as a struggling, Native American learner to help my minority students become successful achievers. There is significant research offering suggestions for reaching minorities, so I draw from this research while developing personal relationships with my students. I believe it is in these relationships that students reveal their talents and exceptional abilities. As a teacher of minorities, I try to enable my students to embrace their heritages by sharing my own stories as an outsider looking in.

The goal of education is for children to succeed in the White world but, at what price? While we as educators can't erase the negative stigmas associated with prior injustices to Native Americans, we can expose the truth and make an earnest attempt to reveal those injustices by teaching what has been left out of the curriculum. Thus I end this paper with Loewen's (1995) invitation:

> If we look Indian history squarely in the eye, we are going to get red eyes. This is our past, however, and we must acknowledge it. It is time for textbooks to send white children home, if not with red eyes, at least with thought-provoking questions. (p. 92)

13. Embracing One's Own Culture and Respecting Differences

Shanedra Nowell

Now this bell tolling softly for another, says to me, Thou must die.
—John Donne, 1994, p. 440

I am always moved by Donne's *Meditation 17*, a piece of prose written in the 17th century, because the words speak loudly of what needs to be heard today. Reading Donne's words, "All mankind is of one author and is one volume," I pause to remember that there is only one race—Homo sapiens, the human race, with no sub-species (Donne, 1994; Dougherty, 1999). The words most often repeated from Donne's passage continue to inspire: "No man is an island, entire of itself; every man is a piece of the continent....Never send to know for whom the bell tolls; it tolls for thee" (Donne, 1994).

Fighting the tide of racial and gender bias is like being alone on an island, trying to survive in cultural ignorance, but Donne's message resonates with me clearly—the interdependence of humankind. We must all rely on, protect, and respect each other in order to achieve anything of substance in this life. This interdependence especially rings true in the goals of multicultural education. My journey through multicultural education leads me down the path of introspection into personal beliefs, guilt, and anger over the past, to reclaim personal pride in my own culture and to glimpse a future that holds promise because of a willingness to accept lessons learned along the way. The challenges are to break away from stereotypes ingrained for generations, to step out of my comfort zone and learn as much as possible about others, and to learn to respect differences as strengths. These lessons also require taking on the responsibility of leading my friends, family, and students onto the path of multicultural harmony. I believe cultural awareness and education are the keys to making America that "One Nation, Under God, Indivisible" that we all pledge to defend.

Lies about Race

Nothing in the world is more dangerous than sincere ignorance and conscientious stupidity.

—Martin Luther King, Jr., quoted in Newman, 1998, p. 124

For years I had been taught the concept of the three races—Caucasoid, Mongoloid, and Negroid. The idea appeared to be based on science and geography, and I took this information to heart as truth. In my mind, all three races were equal in every respect and were different only in appearance. The video *Understanding Race* (Dougherty, 1999) opened my eyes to the complexity of the concept of race, and I immediately felt anger over years of believing in pseudo-scientifically backed lies. We need to reveal the concept of race for what it really is—a societal label, not a biological fact. As Gardner (1995) states, however, "Biological race is dead; social race is alive and thriving." Our modern society created and sustains racial labels, and as teachers—the members of society responsible for educating others—we should do all we can to unveil racial ignorance. We need to replace the lies about race found in school textbooks with the picture of one race struggling to come together after years of segregation, mistrust, and fear in order to create a harmonious future.

Labeling "race" for what it really is does not mean ignoring its role in our society and culture, nor does it erase the threat of racism. Respect for the differences in both physical appearance and culture can be taught from an early age. Fostering individual uniqueness builds confidence in children instead of fear. In our society, "race" has a lot to do with culture, as people tend to closely identify with biological family and others who share the same skin color or social standing. As educators we cannot ignore race, but we should use cultural awareness as a tool to open up communication with and among all students. In this process, teachers first need to understand their own definition of race and culture before trying to help students understand it.

For me, this epiphany occurred as I walked down the halls of Greenwood Cultural Center, viewing the images of early Black communities in Oklahoma. I had never shared my family's views of living in predominately Black communities or their mistrust of Whites, but looking into the past through the old photographs of Greenwood, I came to realize that the close-knit Black families and communities symbolized strength against racism and protection from those who intended harm to prospering African Americans. Considering my family's viewpoints through a socio-historical lens helps me to understand the importance of embracing one's own culture, reconstructing one's identity as a part of that culture, and sharing one's own roots with others. In learning to acknowledge my own culture as an African American, I can teach others how to respect differences in order to move beyond the racism of the past.

According to Banks and Banks (2005), "The human relations approach engenders positive feelings among all students, promotes group identity and pride for students of color, reduces stereotypes, and works to eliminate prejudice and biases" (p. 67). They also suggest using role-playing or vicarious learning experiences in the classroom to help students further understand each other and the world, and hopefully we learn more about ourselves along the way. I believe this approach to multicultural education has great potential for teaching about racial difference through a relational view.

The Power of Women

Southern women are uniquely equipped to juggle apparent opposites. They are molded in a tradition that routinely pairs civility and violence, conformity and individualism.
—Sharon McKern, 1979, p. 18

Although women make up just under half of the world's population (a ratio of 1.01 male to female), the balance of power has traditionally remained in the hands of men (Central Intelligence Agency, 2008). Only in the last century have American women gained much more standing with men, with the triumph of women's suffrage and the widespread acceptance of women in the American workforce. As a young woman, I struggle daily to be seen, heard, and respected. I have experienced life in a male-dominated workplace where a woman speaking her mind takes men by surprise and often receives more scrutiny. While I, as a strong-willed Southern woman, gladly accept the challenge, I do not want my daughters to have to fight this battle. Educating tomorrow's leaders, male and female, to disavow years of gender bias in our society is a challenge equal to erasing racial prejudice. Being female in a male-dominated world, I want to bring multiple perspectives into my workplace and classroom. I believe that a woman's ability to view a problem from many sides and then choose the best solution is a major strength. For me, feminism means sharing power and empowering young women to acknowledge their strengths and assert their opinions. As an educator, I wish to empower my students—boys and girls equally—to raise their voices, do their best, and achieve their goals.

Through women's education, suffrage, and the civil rights movements, women have been gaining a foothold in areas of power such as politics, medicine, and law. With these open doors, the world now sees, hears, and understands more of women's experiences. Research studies into women's issues in medicine and psychology save more lives. Also, young girls now have female role models in almost every profession from astronauts to zoologists, and this aids educators in challenging gender biases through curriculum. In her book *In a Different Voice*, Carol Gilligan (1993) shows us the power of relationships in the development of women's minds and prompts educators to include curricular examples relevant to young women, encouraging them to greatness. Banks and Banks (2005) suggest many ways to infuse the standard curriculum with female perspectives, but I find the gender-balanced curriculum best suited for inclusion. This approach acknowledges the differences between men and women, but "weaves together women's and men's experiences into multilayered composites of human experience" (Banks & Banks, 2005, p. 175). Showing how men and women must work together, the gender-balanced curriculum prevents the gender pendulum from swinging too far toward one gender.

The Place of the South

Because I was born in the South, I'm a Southerner. If I had been born in the North, the West or the Central Plains, I would just be a human being.
—Clyde Edgerton, quoted in Maxwell, 2002

Throughout this journey of multicultural education, I have learned the importance of acknowledging and experiencing my own culture—seeking my own racial, gender, and cultural identity. As an American, I do have a culture, rich in many traditions and ethnic groups, but each of us belongs to multiple subcultures within the American experience. I am an American woman, born out of the traditions of women's suffrage and equality. I am an African American, taught to be proud of my skin color and wear it as a badge of honor instead of shame. I am a Christian, believing that truth is absolute and God given, and believing that we need to love others unconditionally. Possibly above all, I am a Southerner, raised in a place where family, appearances, charm, and spirit matter. I was born in Edenton, North Carolina, a small, coastal town where people still sit on their front porches and greet you as you drive or walk past, and courtesy and poise are the rule, not the exception. In the South, past events, good or bad, bear equal importance with the future. While the scars of racism and slavery are still visible in many southern towns, I believe the South acknowledges its tainted past in order to progress toward a more equitable future. As a Southerner, I take this notion to heart, and I believe that effective multicultural educators must truly embrace their own culture, with all its past flaws, before they can endeavor to teach or learn about other cultures.

Gary Howard (1999) writes about his cultural immersion experiences around the world. After years of teaching multicultural education, Howard recognized that his own multicultural experience was incomplete: "I had been relying on other people's culture to provide me with a sense of meaning" (p. 21). While his studies raised his awareness of other cultures, they did not fill the void of experiencing his own culture. Howard traveled to the British Isles, taking in the sights and sounds of his own Celtic heritage. "At Stonehenge, I embraced my Whiteness, all aspects of it," he explains, and answered the question that he had been pursuing for many years: "How do I incorporate into my own identity these experiences with other cultures?" (Howard, 1999, p. 23). The answer lies in reclaiming one's own roots and connecting one's experiences with those of other cultures (Howard, 1999).

As an African American, the origins of my cultural heritage often elude my grasp. This uncertainty may explain why I feel at home on the sea or by the shore. My hometown sits on the water's edge—a predominately Black community where slaves were once deposited after their journey across the oceans to labor in fields or trade. I consider my identity strongly tied to this place, but I also feel the pull of the water calling me on a journey toward an unknown home. Perhaps this is why the Statue of Liberty, standing in the water, calls all Americans to come and acknowledge our shared national and cultural heritage. I also feel at one with her on the water, looking up at her raised torch with the promise to embrace the people and cultures of the world. On my journey into multicultural education, I have come to terms with my identity—my "Blackness," my female voice, my Southern nature—and have learned to value others' cultures equally with my own. I have also learned the value of incorporating multicultural perspectives into curriculum in order to reach students of every gender, race, and class. Teaching children about their own culture and teaching them about respecting differences are important messages I will take through walking the path of self-understanding. As Americans, we are privileged in many ways, but perhaps most privileged in the fact that our heritage is so diverse and we have the freedom to explore our unique mixture of cultures.

14. Reclaiming My Own Heritage

Julie Macomb

Reflecting on Angelou's (1997/1969) and Rothenberg's (2000) lives and their perspectives, I re-examine my own life in an effort to reclaim that part of my cultural heritage that has been shadowed. While I admire Angelou's affirmation of her Black identity despite obstacles, I struggle with Rothenberg's notion of privilege. However, and most interestingly, reading these two books provokes a deeper reflection on my own journey.

I very much enjoyed reading Maya Angelou's *I Know Why the Caged Bird Sings*. Her narrative form easily lets the reader into her world. It allows me to empathize with her struggles and personal questioning as a child. Although she grew up in a time of American history when racism was prevalent, in this book she focused on her "world," her reality. Two different cultures lived simultaneously in her town of Stamps, Arkansas—the White and the Black. Angelou understood the distinction between the two cultures and wrote about the times when the two sides clashed. One example that sticks out in my mind was when she needed a dentist, but the White doctor refused to see her. He told her grandmother, whom she called Momma, "I'd rather stick my hand in a dog's mouth than a nigger's" (p. 189).

Despite such horrifying events in Angelou's life, she did not allow herself to be defined either by being colored or by what people said about being colored. She had learned not to be ashamed of being Black. Her remarkable journey of rising above suffering and inhumanity is profoundly moving to me. What I admire about Angelou is that she was able to write about racism from her experiences, yet she didn't spend her time pointing fingers. Rather, she let her story speak for itself and let the human side of the reader feel the injustice. I particularly admire her for embracing her difference from the White world at such a young age, something I myself was not strong enough to do as a child.

Although people consider me White, I have Native American heritage. My mother is a member of the Cherokee tribe, the Wolf Clan. My maternal grandfather went to the male seminary school for Indian children in Tahlequah, Oklahoma. His dad was a member of the Cherokee Council and he remembered going to meetings with him as a young child. My grandfather grew up speaking Cherokee in his home until the government forced him and his brothers to attend the seminary school. He told my mother that he remembered his mother's screaming when the White men came to take them to the school. There, he learned to speak English. He and the others would get in trouble if they tried to speak Cherokee. This was part of the assimilation process the White government forced on the Native American people around the turn of the 20th century. My grandfather would speak some Cherokee words to my mother and her siblings, but he didn't remember enough to pass the language on to his children. Therefore, my mother's generation was the first on my grandfather's side not to have spoken Cherokee as a first language. My grandmother was also a member of the Cherokee tribe, but to my family's knowledge, she never spoke Cherokee. She took over the maternal role in her family at the age of eight due to her mother's early death. She was never properly educated in a school. In the Cherokee Community, we take our clan name from the maternal side of the family, which is why I, too, am in the Wolf Clan. The limited education of my mother's family contributed to my view that being Native American is associated with something negative. My grandparents were poor and many of my relatives appeared to have no aspirations in life.

By contrast, my dad's family appeared to be educated, middle class, and completely White. I remember one of my dad's relatives saying they thought we were related to a Kickapoo princess: If we were related to a Native American, there had to be a princess (Native American tribes don't have princesses). This is an example of how the White side of my family showed privilege and status. As a child and a teenager, I was very much into being part of the "in crowd." My parents were not wealthy, but many of my friends were.

My mother is an olive-skinned, dark-eyed, black-haired beauty. My father is the exact opposite. He is pale, blue-eyed, with blond hair as a child and light brown hair as an adult. I am a dark-haired replica of my dad. People have referred to me as Snow White because of my coloring. I have been considered "good looking" and have what society would call the best features of being White: hazel eyes, straight nose, full lips, and milky skin. I also have features of being Native American, which are not as pronounced or considered Native American by some: high forehead, high cheekbones, and dark-brown hair.

No one at school ever asked me if I was Native American, and my appearance indicates little about that part of my heritage. I hid my heritage at school. I always marked White on my standardized tests on the ethnicity section. I never mentioned anything about my family. I was embarrassed to be Native American. Somehow I got the notion that White was better, even though my parents never would have condoned that thought.

In elementary school, there was a federal "Indian Program" that provided free school supplies to students who were card-carrying, registered Native Americans. I would have been horrified if I had ever been sent down to the office to receive the supplies. What would my friends think? We weren't poor, but I had started to associate being Native American with being poor. If you had money, you wouldn't need free supplies. In addition, other students were not receiving anything free, so the free supplies would have made me stand out from the "in crowd." Societal expectations and peer pressure made me feel that if you have money, you are better. If you dress a certain way, you are better. I remember how students were looked down on if they weren't wearing the "right" kind of jeans or the Keds shoes, or didn't have a perm in their hair.

My exposure to other Native Americans, besides my mother's side of the family, was through the federally funded hospitals and clinics that were designated for Native American cardholders to get treatment. Registered Native Americans are provided free medical care, eye care, and dentistry. The closest clinic was in Tahlequah, OK, a 30-minute drive from our home. Whenever we went to the clinic, even though we had an appointment we always had to wait for what seemed like hours. Patience has never been a virtue for me. I used to beg to go to a "normal" doctor. I had looked down on people at the clinics who had to use these facilities. They weren't wearing the "right" clothes, and they all had long, dark, straight hair. Many had few teeth and looked depressed and haggard to my young eyes. They didn't look like me and I didn't want to be associated with them. I wanted to go to Dr. Waters, my dad's White dentist, in town.

I didn't start to embrace my Cherokee heritage until my teenage years. I began learning in Oklahoma history about the Trail of Tears, the Cherokee past my family hadn't told me about, and I was fascinated. I realized I had developed a sense that being White was better, and I had wrongly associated my Native American heritage with being poor. Over the years, I have come to embrace my heritage, although now, some of my own people may not accept me because I don't look Native American enough.

At the beginning of reading Rothenberg's book, *Invisible Privilege*, I did not identify with her at all. I thought she was arrogant. I thought she was trying to speak as if she understood what it felt like to be discriminated against when she clearly could only empathize. All she had was privilege, in my opinion. Looking back, I realize I have more in common with Rothenberg than I first thought. I grew up with the privilege of being "White." I hid my Native American background to appear more "accepted." I took advantage of looking White and ran with the privilege it brought. I probably sound just as arrogant as Rothenberg does when I write about how I perceived Native Americans and being part of the "in crowd." I have falsely felt like I understood minorities because I am, in part, a minority. In fact, looking White and being able to check that I am Native American helped me get my first teaching job. I was living in southern Texas at the time and I remember my White principal saying he was able to check multicultural on that year's report because I was his "token." In Oklahoma, being part Native American is not the exception, but in southern Texas, it was rare.

In my teenage years, when I learned about the atrocities against the Native American people, I started to see my ancestors in a different way. I began to understand why the people I saw at the clinics looked depressed and haggard. They and their parents had been forced through devastating cultural changes and they were trying to hold on to their customs and traditions in a White society. I had started to become more spiritual, seeking God in things, and to care less about what other people, even my friends, thought. I started to empathize with the Native American people. However, as I seemed to feel more comfortable talking about my heritage, I falsely saw myself as a product of mistreatment by the government. I wrote papers in school and spoke about the awful ways the government stole the Native American land. After all, being a card-carrying, registered Cherokee gave me the right to speak out about such things. Or so I thought at that time. My teenage years were the beginnings of discovering myself and my place in the world. I still did not fully understand my heritage, although my growth into adulthood and self-awareness furthered my journey to become who I am today.

I don't think I will ever know what it feels like to be held back by my Native American race. I have always lived the life of a privileged White female, being able to take some advantage of my minority status. I had acted like I understood minorities and often, when talking to some Black or Mexican person, had thrown into the conversation that I was Native American, thinking that linked us somehow. In reality, I was being very disrespectful. My faith in God and Jesus Christ has helped me see people as individual souls and understand that we are all made from our Maker and for the purpose of glorifying Him through our lives. The attitude I had as a child toward Native Americans revealed an elitist, Anglo-socioeconomic view of the world. Although my teenage years and further education led me to understand the circumstances of the Native American past to a certain degree, I did not truly identify with them. Now, as a woman in my thirties, I see my life for what it was: typical; typical of a spoiled, White girl. I had the privilege of looking White in an Anglo society. I had the privilege of getting an education by choice. I had the privilege of being seen as White, yet being a "token" to employers who wanted a White face while still meeting their multicultural quota. I definitely had much in common with Rothenberg and her invisible privilege. How I wish I had been strong enough and wise enough to have been more like Angelou; how I wish I had seen my Native American people for their spiritual, wonderful cultures, instead of for what my Anglo society portrayed them to be! Reading Angelou's and Rothenberg's books gives me strength and wisdom to embrace my dual heritages at a fuller and deeper level. A new stage of life is unfolding before my eyes....

Pedagogical Reflection III:
Reclaiming Roots

Nadine Olson

Who am I? Where do I belong? What makes me the person that I am? Am I a cultural being? What is my ethnicity? A large number of Americans may not be able to answer those questions easily because our modern, national cuture/society has witnessed the phenomenon of smaller ethnic groups becoming so culturally like Anglo-Americans that they also relate to Anglo-Americans, perhaps unconsciously, as their source of ethnic identity (Banks, 2006, p. 81). Various ethnic microcultures in the United States have been subsumed through an acculturation process that involves establishing a set of standards—an operating culture—for interaction and group participation in the national culture. To function successfully in a community dominated by the macroculture, ethnic minority individuals must act within the standards of behavior accepted by and deemed appropriate by the members of that shared culture (Olson, 1989, pp. 32–39). Since the social solidarity of the group is enhanced if members know and share the same language, public beliefs, feelings and operating values, ethnic minorities may even suppress their own language, values, and cultural behaviors in order to operate effectively within the dominant culture.

In analyzing multicultural realities in the United States and in studying the diversity of the population in general, "[T]he appropriate question to ask is not whether an individual is ethnic, but to what extent he or she is ethnic" (Banks, 2006, p. 80). Two essays in this section demonstrate the dynamic nature of individual and group cultures in America. Prevett, in her essay "Growing Up Native American in a White Society," describes the process of internalizing the standards, values, and perspectives of the dominant cultural group in which she grew up. Her autobiographical narrative movingly relates how the strong sense of Native American pride which her grandmother transmitted to her as a young child was gradually eroded by her experiences in school. Not wanting to be singled out as "different," or to be called the derogatory names that her school textbooks associated with Native peoples, Prevett felt embarrassed by her heritage. She began to perceive and judge other Native Americans by the economic yardstick that her White classmates used; her identification with her own ethnic group became weaker as she sought entrance into White society by adopting their operating culture. Nevertheless, Prevett's narrative ends on a positive note in that she was able to recover a sense of cultural pride and to reclaim her roots. The change in school system policies that brought Native arts and dance to the forefront thus acted to enhance the survival of her ethnic culture and enabled Prevett to participate in passing on that cultural heritage to the next generation. She reclaimed what Banks (2006) would refer to as her "ethnicity," a "psychological identification" with her ethnic group (p. 81).

In her essay "Reclaiming My Own Heritage," Macomb, of mixed Cherokee and White descent, recounts denying her Native American ethnic heritage because she was able to—she did not carry strong indicators of Native American physical traits, nor did she or her family members speak any Cherokee. She adopted the operating culture of her White classmates, dressing in the "right" fashion and curling her hair. As a teenager, Macomb, like Prevett, had a crystallizing moment in school when she encountered Oklahoma History and read about the Trail of Tears. She adopted then what might be considered a somewhat ecopolitical (Banks, 2006, p. 80) sense of ethnicity, and saw herself as a "product of mistreatment by the government." It is only as an adult that Macomb now reflects on her privileged, "White" upbringing and better understands how to move more easily and more authentically between her Native American heritage and the White group culture/society in which she lives.

Both Prevett and Macomb point out the importance of schooling in our pluralistic American society and of the role that educators play in helping all students to learn about and to value their ethnic backgrounds. A teacher's ignorance can be detrimental to a child's cultural development, Prevett notes. She stresses the significance of a teacher getting to know her students as ethnic beings, and relates her own commitment to meeting her students' families and learning their beliefs and cultural history firsthand, through conversation. Nowell writes passionately of "Embracing One's Own Culture and Respecting Differences," in part a response to her visit to the Greenwood Cultural Center in Tulsa, Oklahoma. She rejects the outdated, biological construct of race in favor of a sociocultural view of human diversity. By reclaiming her own African American roots as well as her roots as a strong, Southern woman, Nowell feels empowered to teach others how to move beyond racism to respect. In her view, one can only become an effective multicultural educator after first discovering and embracing one's own ethnicity and culture.

The essays presented here deal with reclaiming minority cultural roots, but they challenge me to begin to explore my own Scandinavian cultural heritage more deeply. Both my maternal and paternal great-grandparents and their children passed through Ellis Island in the late 1800s as immigrants from Norway and Denmark and settled in Minnesota. The families soon left the

Scandinavian enclaves in the north to homestead in Nebraska. There it became imperative to learn English quickly, to become economically independent, to form political alliances with immigrant neighbors from other ethnic groups, and to establish new community traditions and practices that helped to bind together a diverse pioneer population that needed to survive in a harsh, new environment. There was little time for grandparents to pass on more than a phrase or two of spoken Norwegian or Danish language, or to practice the music, dance, folk art or other cultural customs of their ancestors. Since my parents and siblings don't carry any physical markers of our heritage—no one in my immediate family has blonde hair and blue eyes—today, the only vestiges of our Scandinavian ethnicity are a few traditional holiday foods.

A career language teacher, I know that studying Norwegian and Danish will be one of the best entrances to learn about my ethnic personhood, for acquiring a second language can expand even further the world views that are embodied in my first language, English. I also understand that a wealth of cultural perspectives can be gained through the study of folk culture, and I am reminded of a technique for learning about folk culture while communicating with native speaker informants. G. Morain (n.d.) coined the name *culture quest* for an activity that asks language students to seek out native informants of the target linguaculture and interview them about their lives and language. (The culture quest can also be conducted in English if informants are fluent in English as a second language.) The study of folk culture reveals many of the components of culture identified by Banks as elements that are useful for interpreting our culturally diverse students' behaviors and for teaching about microcultural groups in America: values and standards of behavior, languages and dialects, nonverbal communication strategies, and perspectives and worldviews (pp.73–77).

Areas of folk culture that are ripe for research include: 1) *how to teach wisdom:* investigating the meaning of common proverbs and folk sayings; investigating manners and social behaviors, such as how to treat your elders; 2) *how to communicate without words:* investigating the use of gestures and facial expressions; investigating the interpretation of signs, signals, and designs; 3) *how to entertain:* investigating games, riddles, tricks; investigating legends, ghost stories, or jokes; investigating songs and dances; and 4) *how to make or do something:* investigating how to cook a secret sauce; how to cure a cold, the hiccups, insomnia; how to celebrate a birthday or other special occasion; how to predict the weather, the future, good and bad luck; how to build something; how to perform a task such as stitching a quilt or branding a steer; or how to create beauty by painting, whittling, or composing.

Personal investigation through face-to-face interviews with members of other ethnic groups will lead students to gain insights into how aspects of folk culture reflect the themes and values of a society. As students compare and contrast their own folk culture to that of the target culture, they will understand both ethnic groups better, and may recognize that individuals can move more easily between their microculture and the society's macroculture because of cultural standards that are agreed upon and shared. It is even possible that individual students will recognize familiar-sounding descriptions of beliefs, values, traditions and meanings from their own heritages, enabling them to reclaim the roots of a family ethnic culture they previously knew little about. It is in the process of discovery that we re-establish the cultural pride that will give us strength to identify psychologically with our ethnic group and will enable us to pass on to our children the values and perspectives that make us who we are.

Part IV

Global Perspectives

15. Out of Place: Teaching Arabic as a Foreign Language in the U.S.

Azza Ahmad

As new immigrants from cultures different than the mainstream culture in the US, we are living beyond our comfort zone DAILY. It is usually considered "brave" for individuals with the mainstream cultural background to step out of their comfort zone once in a life time. Using that frame, we ought to be "heroic" simply by being new immigrants. We have a lot to contribute to the world—especially now in this era of globalization, so to speak, when migration is becoming the norm, not the exception any more. When a community listens to strangers and their "heroic" surviving stories, this community will survive and thrive on diversity. I hope that would be our near future. (Professor Xin Li, California State University-Long Beach, personal communication)

As an Arab-American immigrant woman, I have always been interested in reading about immigrants' experiences of living in different cultures. The opening quote is from a personal email exchange between Dr. Li and me in the Spring of 2006. I read her book, *The Tao of Life Stories* (2002), where she shares her journey as a Chinese immigrant and what it means to live in two different cultures. I was very inspired by the messages of her book and decided to contact her about my admiration and what I have learned from her. Although we come from two different cultural backgrounds, we both found a bridge built through words.

Sometimes I wonder if being a stranger to the mainstream culture—being out of place—motivates people to develop their intercultural understanding and global awareness. They learn to be patient and persistent, as well as open to others. Their stories are tales of engaging in a continuous dialogical exchange between themselves and others. As an educator, I am intrigued by the pedagogical implications of these stories. In order for students to become democratic and global citizens in the 21st century, they need to understand what it means to live in two or more cultures. Furthermore, these stories offer teachers inspiration for becoming healers who encourage their students to discover and reconstruct themselves within caring and understanding relationships. The following story is my attempt to briefly share my learning and teaching experiences that helped me travel through an in-between space for international dialogue.

The Beginning

Perhaps my undergraduate studies in mass communication at the University of Cairo in Egypt, with the focus on journalism and broadcasting, were the starting point for me to experience the process of cultivating multicultural awareness and promoting global consciousness. I had the opportunity to be an intern at one of the major newspapers in the Middle East. I attended the daily meetings where it was determined what would appear in the paper the following day. Through that experience, I realized that news stories are under the control of journalists or editors who select and choose to write about certain stories in a certain way. Sometimes I was able to participate in the discussions about what to add or delete from certain stories. During the process, I was wondering if we were really seeing the world through others' lenses. How can we be certain that these lenses present accurate, and not stereotyped, views? I began to actively seek multiple sources and listen to different perspectives.

My husband and I decided to come to the U.S. to pursue graduate studies in 1987. We were so excited about coming to the "Land of Dreams" where everyone had equal opportunities. We were imagining a melting pot society, where immigrant people of different cultures, races and religions unite and develop a single, multi-ethnic society. However, the first time I was asked to fill out an official form, I was totally surprised and confused by the ethnicity question and I was not sure where to locate myself. I am not White, Black, Hispanic, or Asian and I was unsure about what was meant by the other options, so I put "human being."

Although we enjoyed being members of graduate schools, we were also confronted by the people's ignorance or misconceptions of Middle Eastern culture. Their misconceptions were directly related to the media's negative representations of the Arab world as a place of deserts and camels, as well as of arbitrary cruelty and barbarism. These images included the objectifying of Arab women as belly dancers and harem girls, and Arab men as violent terrorists and oil "sheiks." After my twenty years of living in the U.S. as an Arab American, I believe that no other group has been more vilified in the American media than Arabs and Muslims. Children's cartoons, television series like *Charlie's Angels*, and films like *The Siege* all repeat the negative portrayal of Arabs. Arab American parents have to shield their children from watching these programs. However, their peers at school watch them, and as a result there has been an ever-growing pressure on Arab and Muslim children to deny their cultural identity.

A few months before my graduation as a master's student, the September 11 attacks occurred. There is no doubt that September 11, 2001 will forever be remembered as one of the worst days the nation has faced since World War II. Unfortunately, the deep shock and anger over this national tragedy and the grief over lost lives were compounded by a rush to blame Arabs collectively for the attacks.

This situation was similar to what Ted Aoki (2005) described during WWII when Pearl Harbor was attacked and Japanese Canadians immediately became the target of resentment and discrimination. Aoki, who later became a well-known educational scholar, had a bachelor of commerce degree from the University of British Columbia, but the only job he could find at the time was to work in the sugar beet fields. After the war, Aoki was not permitted to live within a certain city due to his ethnicity as a Japanese Canadian. He considered himself a good Japanese Canadian citizen who was willing to help and serve his country; however, the mainstream culture did not consider him in the same way. The mainstream culture could not perceive beyond Aoki's "whatness," reflected in his inherited Japanese look, into his "beingness," which reflects his constructed Japanese Canadian identity. I can imagine how difficult it must have been for Japanese Canadians during that wartime. The wartime experiences of Japanese Canadians have occupied my thoughts since the time of September 11 as I have witnessed how Arab Americans in the United States have suddenly been put into a position to defend themselves, their families, and their status as Americans.

"Why Do They Hate Us?"

One day I was watching a TV program on Nickelodeon about children's re-flections on the September 11th attacks. A young girl asked a serious question: "Why do they hate us?" This was a question that resonated with many people at that time. I tried to analyze this question. First, the interrogative particle "why" implies that there are reasons behind this kind of hatred act. What could be these reasons? Was it really because the Americans enjoy more freedom than the attackers have in their countries? If that were the reason, why didn't they attack Switzerland, for example, or another free democratic country? Secondly, I analyzed the use of the pronoun "they." To whom does "they" refer: to the attackers? To all Arabs or to all Muslims? Thirdly, I considered the use of "us." Does "us" refer to the American people or American policy or American government?

Although all these questions seem direct and simple, only an in-depth un-derstanding and awareness of historical, linguistic, cultural, and sociopolitical aspects of the Middle East can lead to enlightened answers. What I can perceive from these questions is that the American public is mostly uninformed about many Middle Eastern issues. I think that the media has played an important role in shaping public opinion and has contributed to this information gap. For many Americans, the mainstream media is one of the most powerful sources for learning about what is happening in the world. As an Arab American who has spent quite some time here and quite some time in the Middle East, I can see how the media here in the U.S. create negative stereotypes towards the people of Middle Eastern descent.

The Role of Dialogue

At about that same time, I completed my master's thesis, which highlighted the women's movements in many parts of the Middle East and the misrepresentation of the portrayal of Arab women in the media. I was encouraged by some of my professors to present my study in some of their undergraduate courses as a way to increase students' awareness about global issues. I always started my presentations by asking students to write on small index cards the answers to such questions as "What comes to your mind first when you hear the word 'Middle East'?" "What do you think about the gender roles in the Middle East?" I then collected the cards, continued my presentation, answered students' questions, and finally concluded with the fun part of reading the students' answers on the cards. Overall, they were all wonderful experiences for everyone. I enjoyed most those presentations where I was completely involved and engaged in the discussion, and I could experience the feeling of flow in those classes. I loved the students' questions, as they helped me to have more insights about my own culture. I felt like I was in a different world with new, undefined boundaries.

A wonderful professor in the history department noticed the positive interaction between the students and me in one of her classes. She suggested introducing an Arabic language and culture program at our university and encouraged me to think seriously about designing that course. I found her idea fascinating, and this became a career that I desired to pursue. It could be a great course for fostering the international understandings and dialogues that are essential to promoting peace. Also, at that difficult time, the tension that I had experienced guided me to think of how to encourage students to search, explore and develop their own understandings of the Middle Eastern cultures. I thought about how I could encourage my students to be more aware and familiar with the Arabic culture in a way that could lessen the hostility and fear between the two groups.

I further asked myself several questions. How have I developed a positive attitude towards American people? Why do I have a feeling that I accept them more than they accept me? Do I perceive the American culture differently from how the Middle Eastern people perceive it? Why? Aoki (2005) argues that living in the space between two different cultures has provided him with a hybrid identity. This notion of the in-between space is particularly helpful for me in rethinking about possibilities that international and intercultural dialogues can open up, even during times of conflict and tension, for both individuals and communities.

After this analysis, I realized that accepting other cultures requires some effort, whether through reading their literatures, observing people in their daily lives, or immersing oneself in another cultural setting. Human beings, no matter where they come from, share many commonalties and they also have differences that demand respect. However, this understanding cannot be attained without being willing to learn about others, without communicating through languages that are mutually understandable, or without intitiating constructive dialogues between different cultures.

Freire (2004) stressed the power of dialogue in developing critical thinking, not only about educational systems, but also about different aspects of our lives. Dialogue can build bridges and create connections between human beings. He listed five elements to develop such a dialogue: love, humility, faith, hope, and critical thinking. True dialogue exists when the dialoguers have a profound love for the world and for people, a humility and mutual respect for the other's thoughts and beliefs without having to adopt them, a faith in humans' ability to be more human, a hope that injustice can be overcome, and the willingness to engage in critical thinking.

> Because dialogue is an encounter among men [*sic*] who name the world, it must not be a situation where some men name on behalf of others. It is an act of creation; it must not serve as a crafty instrument for the domination of one man by another. (Freire, 2004, p. 126)

Paulo Freire's philosophy of dialogue for critical education has been influential in my thinking about creating a space for dialogue. Such a dialogue encourages a constructive teacher-student relationship that allows the birth of new thoughts and situates the teacher as a learner.

Initiating an Arabic Program

All of the previous thoughts, emotions, and situations paved the way for the birth of a new idea, which was introducing an Arabic language program at Oklahoma State University-Stillwater. I proposed and discussed the importance of having such a program with the university's administration. After several interviews and meetings, the administration agreed to try it first and see how students would respond. The class was offered through the university's extension program. In the Fall semester of 2003, the first Arabic language class was opened at OSU. I spent the whole spring and summer that year promoting and planning that class, including searching for the best textbooks, attending workshops, and designing the curriculum. My office was located in the Department of Foreign Languages and Literatures, which was my academic affiliation, but financially the university's Outreach Program was in charge. Most of my colleagues in the department were very friendly and helpful; a few people, however, were unwilling to communicate.

The program flourished, with large student enrollments. Our first class was covered by the local and state media. Students were interviewed to reflect upon their experiences and most of them were very excited about taking the class. They also went beyond the class and consulted me on the most useful study abroad programs, and some students visited the Middle Eastern countries. Within the first year of the Arabic program, five of my students went to Egypt and Jordan; in the second year, four students joined immersion programs in Beirut, Egypt, and Morocco. The purpose of these programs is to highlight the realities of cultural diversity, pluralism, and the common heritage in the region from both historical and modern perspectives in order to promote intercultural dialogues.

The course was designed for students with no prior knowledge of Arabic. From the first day of class, students engaged in functional activities such as practicing Arabic greetings and introducing themselves. The five skills of listening, speaking, reading, writing, and cultural awareness were practiced to varying degrees. When I speak about cultural awareness, I mean both the big "C," Culture—including literature, arts, and poetry—and the small "c," culture—including gestures, body language, commonly used proverbs, and idiomatic expressions. One of my main objectives was encouraging my students to conduct a dialogue between their native culture and the Arab culture. Dialogue, based on mutual respect and understanding, stressed our commonalties, acknowledged our differences, respected our identities, and helped us learn the art of living constructively with differences. For that purpose, I invited guest speakers from the Arab world and encouraged students to practice their language with them and to ask them questions. Part of the course requirement was for students to study and present their findings about cultural aspects related to the Arabic language. The cultural presentations of my students inspired me to consider my own culture from many different perspectives. I learned as much from them as they learned from me.

When I started this program, almost everyone from both cultures was skeptical. From the American side, some were skeptical about me teaching such a class as an Arab American, female instructor. From the Arabian side, some were skeptical that I was teaching Americans the Arabic language to help Americans use it against the Arab people. That tension between both sides did not discourage me, but rather motivated me to persist with more efforts to create an in-between space that challenges the either/or position and brings movement across cultures into play. Students who were invited into this space responded positively. In the spring semester of 2004, one of my students, a political science major, said in an interview published by the *Daily O'Collegian*:

> Until two different cultures can communicate equally between each other with full understanding and respect of [sic] each other, they're never going to be able to get along… It's not just a language barrier, it's a cultural barrier for sure. (Quoted in Zavadny, 2004, p. 7)

This statement sums up the purpose of the class. It also indicates our students' ability to understand deeper meanings of language and connect their experiences with curriculum in a new way.

Teaching Arabic as a Lived Curriculum

In general, research seems to support the efforts of teachers of foreign languages to discover and respond to learners' needs and goals when planning instruction (Dörnyei & Csizer, 1998). This is similar to Aoki's (2005) notion of a lived curriculum that connects pedagogy with students' lived experience. I used this approach for teaching Arabic.

On the first day of the class, I started by telling students that Arabic is a widely spoken language, spoken by over 160 million people, in an area extending from the Arabian Gulf in the East to the Atlantic Ocean in the West. Also, Arabic is spoken by the three million people of Arabic origin living in the United States and Canada. Although Arabic is not easy to learn and requires a consistent effort, many English speakers have learned it and some have become well-known scholars of the Arabic language. It is rewarding to learn Arabic not only for building cultural connections and bridges with a large population of the world, but also for seeking promising professional careers. In this way, students were encouraged to make meaningful connections.

According to Alosh (2000), teachers in a functional approach must deal with means of conveying abstract knowledge as well as trying to develop in learners the ability to use this knowledge. In my classes, students were strongly encouraged to use the language through interactions. During this process they recalled vocabulary, practiced conversation, and negotiated meanings in order to make sense of the language. These practices usually brought a lot of fun to our class. Students surprised me with outcomes that exceeded my expectations. Sometimes students asked me about things outside of my lesson plan. Such initiatives brought me much delight, and I tried as much as I could to adapt my lesson plans experientially so a lived curriculum was created by both students and the instructor.

I left the program two years ago in order to pursue my doctoral degree in teaching foreign languages at another university. The Arabic language program at OSU is continuing to grow and has expanded to include intermediate levels of language proficiency. The American Council on the Teaching of Foreign Languages (ACTFL) declared the year 2005 as the year of languages. This initiative highlighted the need for people around the world to communicate with each other across differences. The ACTFL vision statement reads (2005), "All Americans should be proficient in at least one language and culture in addition to English. For this reason, foreign language education must be part of the core curriculum and be treated as central to the education of all children." My students embraced this initiative ahead of its time. Almost all of my students from that first Arabic class have visited the Middle East at least once and they came back with wonderful experiences and great insights. These trips were not necessarily free from conflicts each time, but educative in the sense that participants began to understand how people in different parts of the world live. I told my students: Welcome to the new world, an out-of-place world leading you to find your own paths.

16. Conversation and Globalization: An International Student Advisor's Intercultural Path

Jon Smythe

To be teachers means re-shaping our values as we ourselves are being re-shaped by the newness of a changing world. What we fight for or against continues to change as struggles and conflicts of the world unfold in our place of call and response.
—Dwayne Huebner, 1999, p. 381

Huebner's insightful comment indirectly re-emphasizes the role of teacher as both teacher and learner, continually involved in re/shaping both personal and curricular values in response to the call of a changing world. But shifting one's value orientation in the face of changing circumstances is neither automatic nor easy. It is a messy process involving work, struggle, at times pain, and, of course, the openness and willingness to learn from and with others. To learn from others—especially from students themselves—can prove challenging when the expectation is that the teacher is the expert who must have all of the answers. It is also challenging from the standpoint that efficiency, rather than the exploration of our shared and contested reality, has become the gold standard in the American educational system. In this paper, I go off the beaten path to explore an increasingly complex global reality—a complicated terrain located at the intersection of cultures involving notions of identity, self, and Other. In so doing, I find myself on a shared intercultural path requiring me to speak a new language—the language of conversation—in pursuit of a more dynamic, informed, multi-layered, global sensibility.

Certainly, teaching and learning in the midst of today's unprecedented globalization, which Matus and McCarthy (2003) define as the "intensification and rapidity of movement and migration of people, ideas, and economic and cultural capital across national boundaries" (p. 73), poses great challenges to educators. In the United States, the Center for Immigration Studies reports that the nation's immigrant population (including undocumented immigrants) has reached an estimated all-time high of 37.9 million with 10.3 million of those immigrants arriving within the last seven years (Camarota, 2007), not to mention the estimated 582,984 non-immigrants (Institute of International Education, 2007a) who entered the United States to attend an institution of higher education during the 2006/2007 school year or the 223,534 Americans (Institute of International Education, 2007b) who left the U.S. to participate in study abroad programs during that same period. These figures also do not reflect those individuals who travel in and out of the U.S. for their own enjoyment, nor do they account for the virtual tourism made possible through the surge of such technological advances as cell phones, digital cameras, and the Internet. The world, it seems, is shrinking.

For Smith (2003), such an import and export of people and ideas, aided by the proliferation of technology, creates a tension between global and local self-understanding, an understanding "fraught with various new kinds of identity crises" including "eroding senses of national identity" and involving "difficult questions about epistemological authority, about how knowledge is produced, represented, and circulated, and perhaps especially about the auspices of curriculum work" (p. 36). From my perspective, however, difficult questions about "epistemological authority" rarely get asked and "crises of identity" often lead to paralyzing fear or misguided anger. These feelings, though painful at times, should not be ignored, but used as a wake-up call to rethink our selves and reflect on our curricula.

My own wake-up call from the world at large came early in my role as an international student advisor for a large community college in the Midwest. Asked to develop materials for an international student orientation, I gladly accepted the invitation. Up to that point, I had been an English language tutor, an advertising sales executive, a Peace Corps volunteer (penance for being an advertising sales executive), and an English as a Second Language instructor. Certainly, then, with my experience in international education and the communication arts, I thought developing these materials would prove no difficult task.

I created a handout designed to explain some of the differences in expectations between the American educational system and other school systems around the world. Of course, in the interest of efficiency, I couldn't exactly compare the U.S. system to all the systems of all the other countries in the world, so I created a table with two columns, one labeled "The U.S. System" and the other labeled "Some Other Systems"—thus presenting the United States in clear contrast to all other countries, which had been collapsed into a generic, amorphous mush. I filled those columns with a variety of cross-cultural comparisons based on my overseas teaching experiences, teacher or advisor lore, and popular advisement manuals designed to assist in explaining cultural attributes of certain student groups. For example, I had noted that some international students seemed surprised at the clothing worn by American students and instructors, so one of the items I included was that "in the U.S., students and teachers may be dressed informally" and that "in other systems, students and teachers may be dressed more formally."

While these points seem innocuous, other information was a bit more contestable such as that in the U.S., students "earn" grades and in other systems it may be common to "bargain" for grades. I had heard from a number of instructors and other advisors and had read in a number of advising manuals that certain international student groups were prone to bargaining for grades. So, at the time, I thought it was an important difference to bring to the foreground. It hadn't occurred to me at the time that much of the information I gathered and perpetuated was from a subjective, Anglo-American point-of-view or that, because my educational experience was largely in relation to international students, I had little way of knowing—as I do now after also advising American students—that some American students take bargaining for grades to a completely new level. I have also come to realize that there are many ways of bargaining for grades and that those forms are socio-culturally defined. In short, from a cultural standpoint, there are socially acceptable forms of bargaining and those that are not.

In any event, I used my handout in several new international student orientations. Each time the students sat passively as I read each comparison—with very little discussion and no debate. Of course, I made the disclaimer that some of the information was not pertinent in every situation but that examining these differences could bring various issues to light for "us" to think about. It was not until I was asked to present on international student issues at a faculty meeting that I received my wake-up call. I thought it would be helpful to include some of the information I had created for the orientation in my faculty presentation—especially the educational system comparison handout. The faculty seemed to appreciate the information I provided and shared their international student "horror" stories with great dramatic emphasis. A few days after the presentation, one of the professors who was also a friend pulled me aside to mention that one of the other faculty, who was an international person himself, had mentioned that my presentation was, well, "racist." My friend assured me that none of the other faculty or administrators sensed any trace of racism in the materials I presented, but she felt that I should be aware of this particular faculty member's perception.

I have not seen the instructor since the presentation, and although I have never had a chance to discuss the matter directly with him, I have definitely felt the sting and the weight of the suggestion that my presentation was racist. What was interesting to me was that none of my American colleagues saw any trace of racism; that such a pronouncement came from the only international person in the room, the very population I was trying to "serve"! I was certainly embarrassed and knew that I would never use the document again—even though I thought some discussion of differing educational expectations could be useful. This situation made me ask questions: How do we "teach" difference without insulting or speaking for others? How do we broaden curriculum to include different ways of thinking and being in the world without fixing the world into simplistic categories? And, how do we engage others respectfully in ongoing conversations about our separate and shared subjective realities?

The situation, though seemingly negative, provided a creative opportunity for me to rethink how and why I had developed my orientation materials in the way that I had. Ultimately, I decided that I needed to shift my position from that of teacher/expert/speaker who provides answers for and about students without their input, to that of learner/facilitator/listener who asks students for their perspectives so that we can develop new knowledge in concert. According to Wang (2004), such a "repositioning" requires that the "subjugated perspectives of the marginal members of the classroom get recognized" (p. 77). However, it is often difficult for "mainstream students and teachers, given that they often (unconsciously) feel threatened by socially constructed *differences* [emphasis in original]..." (Wang, 2004, p. 77). In other words, any perspective that offers a different view on the mainstream construction of reality or any shift that requires a change in positionality (and indeed the power structure) from subject/object to subject/subject can be problematic because the "traditional central position of being the subject objectifying a minority other...is no longer secure" (Wang, 2004, p. 77). But Wang argues that it is the mutual respect for the differences of others, rather than a focus on universality, that can open up positive and generative learning contexts for both teacher and students. She suggests that "the world is multiplied because of difference" (p. 132) rather than being reduced to a stagnant commonality. Therefore, I needed to develop a new orientation to limit my voice (limit, but not eliminate it) in order to share the power and responsibility for co-creating knowledge together with students and to recognize our differences as the dynamic springboard for opening up multiple spaces for mutual respect and mutual learning.

For my revamped orientation, I also wanted to enlarge the conversation to include other perspectives that would likely intertwine with the new international students' perspectives at some point. I invited faculty members and administrators to the orientation so that they could share their expectations of students, and I wanted them to hear what students expected of them. I also invited international students who had already been at my school for at least one semester who could share their experiences as well.

The change in the orientation was immediate. For instance, when I asked students about their impressions of the U.S. or Americans (instead of telling them), the students were no longer silent or passive. Since asking this question in several orientations, students have offered up a number of responses such as:

"Americans are very warm and friendly compared to the people in my country."

"Americans aren't very friendly and they don't want to get to know you."

"Americans are friendly but in a strange way. They always ask 'How are you?' but they don't really want to know and they want you to be happy all the time."

"Americans like to hug too much, but I don't like to be hugged."

"In my country, people are always hugging, but Americans can get offended if you hug them."

"People don't hug in my country, but it doesn't bother me and I understand why people hug here."

By listening to these multiple and, at times, contradictory impressions that students are forming, it becomes clear that the U.S., too, does not fit into any simplistic category, but can mean many things to many people as they build personal relationships with American culture through their lived experiences.

I have also asked students to share their fears about being an international student in the United States. The answers to this request are usually more difficult to hear. While some students are fearful about their language skills and others are worried about making good grades and passing tests, a fear that almost always comes up is a fear of racism, of being stereotyped, and that teachers and administrators will fail to see or understand their individual needs. Although it is impossible for me to offer assurances that the students will not experience racism or stereotyping, I can listen to their concerns and I can ask myself (and others) those difficult questions of how it is that "we" come to know or make subjective judgments of the world. Such a shift then creates a new relationship in the teaching/learning dynamic and way of being in the world, in that "one's own culture no longer is the baseline against which normality is established, permitting an enlightened cultural relativism" because "once one's own taken-for-grantedness is seen as strange, it can be much easier to see those who are different as normal" (David & Ayouby, 2005, p. 19).

Through opening up conversations with students, I was able to learn from the students' perspectives and, in turn, they learned that if I could pose the question, I could also be trusted to "hear" the answer. By adopting a position of "not knowing" and "asking," I was able to open what Gough (2003) refers to as an "interstitial transnational space," a negotiated space where multiple "contrasting rationalities" can work together constructively rather than a singular perspective displacing another based on notions of cultural superiority (pp. 66—67). For me, the creation of an "interstitial transnational space" required me to de-center my own socio-cultural understandings so that other voices could be heard and new knowledge could be co-produced in a shared space.

While assuming a position of "not knowing" and engaging others in conversation in order to explore the diversity of thought and experience within the educational sphere may seem simplistic and rather easy to achieve, often it is not. In my experience in higher education, it is neither common nor easy to engage students in meaningful conversation, nor is it easy to hear difficult knowledge in response. Both students and instructors seem to prefer to keep each other at a distance. Instructors complain to me about students; students complain to me about instructors. Sometimes it appears that they rarely communicate with one another. Perhaps this is partly because:

> Conversation is not simply talking. It is talking and listening. It demands internalization of what the other says and reworking one's own thought and being. It requires a willingness to give of one's self and to receive from the other, and an eagerness to bring the I and the Thou together in a significant act of relationship and living (Huebner, 1999, p. 68).

For educators, shifting one's position to a more equitable and ethical relationship with students also involves relinquishing sole epistemological authority for the creation/production of knowledge or, as Huebner (1999) suggests, teaching "in a way that [students] become freer by using knowledge, rather than embedded in new cultural chains" (p. 39).

In my role as international student advisor, I am often viewed as the international student expert and am expected to know the needs and interests of international students. At the beginning of my career, I was a bit shocked to find that well-intending faculty members or administrators called on me to answer questions on behalf of international students without ever speaking to the students directly, as if I alone were the arbiter of truth regarding those students. Imagine the absurdity of a White male faculty member speaking with a White male advisor on the phone attempting to determine why a Japanese student wasn't, in the faculty member's view, "behaving very Japanese."

After many similar situations, I am no longer surprised to find that when asked to speak on international student issues at various meetings, what the participants are really after are simple recipes for dealing with international students without having to question themselves, their subjectivity, their epistemological authority, or their motives within the teaching/learning encounter. They want to know that international students fit into neatly defined categories so that they may anticipate behavior rather than engage the student in front of them. They become frustrated when I explain that I don't "know" what international students think, want, or need, and they become even more frustrated when I suggest that it is their task to investigate, to become vulnerable, to engage students in conversation, to ask students what they think instead of telling them what to think, and to listen. But this seems to be a "non-answer."

There is something more comforting in "thinking," for example, that all Asian students are polite, shy, and studious, and avoid looking directly into the eyes of an authority figure—earning Asian students the weighty title of "model minority." Weighty in the sense that when Asian students don't live up to the stereotype (when they don't behave "very Japanese," for example) they are judged especially harshly as abnormal rather than as complex and as uniquely human as other students. Many people seem surprised, for instance, when I tell them that I work with Asian students who are not polite, who are not good at math, and who have no difficulty looking me in the eye to ask uncomfortable personal questions.

My goal here is not to portray Asian students negatively, but rather to point out that it is impossible to pre-determine students' thoughts, feelings, or behaviors based on popular cultural projections that avoid the complicated work of getting to know students as both products of their cultures and their individual lived experiences. Without engaging students in ongoing and mean-ingful conversation, it is also exceedingly difficult to know how students relate to their own culture, which parts of their culture they embrace or reject, and how they will react at the intersection of cultures as they choose to embrace and reject parts of multiple cultures. An intercultural, conversational approach to curriculum takes into account that cultures are ever-changing and that the fluidity of dialogue among conversation participants provides a means to ex-plore and respond to shifts in cultural understanding and personal experience.

Although inviting conversation into curriculum may be inconvenient, time-consuming, and messy, Huebner (1999) concludes that "if man [*sic*] does not learn to converse with those who surround him and impinge upon him, then he must find other ways of dealing with them; either ignoring them or turning them into objects of use or control" (p. 81). Certainly, examples exist on both the local and the global stages of how a unilateral non-dialogic approach results in misunderstanding, dehumanization, conflict, and violence. Do educators seek to perpetuate this violence? Ignore it? Interrupt it? One of the current mantras sung to the tune of educational crisis in the American school system is that educators must prepare students for "global competition" (especially with China and India), thus pitting the U.S. against the rest of the world once again. Let's imagine that "we," as educators, follow a different path, an intercultural path that embraces the flow of communication and rejects the promotion of fear and educational crises as its motivating force. What if we were to speak of the need for "global participation," "global cooperation," and "global conversa-tion?" What if we as educators invited the Other, non-mainstream voices into curriculum and more importantly, perhaps, into the decision-making process?

As citizens of a new global reality, I suggest that a more enlightened peda-gogical and educational relationship works in tandem with, rather than against, global interests. Just what those interests are cannot be decided by one country, one person, or one cultural group, but must be discussed from a variety of perspectives on a global scale. While conversation is not a cure-all in the pursuit of peaceful coexistence, it does provide possibilities for rethinking both our selves and our curricula. It can also open up new potentialities for working through unsettling fear, identity crises, or the desire to control others as we take our first tentative steps on intercultural pathways in order to greet the world as it arrives on our front doorsteps in the form of globalization.

17. Cultivating Global Consciousness: An Educator's Journey

Ann Marie Malloy

U nderstanding global consciousness presents serious challenges for American educators, especially after the tragedy of September 11, 2001. How do we create a learning environment in the midst of crisis to promote global civility, dialogue, and interconnectedness? I have been committed to teaching for global awareness and consciousness for over twenty years in a community college. From my experience, study, and reflections, I have developed eight steps—not fixed but fluid—for cultivating global consciousness. As we move through these interconnected and evolving steps, circling and spiraling in our awareness and understanding, our capacities for new insights expand, our courage and humility grow, and our connectedness with others who are different from us is strengthened. In the following I narrate my own journey of cultivating global consciousness through these steps, not intending to provide a prescriptive model but to initiate a much-needed educational dialogue on global issues.[1]

Experiential Awakening

My story began in 1987 as I was just starting my career in college teaching while completing a certification program in lay ministry through my Catholic diocese. There, I was introduced to Fowler's *Stages of Faith* (1981) by a female theologian. I recognized that the more mature stages of faith described by Fowler were reflected in the film *Becket* (Wallis, 1964) and started asking my students to analyze the cinematic story of the life of Thomas Becket using Fowler's faith stages. This proved to be a challenging project for the students because they tended to think about faith as something you have rather than as a process of becoming.

At the same time, engagement with global affairs became increasingly important to me and my colleagues in the arts and humanities as we began to change our approach to teaching the humanities. We revised our curriculum to include cultures outside the traditional Euro-American culture in order to expand the perspectives of the students in our classrooms. If learning is "the extraction, from confusion, of meaningful patterns" (Hart, 1998, p. 127), we decided that the confusion of information should be more inclusive if it was going to result in patterns of thinking that would be relevant to the future. We were no longer satisfied with African, Asian, South American, Native American, and other non-Western cultures being reduced to sidebars or endnotes to Western civilization and, as a result, we adopted a global "encounter and re-sponse" approach to the academic study of cultures. These attempts to negoti-ate the expressions of cultures beyond the Eurocentric were causing each of us to re-examine assumptions about canons, aesthetics, the nature of teaching and learning, the Socratic method, dualism, wisdom, and our educational roles. It was confusing, messy, and meaningful all at the same time. I began to call this beginning stage of global awareness "Experiential Awakening."

Interactive Comprehending

My work with the students affirmed repeatedly that the experiences of life and artistic expression were only the beginning of learning. Like many other teachers, I was trained in Bloom's taxonomy (Bloom, Mesia, & Krathwohl, 1964). But when my art appreciation students had trouble with modern abstract art, I looked to Edwards' *Drawing on the Right Side of the Brain* (1986) for a defini-tion of the creative process and drawing exercises that could address aesthetic creativity and its relationship with scientific methodologies.

As I used some of Edwards' drawing exercises to help the students under-stand the expressive qualities of line in abstract art, I began to realize from their drawings that the descriptions of Fowler, Bloom, and Edwards were missing something. They were defining process through foundational building blocks which did not really communicate the energy that I was seeing between the lines and spaces of my students' drawings. In other words, the sense of motion within the steps and stages was not being adequately addressed. So I began to refer to the stages of meaning-making as double-worded gerunds, using verb forms to suggest a sense of movement. Thus, there is not only energy *in* each word, but *between* the words as well.

The second stage, "Interactive Comprehending," is an adaptation of Bloom's "Comprehension" step and Edwards' "Saturation" step to indicate a conscious involvement with information to support successful learning and problem-solving. But as Baars (1997) argues that content and context are twin issues in experience, I became interested in what is beyond the conscious mind in blending content and context.

Global Immersing

I call the third stage "Global Immersing," influenced by Cross' (1995) work on African American identity development, in order to recognize that people respond in real-world contexts in many ways that go beyond the rational. The notion of immersion is embedded in the "merging of the sensual, the logical, and the aesthetic perceptions of the individual" (Erickson, 1988, p. 184), which is important to developing global citizenship. Michelson (1996) pointed out that the West has a bias of separating experiences from critical thought. He says that experience is messy and immediate. In the tradition of Western thought, this messiness is to be transcended through sustained, self-conscious, rational thought, objectivity, and "a rhetoric of order and control" (Michelson, 1996, p. 444). This traditional Western attitude is problematic when we move into the intercultural worlds, and we must change this mindset and learn from a holistic viewpoint.

As I was becoming more sensitive to and less overwhelmed by the incredible diversity I encountered everyday in my huge, multi-campus, urban community college, I also began actively seeking opportunities to open my students' eyes to different worlds and to learn from eye-opening experiences myself. I led students on international study trips to Ireland, Greece, Turkey, Italy, Germany, England, Austria, France, Switzerland, and Spain. We experienced a total transportation shutdown in Spain as well as a car bombing a block from our hotel in Madrid. We saw striking employees marching in the streets of Seville, Spain, and Munich, Germany. We tried to avoid rioting in the streets of downtown Athens when Arafat visited. We were surrounded by soldiers with guns as we boarded a bus for Ephesus, Turkey. We also met the most delightful people, saw dazzling art and historical architecture, sang on beaches, danced in the streets of Barcelona on Pentecost, told our stories on a hillside as we viewed the Parthenon under the stars, and slept on the floors of American airports with a vast array of people from all over the world. These experiences of immersion exploded the preconceptions the students had about the peoples of the world. They also learned a lot about themselves through dealing with lost luggage, local violence, currency and language differences, the poverty of gypsy camps, changed plans, and a variety of cultural expressions.

I also began to go on study trips through the East-West Center on Asian Studies. Immersing myself in global affairs and reshaping the cultural climate of my college, I directed conferences on infusing studies about Asia into the undergraduate curriculum and coursework, and organized international film festivals and intercultural activities. Meanwhile, questions were arising about my own belief systems and those belief systems I was encountering along the way in my global journeying. Since I was serving as an advocate for students of many nationalities, ethnicities, and belief systems, I was, in a sense, embracing them as valuable and important. But, how important could these ways of understanding the world be if they collided with my own traditions and beliefs? The old dualism of the Western tradition with its sense of either/or, right/wrong, self/others became uncomfortable for me. It was time to face the conflicts, paradoxes, and complexities that this interplay of forces was creating.

Reflective Incubating

I turned to the more holistic Benedictine tradition of pre-modern monastic contemplation in which I had been educated, a tradition that had been an intimate part of my life. This return to my own spiritual tradition led me to embrace new insights and the role of contradiction in Benedictine spirituality. As Esther de Waal (1998), an Episcopalian oblate from Wales, writes: "We find that we have to make room for divergent forces within us, and that there is not necessarily any resolution of the tension between them" (p. 23). She describes all of us as people of paradox who can find ways within ourselves to enable the contradictions to become life-giving. This approach of tolerance, patience, and "making room for divergent forces" has helped me in understanding the dynamics of intercultural exchange. Thus, the Benedictine tradition of reflective contemplation inspires me to think that I do not have to live dualistically or break away from the multiplicities in the world, but rather I can live in global consciousness with its confusing array of perplexities and possibilities. "Reflective Incubating" means waiting in responsive receptivity and living reflectively, sometimes unknowingly, but with the willingness to be open to what global consciousness brings on the path of working with diversity.

I began reading about monastic women in the Catholic tradition who were the authors of their own works. Their thoughts were rooted in experiences and knowledge that differed from their patriarchal mentors and predecessors (Lerner, 1993, p. 47). I became particularly interested in Hildegard of Bingen, who chose a life of monasticism and grounded her authority in her own mystical revelations and direct personal relationship with God. She wrote songs, letters, sermons, and scientific studies about her own visions of creation, the cosmos, nature, and humankind in a holistic way, challenging the rationalism and dualism of Christian Neo-Platonism. Her writings reflect her attempts to transcend the limited definitions of the feminine in her religion in order to celebrate womankind as a reflection of divine beauty and creative love.

Creativity involves the ability to embrace all of creation and value the self and others beyond the limitations of one's traditions. In her book, *Women Who Run with the Wolves* (1992), Estes says:

To create one must be able to respond. Creativity is the ability to respond to all that goes on around us, to choose from the hundreds of possibilities of thought, feeling, action, and reaction and to put those together in unique response, expression, or message that carries moment, passion, and meaning. (p. 316)

It appeared to me that creative thinking is responsible critical thinking.

Critical Analyzing

It seemed to me that Estes' definition of creative responsibility, which involves critical analyzing, was the very definition of college teaching. Yet, this was not how I was taught in my undergraduate and early graduate work. I had only experienced male professors and knew no women with doctoral degrees. I had to learn how to be a college professor from my colleagues, students, and other "women who run with the wolves."

I began to question not only the information I had been given in my college learning, but also the ways in which I had been taught. My past experiences with all White, male, American professors were presenting problems that I needed to confront if I was going to continue to develop an understanding of multiplicity in a global context. I became an advocate for actively hiring new faculty from a greater variety of ethnic and international backgrounds in order to ensure that the knowledge we are continually constructing as a learning community has integrity.

From these experiences of considering the importance of gender and then expanding this awareness to other marginalized groups, I began to realize the importance of critical analyzing for cultivating global consciousness. Critical analysis led me to understand that silenced voices must be included if knowledge is to be authentic. The students who develop as the best campus leaders have the ability to thoughtfully and critically analyze their own situations. The more confident they are in this capacity, the more willing they are to include students from diverse backgrounds in decision-making.

Paradoxical Synthesizing

Belenky, Clinchy, Goldberger, and Tarule (1986) explore how women are alienated and voiceless because they are at odds with the traditional male models of knowing, power, and self-definition. In recognizing this sense of alienation in my own educational encounters, I began to realize how many others around the world must also be feeling alienated, voiceless, and powerless. They introduced me to the idea that "teaching can be simultaneously objective and personal" and that "there is no inherent contradiction, so long as objectivity is not defined as self-extrication" (p. 224). This resonated with how I thought, believed, and operated in the classroom. Education is not just about the objective, rational analyzing of a pre-determined canon of information; it is also about a person's ability to respond to the human conditions. It is responsive and thus constantly creative, incorporating experiences, multiple ways of comprehending and expressing, immersing, reflecting, analyzing, synthesizing, and living. It is a flow connecting paradoxical synthesizing with all other stages in which global consciousness evolves rather than a set of foundational building blocks inherited from the ancient Greece.

Reclaiming my connections with women thinkers and creators from my own cultural tradition and critically analyzing the role of gender, I have grown to desire a "both-and" approach to the problems of teaching and learning in society by incorporating multiple perspectives, and creating an inclusive and interconnected community. In this process, I have continued to discover and appreciate worldviews outside of my Euro-American classical training that resonate with ways to synthesize the paradoxes of our lives. In his book, *Creative Unity,* Rabindranath Tagore (1995/1922) of India says:

> The truth of our life depends upon our attitude of mind towards it—an attitude which is formed by our habit of dealing with it according to the special circumstance of our surroundings and our temperaments. It guides our attempts to establish relations with the universe either by conquest or by union, either through the cultivation of power or through that of sympathy. And thus, in our realization of the truth of existence, we put our emphasis either upon the principle of dualism or upon the principle of unity. (p. 45)

I have decided that I want to place the truth of my existence upon the principles of relationship and unity. I hardly understand all that this involves, but in the face of increasing global conflict and violence, I am committed to an ongoing search for such a sense of creative unity, as it is a caring thing to do.

Enlightened Valuing

The essence of "Enlightened Valuing" is empathy and concern for others. I studied Starrat's (1994) "multidimensional ethic of care" with its three frames of justice, care, and critique and was struck by these alternative ways of viewing global ethical dilemmas. Caring about others involves the search for justice from multiple perspectives, not just from one's own, if an appropriate critique of a situation is to be developed. I also explored Noddings' (1984, 2002) theory with her focus on the consciousness of "caring for," which requires listening, self-awareness, and responsiveness to expressed needs. We need to continue to monitor the effects of our actions and react anew to the responses of those we care for. Thus, an energy system develops that requires not only the establishment of global relationships of caring but also the maintenance of the environment in which caring can be effective (Noddings, 2005, p. 7).

This notion reminds me of how important college teachers are in developing and maintaining civil, caring environments where diverse people can come to know and understand each other better through the juxtaposed narratives of their many perspectives. I remember a young male student in one of my classes who, shortly after September 11, announced that all Muslims are crazy. An older Muslim student, who always sat in the back and participated in the class with elegant reserve and quiet respect, responded, "I am not crazy." I was afraid that one or both students would withdraw from the class after that, but they both stayed and participated, contributing to the creation of a caring, enriched learning environment that fostered civil discourse and ethical inquiry. Noddings (2005) argues that peace and global citizenship are intertwined and suggests that "peace may be a precondition for global citizenship" (p. 17) because it is difficult to teach global citizenship when war threatens. But when war threatens, global citizenship is also needed and can be cultivated in the midst of conflict to generate greater understanding in the promotion of peaceful alternatives and resolutions. "Teaching for global citizenship may help promote peace" (Noddings, 2005, p. 17). We need to actively create an environment in which such teaching and learning can happen. More importantly, we need to foster the students' desire for study because for every individual, "education is a private engagement in a public world for the redemption of both" (Block, 2001, p. 37).

For developing global citizenship, McIntosh (2005) advocates the "capacities of the heart," which include the ability to respect one's own feelings and delve deeply into them as well as the ability to become aware of others' feelings and to believe in the validity of those feelings. It is also a capacity to experience in oneself a mixture of conflicting feelings without losing a sense of integrity in the self and a good wish for competing parties. Furthermore, she calls for the ability to balance "the heartfelt with the felt knowledge of how embedded culture is in the hearts of ourselves and others" (p. 23). All these capacities are what global education needs to cultivate. It seems to me that the caring capacities of the heart help us overcome our localized feelings and reach out to the world with universal love.

Universal Loving

Universal loving as authentic compassion is not just a personal feeling or sentiment; it is energy that relieves the pain of others through public actions and works of mercy. What else but the energy of love can inspire people to rise above their fear, despair, anger, hatred, and desire for retribution in order to come together in civil discourse? The only power on earth that can overcome extremism is love. When teachers profess to serve by providing a safe, ongoing environment for civil discourse, they are participating in creative love. They are choosing to live affirmatively in the belief that education is a viable alternative to violence. Protecting the process is a faithful daily offering of love and hope. Resonating with this is peace activist and founder of the Boston Research Center for the 21st Century, Daisaku Ikeda, who says that "the key to the formation of global citizens is the education" (2005, p. vi).

The recovery of humanity in peaceful community requires educators to journey beyond the borders of nationality, gender, and ethnicity in order to contribute to the construction of a responsible international environment. This is a complex process requiring knowledge, attentiveness, skill, patience, love, and the will to live in the tension of the intercultural questions. Thus, universal loving is not possible without critical consciousness that broadens the path of understanding by combining experience, rational investigation, adaptive knowledge, aesthetic responsibility, imagination, reflection, emotional sensitivity, creativity, empathy, and loving action into an energy system that is helpful for people around the globe.

Summary

I have narrated my own story of being and becoming a college teacher who is committed to cultivating global consciousness in my life and in my teaching. These stages of growth as I describe them serve as markers of my journey, and are always overlapping and flowing around and within each other. Since the importance of global consciousness is just beginning to be acknowledged in American higher education, we need to further such efforts in individual and collective journeys of opening up possibilities for global understanding, compassion, and justice. May my stories invite fellow educators to embark on their own journeys to global consciousness.

Notes

1. This paper is a revised version of Chapter 2 of my dissertation (2006) titled "Fiery Formations of Global Citizenship in Higher Education: The Teacher as Vessel."

Pedagogical Reflection IV: Connecting Global Perspectives and Personhood

Nadine Olson

The vision of the College of Education at Oklahoma State University articulates a sentiment shared, perhaps, by many institutions of higher education at the dawn of the twenty-first century: to prepare life-long learners to serve and lead in a complex, global society and to promote a culture that respects diversity (Oklahoma State University, College of Education, n.d.). To fulfill that vision, both pre-service and in-service teachers need to become culturally responsive educators and world citizens who contribute to the reduction of prejudice and discrimination in their schools, their communities, and the nation. It is significant that institutions are striving to raise the global consciousness of the general population, for we are beginning to recognize that successfully meeting the challenges of this century will require globally aware—and even multilingual—scholars, businessmen, politicians, and educated citizens.

The question, then, is how to accomplish the task of educating for global understanding. The answer may include a variety of institutional policy actions: requiring international studies programs in American schools; requiring language and culture studies in the K-16 grades; internationalizing the curricula of the nation's business schools; or making study abroad programs an integral and affordable component of post-secondary education. However, institutions must also recognize that *understanding* others—particularly understanding their unfamiliar cultural practices and perspectives—is an intellectual and psychological process that occurs over time and through personal, social contact with culturally different others. In short, developing a personal global perspective is an act of cultural discovery and self-actualization. Trompenaars and Hampden-Turner (1998) reference how successful Japanese business managers approach the challenges of globalization by saying:

> In the process of internationalization the Japanese . . . were not the first to observe "When in Rome, do as the Romans do," but they seem to act on this more than Westerners do. The Japanese have moreover added another dimension: "When in Rome, understand the behavior of the Romans, and thus become an even more complete Japanese." (p. 4)

Their statement is perfectly in tune with the philosophical stance of language educators, who believe that as we become competent in other lingua-cultures, we will develop deeper insights into our own language and culture and become more fully conscious of how we relate to other cultural beings. In fact, two of the five major goals of the National Standards Project (1996) are understanding the cultural products, practices, and perspectives of a society, and understanding linguistic and cultural comparisons of one society to another. As A. E. Fantini (1999) states:

> Experiencing a different culture . . . surfaces provocative questions, not only about the new experience at hand but also about what one has always taken for granted—one's own language-culture. While exploring the new LC, the learner is able to look back on his or her own from a new vantage point. (p. 168)

The authors of the three, thought-provoking essays presented in Section IV, Ahmad, Smythe, and Malloy, have all intuited and made operative in their own lives the belief that understanding another's culture—culture being the essence of how a society understands and interprets the world—lies at the heart of all effective human interaction. Their essays describe very personal journeys on the path to self-awareness and awareness of the Other.

Ahmad speaks eloquently about the personal pain that she and other Arab Americans felt after September 11, 2001, having "suddenly been put into a position to defend themselves, their families, and their status as Americans." She determined, however, to be an agent of change, breaking down stereotypes by becoming a teacher of Arabic to American students. Ahmad was consciously introspective in analyzing the cultural space in which she lived before she embarked on the development of the curriculum for her new program: she contemplated the areas of commonality and of difference between her native culture and American culture; she committed herself to forging cultural bridges through constructive, cultural dialogues; she acknowledged her own profound love for people and for the world; and, she imagined herself as a teacher-learner, an ideal position for one who actually lives between two cultures and maintains respect for both. It does not surprise me that Ahmad's "lived curriculum" was successful and that the majority of her students ventured abroad, returning with greater, personal insights about themselves and the peoples of the Middle East. In fact, Ahmad was developing in her students what Fantini (1999) describes as intercultural competence, "an ability that enables individuals to operate effectively and appropriately in more than one language-culture, and an ability that is increasingly valued and needed in today's world and in the years ahead" (p. 167).

Smythe also related a very personal journey toward reshaping his curricular values based on his own deepening intercultural competence. Like Ahmad, he found himself at the complicated "intersection of cultures involving notions of identity, self, and Other." Smythe described the process of navigating this terrain as messy, recounting in clearly painful detail various international student orientation sessions and one particularly disconcerting faculty presentation. However, his response to difficult situations demonstrated Smythe's dispositions for intercultural success: he embodies the necessary behavioral attributes that are most commonly cited by interculturalists, namely "respect, patience, a sense of humor, tolerance for ambiguity, flexibility, empathy, nonjudgmentalness [sic], openness, curiosity, and motivation" (Fantini, 1999, p. 175). Smythe opened himself up to learning from his international students, to listening to their voices, to respecting their views about American culture as contrasted to their own; as a result he revitalized an entire curricular approach to his orientation classes for international students and American faculty members. Smythe urges others to change their teaching goals, also, from preparing American students for global competition to preparing them for global conversation and participation.

Malloy narrates in almost fervent tones her journey to global consciousness. She has dedicated much of her adult life to promoting global dialogue and she shares the very specific processes that helped her achieve such dialogue in her own teaching of the arts and humanities. Her steps to self-awareness are dynamic, engaging, and challenging of traditional, Western ways of perceiving the world; her path required her to face "the conflicts, paradoxes, and complexities" that she herself was creating along the way. Malloy embarked on a journey in search of cross-cultural meanings in her daily life, and discovered that *ways of meaning* are myriad. Her semiotic view of culture offers a fresh perspective on an important goal of cultural learning: to measure one's skill in interpreting cultural meaning from an *etic* perspective (the outsider's view) in terms of one's accuracy in making judgments about a given context that are similar to those made by members within the native cultural group (the *emic* perspective). Malloy's hope is that countless more people develop such interpretive skills and use them in the employ of building a responsible global environment.

Either implicitly or explicitly, all of the essayists ponder how they can be instruments of change, helping others to mature as world citizens and to become more complete human beings. Each provides telling examples of how such growth can be nurtured in and out of classrooms by caring and culturally responsive educators. Experiential learning such as they describe has proven to be very important to the emergence of global perspectives, and we teachers can provide unique opportunities for our students to engage directly in interaction with other cultural groups. However, we can enhance the probability that those intercultural encounters will be more successful (*i.e.*, meaningful) if, before sending our students off on adventures abroad, we focus on preparing them for target-culture exploration. I would, of course, emphasize the benefit of gaining a functional level of proficiency in the target language before sojourning abroad, as language and culture are intimately entwined. Nevertheless, even monolingual teachers and students can work to identify and strengthen the dispositions, the interpersonal skills, and the interpretive skills that will increase their intercultural success and their growth as intercultural beings. The following is the description of three teaching strategies that I have used effectively with both secondary students and college undergraduates who study languages and have aspirations to travel abroad.

Dispositions. Many teachers and professors become international travel guides for student groups during the summer months, and it takes great courage, energy, and commitment to plan student trips and to prepare students for the cultural shock that they will surely experience. M.B. Cassidy (1988) believes that "how students prepare themselves for a trip determines what their experience will be" (p. ix). Her helpful guide includes instructions for students to actually role-play situations they will encounter abroad. The teacher acts as a coach, suggesting appropriate cultural behaviors and language that students can practice to carry out daily life activities in the target culture, such as using the phone, dealing with a medical emergency, or using appropriate courtesy. Discussing their faux experiences and reactions in a safe environment at home helps students to reduce their nervousness about the new realities they will face later. Through simulations, students have the opportunity to develop confidence, a sense of humor in awkward situations, resourcefulness, flexibility, curiosity, and patience—all attributes or dispositions associated with successful cultural interactions (Fantini, p. 175).

College professors, too, feel responsible for the safety and emotional well-being of their adult students. Surveying adult students by means of a cross-cultural inventory can highlight areas of concern relative to adults' personal attitudes about cultural differences. K. Cushner (2003) developed a useful Inventory of Cross-cultural Sensitivity. Individuals rate their agreement or disagreement with 36 statements about intercultural experiences, such as:

> It is better that people from other cultures avoid one another.
> It makes me nervous to talk to people who are different from me.
> The way other people express themselves is very interesting to me. (pp. 5—6)

The inventory is scored by five, pre-established sub-scales: Cultural Integration, Behavior, Intellectual Interaction, Attitude Toward Others, and Empathy. Thus, relative strengths and weaknesses of individuals can be identified and planned for. Cushner's Inventory has been routinely used since 2006 in screening pre-service teachers at Oklahoma State University who are applying to complete their student teaching internship in Costa Rica, and the instrument has provided university supervisors with insights that have allowed for some intervention and support activities to help particular students deal better with the culture shock they experienced upon arrival in Costa Rica.

Interpersonal skills. If a cross-cultural interaction is to be successful, each individual must be aware of the social processes being practiced by the other, *i.e.* his or her interpersonal communication skills. Interaction is further complicated by the fact that such processes are culturally bound, yet also mediated by individual personalities. If one participant is operating from the basis of stereotyped assumptions about the other, dialogue can be stymied. The authors in Section IV eloquently described how false stereotyping can interfere with cultural understanding, and it strikes me by leading classroom activities directly confronting the process of stereotyping, teachers can provide another important training opportunity for their students.

Y. Nakata (1997) developed a learning activity that she calls "Turn Off the Stereo(type)." Students who may already be operating on false assumptions about others stand to benefit most from the activity, so it will be most successful in a local community with a culturally diverse population. Students are initially asked to complete several open-ended sentence starters about a number of the various cultural groups in the community, using the pattern: "Australians (for example) are always . . . ; never . . . ; sometimes . . . ; like . . . ; don't like. . ." One of the sentence prompts can certainly be "I am . . ." or "We are . . . ." Then, students compare their responses with others in small groups and, based on the statements they have shared, develop a questionnaire that they will use to interview real people from the culture being stereotyped to find out if the stereotype seems valid to those informants (p. 206). When field interviews are complete, groups report their findings and the teacher guides a large-group discussion on the validity of stereotypes. With this type of activity as background, the teacher can then introduce various positive and negative stereotypes that others hold of the majority cultural group in the community, and encourage students to explore the possible sources of the stereotypes. Students may be completely unaware of the behaviors that others have observed in their cultural group, since they tend to see themselves as fully independent individuals acting with complete freedom from negative group/peer influences. Oh, to see ourselves as others see us! Through these activities, students can be guided to understand that stereotyping, "using extreme, exaggerated forms of behavior . . . is the result of registering what surprises us, rather than what is familiar. . . . It exaggerates and caricatures the culture observed and, unintentionally, the observer" (Trompenaars & Hampden-Turner, 1998, p. 26).

Interpretive skills. An effective instrument for practicing interpretive skills is the Culture Assimilator, or Intercultural Sensitizer. Albert (1995) succinctly describes the instrument as one "specifically constructed to sensitize persons from one cultural group to the assumptions, behaviors, norms, perceptions, interpretations, attitudes, and values . . . of persons from another cultural group" (p. 157). In essence, the Sensitizer is a short narrative that describes an episode or critical incident that typically occurs when an American (culture A) interacts with a native from culture B. The incident causes consternation in the participants because the situation, based on key cultural differences, can easily be misinterpreted if one or both parties have insufficient knowledge about the other's cultural practices and perspectives. Albert explains the interpretive task that is presented to students:

> Each story is followed by one or more questions about the behavior, thoughts, or feelings of the person from culture B. . . . After that come four . . . alternative interpretations which might be given in response to the question. Trainees must select the . . . interpretation that makes the most sense to people living in culture B. . . . Once trainees have chosen an attribution, they are instructed to turn to a given page . . . that discusses the interpretation they chose to determine if it is the attribution made by persons in culture B. If the attribution selected was not one favored by persons in culture B, trainees are told so and are asked to go back to the story and make another choice. They keep doing this until they select the attribution which is preferred overall by persons in culture B. At that point they are given an explanation for the behavior and additional information about culture B. (pp. 158–159)

Culture Assimilators or Sensitizers involve students actively in the interpretive process, and they can easily be used for individual study or group discussion. They make learning more enjoyable than textbooks, and Albert reports that "numerous evaluation studies have shown [the Intercultural Sensitizer] to improve not only the trainee's understanding about patterns of behavior and thinking in the other culture, but also task performance and adjustment" (p. 158).

By practicing the components of cultural interaction through performing simulations, identifying stereotypes and turning them off, and interpreting unfamiliar situations before directly engaging with international counterparts, students of culture will have an opportunity to develop the skills they need in order to become citizens of the world, able to embrace cultural globalization, but confident in their own personal identity and selfhood.

Part V

Do I Have a Culture?
Understanding Whiteness

18. *The Color of Fear,*
the Change in David, and Racial Identity

Tracey Roberson and Stephani Allen-Brown

This essay is a dialogue, across the racial line, on the film *The Color of Fear* (Lee, 1994), which describes a weekend retreat where a group of men come together to discuss and debate the issue of racism and its role in each man's life. It is highly emotionally charged as the men of the minority group—including two African Americans, two Mexican Americans, two Asian Americans—try to make the two White men understand what it means to be a minority in a White man's world. The character of David is particularly significant for our analysis, as he is initially quite stubborn in denying White privilege, but finally begins to reach a certain understanding as a result of engaging in the group discussions. As a White and a Black American, respectively, we discuss what we have learned from David and his interactions with others to inform our own conceptions of what it means to be White. We first offer independent accounts and then initiate a conversation with each other.

Tracey's Story

Over the course of a semester in a multicultural education class, I began a journey of reflecting on both who I was as a child and who I have become as an adult. The most powerful tool in taking this journey was *The Color of Fear*, an amazing film that empowered a group of participants.

Running parallel to the transformations in the video were transformations within the class as well. The students in the class, of both males and females and various cultures, included African Americans, Japanese Americans, Native Americans, and Hispanic Americans, with the majority being Caucasian. The instructor of the class, Dr. Wang, is Chinese, which also made the teacher's perspective on the whole issue of racism in America interesting. It seemed that many of the feelings and thoughts of the men in the film intersected with the various racial groups in the class. Particularly significant is that the film mirrored Whiteness back to the White students, including me, in what was not a comfortable experience. One of the two White men, David, underwent the most transformation during the weekend, and his change challenges me to understand and transform my own racial identity.

Throughout the film, the men of the minority groups shared their stories of racial discrimination and oppression in their daily lives. David, however, initially refused to believe that there was a racial dimension to everyday reality. He could not understand others' experiences and feelings. David did not see "race" and did not see any racist aspect in himself. This became very frustrating for those who suffered from racism. David is not alone, as many White Americans, including some of the students in class, share similar sentiments.

As the weekend continued and more emotions were shared in the group, David finally started to "see" others' viewpoints. The intense discussions and continual encounters with others' painful experiences finally led David to lift the guard that he had used to cover his own childhood of abuse by his racist father. As those harsh memories came back, he finally could feel the pain of others as he opened up to his own. This brought about a huge breakthrough, and a healing process began. But this breakthrough was only a beginning: Now that he had made this discovery about racism and the invisible privilege he had enjoyed, how could he begin to mend fences and struggle against racism?

At this point the class began to draw parallels to their own lives. With the diverse population of the class, many emotional and heated discussions transpired as the minority students related to the feelings of the men of color in the film, while the White students examined their roles in preserving or going against the system of racism.

During this time, I began to explore my own background. I grew up in Louisiana in the 1970s and 1980s. Looking back, I am very aware of the racial lines that existed. One of the towns I lived in for a few years was openly divided. When my sister graduated from high school in 1977, the school held separate proms for Black students and White students. Ten years later when their reunion was held, there was a White student reunion and a Black student reunion. Finally in 1997, another decade later, the two groups decided to merge and hold an integrated, twenty-year reunion. Ironically, attendance from both groups decreased because of the integration. This demonstrates an immense amount of prejudice still existing in the late 1990s.

By the time I went to high school in the 1980s in a larger town in north Louisiana, things had improved, yet I was still exposed to elements of racism. Although there was more institutional integration of the two races, there was still not much mixing of the groups socially. The only Black students consistently welcomed into White social groups were the athletes. Most of the area schools had one "token" Black cheerleader so that the school could not be accused of discrimination.

Unfortunately, because I grew up in a place where this type of racism was the norm, I had no idea how inhumane and disgusting these practices were. It was just the way it was, and we did not question that it could possibly be wrong. Then I moved to Oklahoma in 1988. While many people including me recognized that Oklahoma was still a fairly racist state, it was certainly an improvement from Louisiana. My parents had instilled in me some values of equality and dignity for the human person regardless of race, so when I moved to Oklahoma and experienced a better racial situation, I quickly adapted and changed my way of thinking to one that was more open-minded and inclusive.

As I watched and reflected on *The Color of Fear,* I was forced to think about my role in society as a White person of privilege. Growing up in Louisiana around so much racism, I never considered myself superior or racist, but when I heard so much from people who had experienced the trauma of racism, I started to realize that while I never intentionally mistreated or avoided people of color, I also never stood up for them. Throughout the course of the semester, as the class kept returning to discussion of this film, I psychologically dealt with how much I was like David in his oblivion to racial reality. As a result, I grew as a person and became aware of my own privilege, previously invisible to me. One crucial revelation is that even though I was not explicitly racist, I had not done much to defy racism.

Like David, I had to ask myself, "Now what?" Now that I had come to this realization about myself, what could I do about it? How could I combat racism and prejudice? The most powerful avenue I could take would be in my role as an educator. I teach part-time and serve as an assistant principal of a small Catholic school where there are very few minorities. With new understandings of race and racism, I realize that it is imperative to help students, most of whom are living in invisible privilege, to understand the notion of privilege, the manifestations of racism, and the need for multiculturalism.

This is an area where our education system, as a whole, fails. Little bits and pieces of multiculturalism are thrown in the margins of a teacher's textbook, but this is far from teaching true self-awareness and understanding of others. As educators, we are challenged to make stories, poems, and films about racism come alive for our students in order to touch them and encourage them to reach out to others. We must put real faces, personalities, and emotions to these stories. Reading non-fiction accounts such as *I Know Why the Caged Bird Sings* and having guest speakers come in and share their real-life stories can be powerful ways to reach into the hearts and minds of students. In Oklahoma, we have the Greenwood Cultural Center, The Jewish Holocaust Museum, and various Native American cultural resources. Using these resources can provide powerful, educative, and enriching experiences for students. Sitting eye-to-eye with people who have suffered from racism, just as David did in *The Color of Fear,* could break down racial barriers for students. These lessons prepare them for the multicultural world they live in and educate them to become open-minded individuals who welcome others and thus enrich their own lives.

Stephani's Reflection

Watching *The Color of Fear* is an experience that forces introspection. The film is provocative. From the very beginning, it is clear that as the men gathered in the room and exchanged pleasantries, the mood quickly changed from easy-going to intense, from peaceful to angry, and from angry to understanding. But that is what happens when we discuss race. The word "race" has another definition: a competition for a prize and supremacy. If we borrow this definition as a metaphor to discuss race as a social category, someone must finish in first place and someone must finish in last place; someone must win and someone must lose; there is only one winner in every race. While the race track looks as if everyone has a fair chance, the pole position has its advantages, for the inside lane has the shortest distance. Because of the unequal starting points, participants have different relationships with "race," and to open up dialogues on such differential positioning is not easy. As the film shows, for David, one of the two White men in the group, and for Victor, one of the two Black men in the group, the journey to openly communicating their deepest issues began with anger, hurt, resentment, and ignorance, but the two men finally reached a certain understanding.

To be White in America is like running in the inside lane. It is like being born in pole position. In *The Color of Fear* there were two White men—Gordon and David. Gordon admitted that he was a racist. He owned it as a problem, and it was not something he was proud of. He was a work-in-progress toward acknowledging White responsibility for racism and being willing to participate in dismantling racism. Then there was David. David did not think of himself as a racist. He believed that he was a fair person who did not have any misgivings about other people based on race. He acknowledged certain stereotypes about some groups, but he believed he accepted everyone for who they were. David represents the mindset of so many who do not understand how racism has impacted American society. They believe that racism exists only in the minds of those who explicitly express racial superiority or take racist actions. The Gordon types can become allies for anti-racist collective efforts, but the David types stay as part of the problem rather than become part of the solution.

In the beginning, David refused to accept the role that racism plays in keeping minorities disenfranchised. He wanted to believe that people have not achieved simply because they do not desire to achieve or do not work hard.

Even in the process of interacting with others in the group, hearing their stories, and learning more about their individual and collective experiences, David had a hard time recognizing the existence of racism. Only when the film approached the end was David able to see what had been invisible. The heated discussions finally led to a breakthrough moment when David was asked how he would feel if his own daughters could not get into certain universities and others simply said to them, "Maybe you should work harder." It was difficult for David to learn that personal accomplishment is not exclusively a matter of hard work and willingness to achieve. Unfortunately, David's viewpoint is consistent with that of the majority who believe that racism is not real and that each person is responsible for his or her own personal success. It is extremely difficult for the Davids of the world to imagine that external forces can block someone's way. However, we are only half right if we think we are in charge of our own destinies.

Victor knew all too well the struggles that come with being a minority—especially an African American man. His response to David was often laden with anger, and it is easy for me as an African American to understand why. Victor knew what it was like to put his best foot forward, to run faster and to work harder, but still get nowhere because of racism. Victor told about how he was automatically placed into the lowest-performing group on his first day at a new school. His performance quickly indicated that he belonged in the highest-performing group. Because he was African American, his teacher responded not to his ability, but to the stereotypes about his race. This situation is common for many minority people. Their whole educational experience is marred by such bias. As a result of their tremendous struggles with school, teachers, and the educational system, some of them just stop going to school altogether.

Racial relationships in this country have a long history, and African Americans have had to fight for their very survival. African Americans first came to America as slaves. We were told what we could and could not do. We were programmed to do, think, and be as the slave owner instructed. After slavery was over, the mindset did not immediately go away for Blacks or Whites. Owning another person as property became illegal, but that does not mean that the racism that established and supported slavery as an acceptable and necessary process has disappeared. Slavery simply went underground. As a result, there are still White people who consciously or unconsciously believe that Blacks should know their place. They believe that Blacks should not be too high-minded. The basic logic is that you must work hard and earn your way, but you cannot feel too good about yourself while you are doing it. This is a slavery mentality that becomes a hidden agenda, and it is still at work.

In *The Color of Fear*, Victor became frustrated with David's inability to accept the role that Whites play in the racist constructs they created in society.

Victor's frustration only grew stronger because David refused to acknowledge that race is a social and political reality for many. David could not imagine what life was like because he was in the majority group, the yardstick by which everybody else was measured. He did not have to worry about meeting the standard, because he was the standard. He did not understand the racial bifurcation in this country where one is in direct opposition to Whites if he or she is not White. In the end, after spending the weekend exchanging stories of hurt and of pain, Victor believed that he had developed more trust. Finally, David realized that his unwillingness to recognize the impact of racism came from his unwillingness to see that life can be so cruel and unfair, and Victor responded with his hands stretched out, "Now I can work with you from here." David's attitude in the end represents what many African Americans hope for. It is not reparations or welfare we want to make up for our struggles; we simply want others to acknowledge that there is a struggle. It is very difficult to run a fair race when someone else has such a gaping head start. Is it too much to ask to simply level the playing field and make the rules the same for everyone?

A Dialogue on Whiteness

Tracey: My understanding of my Whiteness continues to grow as I spend more time in reflection as a contributor to this book. Both my memories of and reflections on *The Color of Fear* and my understanding of Stephani's feelings lead me further down the road to understanding racism in our country. One assessment that really sparked my comprehension of Victor's anger in the video was Stephani's explanation of Victor's frustration with David. She explained that Victor's frustration grew not so much from the racism of the past, but from David's inability to accept the role Whites have played in forming this racist society. At the moment I read this, it became clear that for me and others who have played a similar role in racism, the issue is admitting the role we have played. We can not change the past, but we can contribute to making change by admitting the past. Stephani's writings further opened my eyes and her metaphor of the race sparked a deeper understanding. Her description of White people being in the pole position or the inside lane while people of color begin at an unequal starting point is such a vivid illustration of the battle that people of color face. As stated earlier, I never really thought of myself as starting ahead or having all of this privilege, but the visual image of the race with me and other Whites standing on our mark ahead of others really made things clear for me.

Once I grasped the clarity of this image, I again reflected on Victor's thoughts and emotional responses. His story of being placed in the lower reading group in school simply because he was Black evoked a true sense of guilt in me. It was not guilt just because of what happened to Victor and other people of color, but guilt from a life of taking my Whiteness and privilege for granted while so many other people in our society suffered injustices. While I did feel bad about Victor's experience as well as about the hundreds of thousands of injustices that people of color have faced over the years, I again thought back to my childhood and realized that I was given so many opportunities simply because I was born White.

Stephani could relate to Victor's anger and frustration with White people. In stating, "We simply want others to acknowledge that there is a struggle," Stephani's feelings merged with Victor's. This request is valid and necessary if wounds of the past are going to begin to heal.

Stephani: I grew up in Tulsa, Oklahoma. Every school I went to was integrated and I always went to magnet schools. This was significant, I believe, because I did not see the impacts of underfunding and poverty. It was not until I was in middle school that I first experienced racism. Interestingly enough, it was not with more affluent Whites, but with poorer and often undereducated Whites. After that experience, I saw it more often. Then I went to a high school which excels in academics and athletics and all other aspects. My high school experience taught me more about the hidden undercurrent of racism than any other institution. It was an African American high school and the best in Tulsa. Then in the 1970s, almost forty years after opening its doors, the high school was turned into a magnet school and the student body had to be fifty percent White and fifty percent Black. Many in the African American community believed that the integration was not designed to break racial barriers in the city. Instead, White powers could not handle a Black school in north Tulsa that was better than all the other schools in the city. This institutional racism, as some may call it, is what I have grown the most familiar with.

I agree with Tracey when she says that we all have a role to play in improving racial relations. If racism exists at the institutional level, we all have responsibility for creating a better system. But Whites and Blacks have different relationships with the system and this difference must be acknowledged before we can make any progress. Most White people are unaware of the privilege they are afforded, but Tracey is willing to accept what so many Blacks feel to be true about White privilege. I think this acceptance is a major step toward healing. It is very difficult to be engaged in a discussion where the other party refuses to acknowledge what is wrong about the situation; and as long as that person holds fast to what he or she believes to be true, there will never be an authentic dialogue. While I don't wish Whites to feel guilty for just being born White, I do believe that recognizing the benefits of being White due to the system of racial inequality is the first step toward making amends and leveling the playing field. I wish that David's epiphany had come more quickly, but it did at least come. Perhaps his change speaks for the possibility that all people can challenge themselves to confront their own racial and cultural ignorance. My hope is that as long as there are Traceys in the world, there will be healing.

Tracey: There are several steps in dealing with this societal issue of racism. The first step for White people is to acknowledge invisible privilege. Through my journey with Dr. Wang, I accomplished this step. The next step for me is combating racism through the institution of education. I feel fortunate to be in a position, professionally, where I have the opportunity to open students' eyes to diversity issues. Not only is it my opportunity, but it is my responsibility.

Throughout the class, I kept asking myself why this type of class was not required at the undergraduate level, particularly for students studying to become teachers. I strongly feel that multicultural education needs to be integrated into curricula long before the graduate level of education. I have now come to realize that even waiting until students are in college is way too late. This type of education needs to occur very early on, before habits, beliefs, and actions are so embedded in our children.

As an administrator in a small Catholic school where over 90% of our school population is White and middle to upper-middle class, I feel a huge need to make our students understand Whiteness and become leaders of change. We have already begun units that we hope are the start of making these children more aware and proactive in the fight against racism. Last year our principal taught a unit on racism using a powerful documentary about Rosa Parks as the introduction. After several sessions of meaningful discussion, the class culminated with a trip to the Greenwood Cultural Center, where students learned about the Tulsa Race Riot, which took place just a few miles from where they live and go to school. This year we have started a similar class with a documentary on the Holocaust. The students will have an opportunity to visit the Jewish Cultural Center at the end of the unit. Every community has places that afford students the opportunity to witness firsthand the inequality of our society. Our school also has a service requirement that encourages our students to go out into the community and not only see this inequality, but work to change it.

This has been a personal journey for me. It began about five years ago and will continue for many years to come. I am thankful I was able to experience the class at Oklahoma State University and the opportunity to have a dialogue with Stephani about these issues. I will continue to work for change and bring others along to do the same.

19. My White Identity:
A Self-Awareness Revelation

Kerri Bury

Having taught in both an underprivileged, diversified public school district and a privileged, predominately White public school district has forced me to realize something about myself: There remains a great deal of room for me to broaden my understanding of, respect for, and interaction with other cultures. College was perhaps the first place I began awakening to new ideas and comprehending new concepts—by "new," I mean "new to me." Nine years of teaching, along with graduate studies which continuously challenged my previous assumptions, have taught me important lessons about self-awareness.

Early on in my graduate studies, I was challenged to understand myself in a different way. I'm not sure how intentional some of our choices in life are and how many can be attributed to learned behavior, but I believe that I may have been and may still be passively contributing to prejudice by disassociating myself, intentionally or unintentionally, from others who are culturally different. Not only do I teach in a predominately White public school district, but I also live in a predominately White neighborhood less than two miles from the school where I teach. We chose to move to this neighborhood because we believed it to be "safe," and it is. My kids ride their bikes up and down the streets and play with the neighborhood children, and everyone honks or waves when driving or walking by. However, there are only two Black homeowners and one Asian family in my large neighborhood. Everyone else is White! My children attend a predominately White school just a few blocks from our house; in fact, they've never been in a class with students of other cultures except for one Asian boy in my daughter's kindergarten class. I also don't have many friends of different cultures. I never thought about the fact that I was actually contributing to prejudice; I would have denied that but I realize now that I have made choices to disassociate myself from others, even though I didn't know exactly what I was doing. I was just staying in my comfort zone and trying to make good choices for my children.

In my elementary and middle school years, I think I only recognized "Black people" and "White people." I recall learning early on that a person's "race" meant the color of his or her skin. I can also remember learning that everyone was "equal." However, I sensed a certain contradiction in those kinds of statements as it implied that inequality did exist. In my schools, the racial minority is obvious: in a class of twenty students, there may have been two or three Black students; in high school, an Asian student might have been added to the mix. Although my middle school social studies teachers did lecture about things like slavery, the Civil War, and the Civil Rights Movement of the 1960s, the messages of those lectures failed to reach me in the passive mode of teaching and learning.

When I began my graduate work, only two years into my teaching career, I was rather concerned about myself, about how other people would react to me, how they would react to things I might have to say, and whether I might offend people when discussing controversial issues. However, I found most of my graduate professors and classmates to be particularly accepting and open. It was this atmosphere that helped me feel more comfortable with being myself. For one class in particular, a class on multicultural diversity, "being ourselves" was somewhat a prerequisite; if I (and others in the class) wanted to gain a greater understanding of diversity and its implications for our lives and for our careers as teachers, we had to be honest. In the beginning, I felt overwhelmed—overwhelmed at the thought of combating prejudice and racism, overwhelmed by the emotions we watched others experience, and overwhelmed with the goals I had set for myself. But one thing I've really tried to change, with modest success, is maintaining a consciousness about my actions, my words, my thoughts, and my encounters with others. Although I don't know all the answers, sometimes I find myself questioning how my own actions, words, and thoughts indirectly impact others' lives either positively or negatively, especially where my teenage students and my own two small children are concerned.

One of the important lessons I have learned is the notion of privilege. I begin to realize that whether or not Whites *feel* privileged, the potential for them to benefit from "privilege" is undeniable. Even righteous attempts to disassociate oneself from the White culture do not negate the abundance of opportunity given to White people. Although I am still working on gaining fuller self-awareness, I begin to comprehend the importance of understanding what roles the privileged and underprivileged aspects of one's life play in order to deal with the confusion that accompanies oppression, racism, and prejudice.

According to Howard (1999), perhaps our greatest means or chance of achieving any kind of transformation or social change lies in the healing process we must experience. I believe we first have to experience personal healing, and eventually, we'll be able to progress to a more collective process of healing as a culture. The first step to healing has to be acknowledgment—acknowledgment of our past—however painful it might be, because we can't change what we are not willing to acknowledge. In order to become more aware of myself, of the role I may be playing in perpetuating prejudice, and in order to heal from the wound of the past, I see nowhere else to begin but with acknowledgment. It is only a start, however, as the "White Identity Orientations" presented by Howard (1999) demonstrate, cultivating racial self-awareness is a complicated and multilayered journey.

Howard (1999) describes three White identity orientations—the fundamentalist, the integrationist, and the transformationist—and discusses them through different ways of thinking, feeling, and acting (p. 100). Fundamentalists are characterized by upholding White dominance in their minds, emotions, and actions. Integrationists begin to acknowledge different perspectives, but their emotional awareness is accompanied by negative feelings of shame, guilt, and confusion. They are willing to help others and make efforts to learn about other cultures, but don't realize that they are still implicitly Eurocentric. Transformationists, on the other hand, challenge Eurocentric perspectives, learn from others, and engage in self-reflective critique. They show appreciation for cultural differences, have a sense of responsibility without guilt, and actively participate in social and collaborative efforts to struggle against racism and oppression of all forms.

Studying Howard's theory helps me to locate where I stand currently. I have to say that I am not a true "transformationist." While I do fall into that category on some levels, I realize—honestly—that I am still an "integrationist" in other respects. On an emotional level, for instance, I mostly experience feelings of shame and confusion. I'm really trying to reach acknowledgment, empathy, and a sense of responsibility without negative feelings, and I think I'm nearing those thoughts and feelings but have not completely arrived. When I visited the Greenwood Cultural Center, I was consumed by feelings of shame. The devastation and destruction and sheer annihilation were overwhelming; it's one of those things that are too sad, too troubling, too disturbing to think about, so most people don't. I was so ashamed that I didn't really want to acknowledge what happened; I was ashamed that "my people" could have been solely responsible for such a tragedy; I was ashamed that this had happened in the very place where I was born and raised. Then, how does one deal with such shame so that he or she is able to move beyond it and onto a more active level? For me, it has to do with the ability to separate myself from the racist past and claim my own agency for working toward racial equality. I did not shape the past, and I certainly cannot change it. I do, however, have power in the present to make my contributions to social change. Such a separation, based upon acknowledgment, rather than denial, encourages me to move beyond those feelings of shame.

I see myself as an "integrationist" on an acting level in many aspects. I am usually compliant, and I have not been really learning *from* other cultures as a "transformationist" would but rather, I have been learning *about* other cultures. To learn *from* others rather than *about* others means being able to change myself as a result of interaction—taking something from others and giving part of myself to others. These are things I'm still trying to work on in both my personal and my professional lives. I couldn't agree with Howard (1999) more when he claims that "the assumption of rightness and the luxury of ignorance" are what have maintained and perpetuated a dominating prejudice. Only in seeing through the racial arrogance of such an assumption and luxury can we truly embrace differences for what they are rather than what we want them to be and engage social actions that challenge rather than reinforce racial inequality and inequity. I wonder if I'll live to experience Howard's (1999) vision: to live in a multicultural world "where the true spirit of diversity reigns and where *E Pluribus Unum* is a lived reality" (p. 119). What can I do to reach such a visionary stage? Teaching becomes an important site for my further growth.

As a teacher, I wonder how I might be able to teach self-awareness and the importance of acknowledging our pasts, including their positive and negative aspects. How can I reach my students on these levels? The best place to begin may be sharing my own self-awareness with them and encouraging them to share their own stories, lives, and histories, when they feel comfortable. Using literature can also be a means of furthering self-awareness—mine and theirs— and a way of teaching empathy. Perhaps the best literature to begin with for teaching this concept is autobiographical writings. I've found that students are much more receptive to what we're studying if they know that it is true—that it really happened, that the people it happened to are real people. Eventually, fictional accounts will also work provided they are "true to life" situations. Role playing activities usually make fictional characters come alive.

I am also drawn to Carnes's (2004) idea of liminal teaching—a method of teaching whereby traditional, structured (and sometimes rigid) procedures are abandoned and replaced with an atmosphere that allows students the liberty to discuss, propose, imagine, and re-enact a world that is different from their own world. I see students becoming their own "thinkers" in using this approach— figuring things out for themselves, not believing or jumping to do everything they're told. Not only does such an approach hold great potential in terms of teaching students about difficult knowledge, but it also helps them develop much-needed critical thinking skills that are seldom cultivated in the traditional classroom. I also hope that if and when students learn such skills and develop diverse modes of thinking, they will be more inclined and equipped to discuss difficult issues with their parents and thus make positive contributions to the atmosphere of their community.

Teaching in a predominately White, very privileged, yet sadly sheltered district is a current challenge. As a teacher and as a parent, I realize that we have the responsibility for raising children to go beyond tolerating others to engaging in meaningful interactions with others in a "give-and-take" manner. I know how much students look up to me as a person—from the way I speak to the way I behave to the way I react. I'm trying to be an honest, accepting person with whom they can interact and share thoughts and feelings regardless of the topic. Perhaps the more I trust them with the person I am, the more likely they'll be to trust me with who they are, and hopefully, in my next nine years of teaching, I'll have discovered more tools to encourage their own self-awareness.

I don't expect to wake up tomorrow and be a "transformationist"; I realize it's a lifelong process of growth and change, one that constantly presents me with challenges, frustrations, excitements, and epiphanies. Knowing that there's always something more I can learn from others keeps me going.

20. A Personal Journey from Colorblindness to Anti-Racism

Melanie Burgess

My multicultural journey began when I became conscious of my own colorblindness. I was treating all people the same and ignoring their racial backgrounds. It seemed reasonable at the time, but then participating in racial jokes, watching movies that marginalized minorities, or ignoring the wrongs committed by Whites started to not "feel right." Through many discussions, various readings, and self-reflection, I began a journey of recognizing that colorblindness, although it seems to be a "gentle" view, can be a form of racism. I had unwittingly been promoting racism by my treatment of others, my ignorance about my own Whiteness, and a fear of acknowledging color. In turn, I lacked connections with cultures different from my own. My desire to make those connections inspired me to transform my past position of colorblindness into a permanent growth pattern toward anti-racism.

The evolution of my thinking began with defining "colorblindness." Colorblindness happens when a person does not recognize another person's race. For example, one does not acknowledge a Black person as being Black. It took me quite some time to change from that position to a new understanding that only by acknowledging difference can we relate to others on a firm ground. The next part of the journey was exploring my White identity. I had to acknowledge the privileges that come with being White, and understand how the acts of marginalization, oppression, and racism at a system level may have impacted my own perspectives and outlook.

I recall one critical incident that influenced my thoughts and attitudes. When I was in the 7th grade, I was bullied by a group of female (American) Indians. At lunchtime one day, I sat down at the only seat left in the cafeteria. As I sat down, one of the girls said the seat was saved and I needed to move. I replied that there wasn't another seat and continued eating my lunch. She then threw food at my face, and the whole table laughed. I felt humiliated, embarrassed, and fearful of these girls. I left the table, threw my lunch away, and went outside. The group followed and surrounded me in a circle. They began a verbal attack and started to push me around. As I attempted to move out of the circle, they made more efforts to keep me in it. The bullying continued during lunch most days, so I avoided eating and socializing in the cafeteria as much as possible. I hated lunchtime! The bullying eventually stopped with intervention from the principal, but I didn't resume normal lunchtime activities.

Being singled out by a different racial group was extremely uncomfortable, very personal, and quite lonely. Being only twelve at the time, I did not have the maturity to know this incident was not about me, but about my Whiteness. Inflicting pain onto a White girl reflected a displaced anger about the collective suffering of Indians. In retrospect, I do not want to justify their actions, but I do want to recognize the pain in their history and how it might have influenced the hostility they held towards me in their act of discrimination. The Indian girls judged me for my skin color without personally knowing my history or me. The irony of this incident is that my grandfather was half Cherokee Indian. Just as the Native American adage says, one should not judge another person without "walking in another person's moccasins" (Quoted in Allgood, 2001, p. 193).

An unfortunate aspect resulting from this incident was that my mindset changed. I became fearful and timid, lacked self-confidence, and wanted to be invisible. If I didn't acknowledge another person's difference, that person wouldn't acknowledge me as being different, or so I thought. Thus, I adopted a colorblind approach to racial diversity. However, what I did not understand at that time was that choosing to ignore others is choosing to ignore myself.

This line of thinking continued for a long time, but as my education and maturity increased, so did my knowledge about racism and colorblindness. Howard (1999) describes colorblindness as assuming "that we can erase our racial categories, ignore differences, and thereby achieve an illusory state of sameness or equality" (p. 53). That was my assumption in the past. Further, I naively thought that recognizing others by their skin color was a form of racism. Christine Bennett (2003) addresses this conception well: "Some people mistakenly believe that simply recognizing a person's race is racist" (p. 85). After reading these authors' critiques, I have realized that thinking we are the same and fearing to acknowledge a person's racial difference can actually contribute to racism. Now, instead of shying away from differences, I choose to see, appreciate, and respect them. We are different, but also related to each other.

I also learned from Howard's (1999) book that I need to understand what it means to be White. This includes recognizing the entitlements and freedoms my Whiteness has afforded me and to what extent those entitlements and freedoms come at the expense of others. The Indian girls used my ignorance as an advantage to voice their angst about being oppressed by Whites. Their verbal attack included calling me "weak" and repeatedly asking if I knew it. Being dominated and outnumbered, I didn't have much choice but to answer, "Yes." They knew what it was like not having a choice and, at that moment, so did I.

To live a multi-culturally rich life, I must understand Whiteness from both non-White and White standpoints. In particular, Maya Angelou's (1997/1967) book, *I Know Why the Caged Bird Sings,* offered me an opportunity to learn, from a Black woman's perspective, about racism, oppression, and White superiority. Her remarkable journey sets an example for how to treat others, while also teaching Whites about their ignorance and fear. Howard (1999) presents his own journey of transforming his White identity in thoughts, feelings, and actions. Through relating to both perspectives and being emotionally moved by their stories, I began to make efforts to understand my own White identity, of which I was not aware before.

Identity of any sort not only relates to words and thoughts but also relates to emotions and actions. Howard (1999) emphasizes the role of empathy and defines it in several ways. The definition that stands out to me is: "empathy is the antithesis of dominance" (p. 73). Once a White person allows a genuine sense of empathy toward anyone, White dominance is confronted. I say "toward anyone" because empathy is a human feeling. If one genuinely feels, then one will begin to understand that feelings come from shared humanity.

Another emotion important to multicultural awareness is trust. The issue of trust and distrust certainly played a role in the lunchroom incident from my childhood. The cafeteria was crowded that day. As I looked around, the open seat caught my eye and I hurried over to sit down and eat. It didn't occur to me to look around at who was seated there. Did I appear to be a White girl who had confidently invaded the Indian girls' area? I was a stranger they did not know or trust. My Whiteness was not welcomed or wanted. Perhaps, if I had gained their trust first, by *asking* instead of *taking,* the incident would have turned out differently.

Confronting ignorance and fear helps to deal with the issue of trust and distrust. The various perspectives on this issue, from history, personal experiences, and current race relations, need to be acknowledged, respected, and explored. I am still reconciling this difficult issue because I must not only fully explore the collective history of Whites and how our words and actions have affected other cultures, but also realize my own distrust and attitudes toward other cultures. Reflecting upon and coming to terms with my behavior and my culture's action will help me achieve knowledge, understanding, and empathy toward different cultures. Making a conscious decision to find ways to gain trust will help reconcile the issue of distrust.

Furthermore, it takes more than critical self-reflection and a shift of perspective to overcome racism. It is essential, as Howard (1999) suggests, to put thoughts and words into action and to achieve a multicultural way of life that integrates thinking, feeling, and acting. I find this step to be challenging because each situation dealing with racial issues is different. It's difficult to decide when to speak up or when to walk away. For example, at my daughter's soccer game, one of the mothers from our team was questioning the name of a player from the opposing team. The girl's name was Majesty. Later in the game, this mother commented that the other team was not performing as well since they had taken "her majesty" out of the game. I decided not to speak up, but, because the girl was Black, in my mind I was questioning if race were an issue. I don't have the answer, but I can actively reflect on the experience to make it a teachable moment.

For me, to cultivate multicultural awareness, I had to go through a process of acknowledging and respecting different cultures, making connections to others within those cultures, and overcoming colorblindness. The process was centered on thoughts and actions, plus the development of empathy. I do not consider my journey towards anti-racism complete, but I have identified these steps thus far:

1. Honestly acknowledging that racism is a reality in which we live
2. Recognizing my colorblindness
3. Being willing to engage in continuous and thorough self-reflection
4. Beginning to comprehensively explore, understand, and transform my racial identity
5. Quelling my fear and ignorance by reading from a variety of authors, having many discussions with others, and exploring my personal history
6. Welcoming the different points of view of other races and cultures, which will lead to developing empathy toward others
7. Practicing daily acts of anti-racism based on what I have learned
8. Keeping the process evolving

My journey toward anti-racism has not been long thus far. It will be an ever-evolving process for personal growth. As I shed my cultural encapsulation, I have set the tone for intolerance toward racism. Further, I am exposing my children and students to our colorful, diverse society and am encouraging them to discover their connections to others. Hopefully such efforts can bring them into a life of anti-racism from the beginning. Together, we are creating the antithesis of racism instead of perpetuating racism through fear and ignorance. What an exciting time in our lives to be proactive participants in our multicultural world!

21. Seeing Others, Seeing Myself

Sean Kinder

Approaching my grandpa quietly, I asked: "Is Grandma asleep, Grandpa?" Sitting outside her hospital room door, he softly lifted his head and muttered: "She has been for the majority of the day." My grandma had brain cancer and was expected to pass away within a few days. Family visited her frequently. Obviously, my grandpa was in pain, so I tried to talk to him to comfort his mind. "Hey grandpa, tell me what it was like to fight in WWII?" His surprising answer has remained vividly in my memory. "Sean, I did many things that I am not proud of. Killing Japanese or any other man is nothing to brag about. I would rather not talk about my time in the war." His face was serious and I could tell that my question had struck a chord that he himself had struck many times before. My grandpa had been a fighter pilot and had developed a reputation in his unit as one of the men with the most kills.

I start with this short story because my grandfather's reaction illustrates the change of my own mindset in a multicultural education class in which I have become less defensive and more aware of racial differences. In this writing, I highlight the important moments of this process.

I was raised in Glencoe, Oklahoma, a small community just about ten miles east of Stillwater. My family lived in the country, so growing up I was never surrounded by any other people except my family and a few neighbors. My social milieu was predominately White. The school I attended was the same, in that its ethnic minorities consisted of three African Americans and a few Native Americans. My family was replete with war veterans. Just like my grandfather, my dad and uncle also are veterans. I could not be more proud of my family and their service. On the other hand, they don't seem to have enough tolerance for diversity outside of their group. For example, I have a cousin who married a middle-Eastern man, and to this day my uncle, among others, disowns her. When I was four, I played with an African American girl and watched movies with her, but abruptly I was not allowed to play with or visit her anymore. Suffice it to say, I was raised in a homogeneous environment with little opportunity to interact with individuals other than Caucasians.

Thus, I believed that it was a good idea to strive for equality, but merely to the degree that minority groups were appeased. My view on diversity was rather narrow-minded. Reading *I, Rigoberta Menchú: An Indian Woman in Guatemala* (1988) has changed my perspective. The book narrates Rigoberta Menchú's life as a young Guatemalan peasant woman and her struggles as a political activist against the brutality of a government that oppressed indigenous people and wiped out indigenous cultures. I began to think outside of my "White" perspective. The suffering that the Guatemalan community went through and the trials they repeatedly faced have profoundly moved me. My thought process began to broaden in reading chapter XIV of the book, where Rigoberta describes her work as a maid in the capital.

Rigoberta worked as a cleaning servant for an established family in town. With her clothes torn and tattered and wearing no shoes, Rigoberta slept, uncovered, on a blanket next to the trash. Her dinners were extremely meager, at best. Often she was given a few beans and stale, hard tortillas, whereas the dog ate bits of the same meat and rice that the family ate. The mistress was disgusted at the sight of Rigoberta and treated her very badly. The family's three sons made her work more difficult by throwing dishes in her face and consistently insulting her and her culture's work ethic and economic misfortunes.

There were times when she felt really depressed and lonely. Rigoberta spoke to herself in sadness, "The mistress used to watch me all the time and was very nasty to me. She treated me like...I don't know what...not like a dog because she treated the dog well" (1988, p. 94). I could not help but ask: how can a human being treat another so terribly? Then it hit me: because I am White, racially I am related to the offensive woman more than to Rigoberta! This epiphany was startling, really kicking to evoke new understanding. I realized that to understand Rigoberta and her story, I must first evaluate my beliefs regarding others not of my ethnicity. More specifically, I needed to expunge the underlying prejudices I had in order to learn how to accept individual and collective others and become open-minded to racial issues.

My next epiphany occurred shortly after reading Rigoberta Menchú's book. In class, we watched a video titled *Understanding Race* (Dougherty, 1999), and in one scene in the film a variety of individuals were asked: "What is your race?" Everyone responded "Asian," "African American," "Caucasian," "Native American," and so forth. I remember answering along with the film, thinking to myself "I am White." As it turns out, the concept of race is much more complicated than that. The film discusses race as a socially constructed notion. Genetically, we are almost identical. This understanding helped me unlearn the superiority that the people of European descent feel, consciously or unconsciously, about themselves.

Another awakening moment happened when the class visited the Greenwood Cultural Center, where I witnessed and felt the painful reactions of an African-American classmate. His emotional reactions had a drastic impact on me. I stood next to him and saw the shifts of his countenance from calm to anger, evoked by brutal scenes of destruction, and from sadness to amazement, evoked by survivors' stories. This remains an unforgettable memory for me. Far too often we read about tragedies in books and see them on television, only to superficially and arrogantly show our sympathy. A great majority of individuals do not get a chance to closely observe the impact of historical traumas. But at this moment, I felt with my fellow classmate the depth of his pain. A range of emotions stirred in my heart. I felt ashamed, because the Center was replete with images of the atrocities perpetrated by people sharing my skin color. The fact that White people were directly responsible for this infamous historical event was outrageous to me, and I felt anger blending with shame. My class-mate's long gaze at the images and stories recorded on the walls moved me to profound sadness. These emotions shocked me into new awareness and posed a challenge for my further growth.

As I engage in understanding others whose lives are different from my own, I begin to see myself differently. Gary Howard's (1999) book produced a lot of uneasiness in the beginning when I read his White identity theory. Ini-tially, I had a hard time accepting that I, as an individual White person, had a duty to be a part of the solution; I felt I was being wronged just because I was White. However, as I further read Howard's discussion, I began to realize that I was not alone in all the emotions I was experiencing, and that these reactions could be worked through to reach a higher level of understanding.

Howard (1999) discusses two phases (each including three stages) of devel-oping a White racial identity, (pp. 88–94). The first phase, abandoning a racist identity, includes the stages of Contact, Disintegration and Reintegration. In the Contact stage, Whites begin the process by encountering racial others, but the orientation in this stage is colorblindness. In the Disintegration stage, Whites begin to question previously learned racial socializations and acknowledge society's unequal treatment of people of color. As one experiences this discon-nection, one feels anxiety, shame, and guilt. Reintegration is the stage where Whites regress to previous prejudices in order to relieve the negative feelings provoked by Disintegration. The Reintegration stage happens to some Whites, but others don't let the dissonance prevent them from moving to the next phase of developing their White racial identity.

The second phase, establishing a non-racist White identity, includes the stages of Pseudo-independence, Immersion-emersion, and Autonomy. In the Pseudo-Independence stage, Whites confront overt and covert forms of racism and take on White responsibility. In this stage, Whites frequently offer help to people of color, but there is an implicit denial of one's own Whiteness. In the Immersion-emersion stage, Whites move away from paternalistic efforts and turn inward to change themselves and encourage other Whites to do the same.

In the Autonomy stage, "a new and positive definition of Whiteness has been emotionally and intellectually internalized" (p. 93) and race is no longer a threat. In this stage, anti-racism is combined with efforts to go against all forms of discrimination, including sexism, homophobia, classism, or ageism.

Such a model on developing a positive and non-racist White identity helped me to situate myself in a broad framework and to understand where I was and what direction I would like to go in the future. I also realized that a person can have qualities from different stages at the same time. While I had those feelings of dissonance, guilt, and shame that accompanied the Disintegration stage, I am moving beyond these defensive emotions and am striving for a positive White identity. I am at the point where I am questioning many moral dilemmas concerning race, and can safely say that I do not feel threatened by race. To reach the Autonomy stage, I will need to actively seek out opportunities to learn from others and to make a commitment to confronting racism in all its forms.

What is most interesting is that I believe this next step is already implicated in my own experiences. Due to physical disability, I intuitively understand what it means to be different. I hope to be accepted by others, even though it does not always happen. When I tell people that I am different because I am in a wheelchair, they do not like my obvious observation. Howard (1999) describes a conversation with an African American colleague in order to illuminate the limitations of the colorblind approach. He asked: "Jessie, if I tell you that I don't see your color, how does that make you feel?" In turn, Jessie quickly responded, "Then you don't see me" (p. 54). The inability of people to recognize my disability also makes me feel that others "do not see me." As a result, I feel disconnected socially, and it is difficult for me to accept myself. These experiences of being a minority myself help me, upon critical reflection, to dissolve my defensive feelings toward racial differences.

From my grandfather's reaction to my question, I think that he had gone beyond the ethnocentric "us versus them" mindset before he died. My own implicit ethnocentrism has been challenged and transformed through developing multicultural understanding. My wheelchair also has helped to shape my perspective about diversity and difference. I hope that others accept my disability by "seeing" it, rather than ignoring it, and by the same token, I will also educate myself about racial differences to continue the journey of learning in multicultural education.

26. The Chicago Experience: Transforming Identity

Brian Payne

I have always felt closer to my friends than to my own family because of the experiences shared with those I call "friends." Many of my very close friends claim a race other than White. I have used these relationships to develop my own character as well as the approach by which I choose to live my life.

The small, Oklahoma college town where I grew up offered very few experiences that promoted the acceptance and comprehension of diversity. Despite the university's somewhat diverse student body, the community was not known to embrace different races or cultures, thus marginalizing those who were "different." Although in high school my friends were of Hispanic, Middle Eastern, African-American, Chinese, and Philippino descent, preceding high school I had only had White males as friends. I was comfortable in my own world of Whiteness and felt as though I had nothing in common with those who were not in my "world." To use Howard's (2006) White Identity Orientations theory, I was stuck in a Fundamentalist state of White identity without knowing it.

After I began developing friendships with people of different races, I became comfortable with who they were as people, but not comfortable in understanding their history and differences. I had begun to develop an Integrationist view (Howard, 2006), viewing the people around me as my friends, but not wanting to classify them by their racial or cultural upbringing. It was not until I moved to Chicago that I began to fully understand the struggles of those labeled as "minorities." More importantly, based upon experiences of encountering diversity on a personal level, I began to see my friends for who they were.

I moved to Chicago in the fall of 1999 after transferring to Loyola University at Chicago, a small Jesuit school. The school is set in the fairly diverse neighborhood of Rogers Park on the edge of Lake Michigan, and is home to a wealth of vibrant and diverse communities. After several days of exploring my new surroundings, I had discovered that I lived in an area with a large Hispanic and Indian population. Other ethnic groups were dispersed throughout the area as well, and added to the appeal of the neighborhood. This was a welcomed change from the predominantly White, Protestant region of Oklahoma where I had lived all of my life. This diversity was part of the reason I moved to Chicago.

However, my romanticizing of this cultural carnival ended shortly thereafter, as I soon began to see how the different races and cultures interacted with one another. People of the same race treated each other, for the most part, with respect in informal daily interactions. However, with someone of a different race, that mutual respect often turned into impatience and hostility. Blacks were impatient with Whites, Whites impatient with Hispanics, Indians impatient with Asians, and so on. These interactions were seen on the elevated trains, in buses, grocery stores, and in gas stations and often when people walked alongside one another downtown. Impatience and hostility were not confined to one particular race; rather, the behavior was alarmingly consistent when it involved heterogeneous ethnic groups.

In high school and during my first few years in college, I had been stuck in an awkward stage where I was comfortable with other ethnicities, but did not fully understand their plight and place within society as they related to me. However, an incident on a public bus in Chicago forced me out of my awkwardness and into a different realm of thinking.

I had just boarded the bus and was having difficulty with the fare machine. I repeatedly put quarters in the machine and they were promptly spit back out. The Black bus driver looked at me and said, "Hurry up, would you, and sit down." Her words seethed with contempt and I felt she was impatient not only with my inability to properly pay, but with another aspect of my persona: being a young White male in khakis and a dress shirt may have screamed "upper-middle class." I quickly apologized, and the machine finally accepted my fare. I then walked to the middle of the bus, where I found a seat facing the front where the driver sat. I didn't really pay much attention to her tone, as I was becoming more familiar with the rougher-edged tone of voice that I discovered people in a large city develop. I had simply assumed that she had been having a rough day and was ready for her shift to end. Yet, at the next stop, a Black man roughly the same age as I got on the bus and began to have difficulties with the fare machine as well. This time, the driver was much more patient and willing to help him pay the fare. I found this odd. Why would her tone and personality change so dramatically when someone was having the same difficulties that I had encountered only minutes earlier? After a moment, I was taken aback and immediately thought, "So this is about 'race.' This is what I've been personally sheltered from my entire life." Had I acted in a way that placed a barrier between us? Had I unknowingly expressed a racist demeanor toward her as I boarded the bus? Having experienced this brief awakening of thought, my mind was clouded with confusion for the rest of the day.

After that incident I continually found myself watching different races and cultures and attempting to analyze why groups of differing ethnicities failed to communicate on the same level with one another. In turn, studying the actions of others made me more aware of my own behavior and attitudes in regard to race, gender, and sexual orientation. Having the opportunity to live in a metropolis with such a strong cultural foundation based on diversity persuaded me to discover who I was in terms of understanding race. Rather than becoming frustrated when confronted with cultural differences or misunderstandings, I began to view those around me with a newfound sense of awareness, compassion, and cultural insight. I had become more empathetic toward those encountering racial prejudice, rather than simply placing myself outside racism. For years, I had been an Integrationist without the vocabulary to express my feelings toward diversity. However, the incident on the bus, along with my cultural observations, enabled me to transcend Integrationism and move toward becoming a Transformationist thinker.

Aside from attempting to comprehend the differences among others, I specifically began to re-approach the way in which I viewed my friendships. Previously, I had never spent time discussing with my friends how they felt when confronted with situations concerning diversity or having to grow up in a small town as a minority. As mentioned above, I had failed to recognize individual differences in regard to race. I was afraid of emphasizing physical characteristics and societal labels rather than treating them simply as friends. I was unaware of these actions and the possible ramifications that this colorblindness could have had on my friendships (Nieto, 2004).

As I moved toward the Transformationist realm, I began to understand diversity, as well as the subtle ways in which discrimination takes various forms. I realized that many schools practice forms of institutional racism unbeknownst to most of their administrators, faculty, and students (Bennett, 2003). The public schools that I attended were no exception to this practice. Although I was unaware of it at the time, several aspects worked against my friends of color: racially biased curriculum standards, achievement differentials, and an overall absence of an appropriate and fair learning environment for students of different races, cultures, or ethnic origins. Not only did these factors work against my friends, but they did not serve me well either because this white Anglo-Saxon Protestant pedagogy encouraged ethnocentric views.

Another form of racism that I noted while in school was positive discrimination (Clabaugh, 1995). This racism was more apparent with my friends of Asian descent, as they were automatically labeled "smart" based on the stereotypes often associated with Asian Americans. My friends of Asian descent recently informed me that most of this pressure in high school was placed upon them by the faculty and students. The label placed on my friends was unfair, as it created a need for them to perform at higher levels of academic proficiency than their peers. This form of racism was also unfair to non-Asian students who were not perceived as being as smart as Asian students. This discrimination made students like me feel as though we had to work harder in class to gain the respect of teachers and fellow students.

In regards to my future career as an educator, one of the primary concepts taken from my experience in Chicago is that I must remember that the upbringing and culture of each student can be different. I must be able to develop a sense of awareness for each student, which they, in turn, will develop for themselves and for their peers. Homophobia, racism, religious intolerance, and sexual discrimination are all common examples of bigotry, and a prepared educator must be able to address these issues. Students must feel comfortable with themselves as well as their peers in order to have a positive learning experience and to establish an environment promoting compassion, empathy, and understanding.

23. Beyond Silence and Denial: Overcoming Institutional Racism in the Schools

Kristen Nelson

In the small New England town where I grew up, I could easily count, on one hand, the Black students in the public school I attended. Likewise, I had only one Black teacher. For the most part these numbers were consistent with the racial make-up of the predominantly White town. Despite these demographics, or maybe because of them, the assumption existed, and still exists today, that racism is not a real problem in the northeast. Whether New Englanders feel akin to their Union forefathers, bravely battling the evils of slavery, or whether they simply lack the personal experience of routine interactions with individuals whose race or culture varies significantly from their own, for the average White citizen in New England, racism seems a distant topic reserved primarily for the deep south or the streets of Los Angeles. For this reason, the issue of racism is often met with surprise, confusion, indifference, or even denial.

An incident in my junior year of high school was a good example of such reactions. One afternoon between classes, two young males, one White, one Black, got into a rather intense fistfight on school grounds. As is often the case when young people fight, a large crowd of onlookers soon gathered. Some simply lingered out of curiosity, looking for any excuse to avoid their next class; others yelled and cheered, enjoying the ruckus, but one, a White male, who was never actually identified, yelled a racial slur at the Black student. Soon school administrators arrived and broke up the fight.

Later, word spread that the White student involved in the fight was suspended from school for inciting racially-motivated violence. This news came as quite a surprise to those of us who were familiar with the two students who fought. It was clear that many in the crowd, as well as the teachers and administrators, did not know that the two boys were actually very close friends and had been for many years. With one word, an uninvolved bystander in the crowd mistakenly turned a schoolyard scuffle into a racist incident. But what angered many of the students, including me, was that the administration refused to believe that anything but prejudice and racial hatred had fueled the argument and in doing so, actually promoted racial discord within the school.

What I didn't know then, and would not learn for many years, is that racial lines have been drawn so distinctly in American tradition, history, and culture that racial tension comes more naturally to many individuals than racial harmony and, to a large extent, the White population is completely unaware of its own participation in and perpetuation of the divided society in which we live.

How is it possible to participate in racism and not know it? In order to answer this question, it is important to examine briefly the two types of racism in this country and how they differ. The first type of racism is individual racism. This is the more overt and obvious form with which we are most familiar. It consists of "prejudice [by an individual] against one or more racial groups that manifests itself in hostile behavior toward all members of those groups" (Levine & Pataki, 2004, p. 28). We can generally recognize this form of racism by a person's attitudes, comments, and actions toward members of minority groups. The second type of racism, institutional racism, is often not as recognizable or obvious as individual racism but it is equally, if not more, damaging. Institutional racism refers to "the complex of institutional arrangements and choices that restrict the life chances and choices of a socially defined racial group in comparison with those of the dominant group" (Pettigrew et al., 1982, pp. 4–5).

For many White people, especially those who would not consider themselves racist, being White is viewed neither as a help nor a hindrance in their lives: Their Whiteness is simply a neutral fact. In their eyes it does not define them, but rather provides a starting point on which their identity is constructed. Their individual heritage (e.g., Scottish, German, French), religion, values, upbringing, familial relationships, social and political affiliations, interests, education, and a variety of other factors help to define them. In contrast, for Blacks and members of other minority groups, race is an undeniable facet of their identity. It is the result of the larger cultural experience and history of their particular group in the United States. For example, an African American male may be described as a "Black man" before he is described as a Christian, an architect, or a Republican, whereas for Whites, skin color is viewed as invisible and other cultural, personal, social, or political. descriptors are used to identify them. In *White,* Richard Dyer (1997) says,

> Research into books, museums, the press, advertising, films, television, software—repeatedly shows that in Western representation Whites are overwhelmingly and disproportionately predominant, have the central and elaborated roles, and above all are placed as the norm, the ordinary, the standard. (p. 3)

If, however, our society is set up in such a way that Whiteness is the invisible norm while all other races are separate, then by no means can Whiteness be considered neutral. It automatically assumes a certain amount of power, influence, and dominance within the society. And when the dominant group holds the power to establish the major institutions within society, these institutions and the ways they operate reflect its attitudes and beliefs. This is institutional racism. Institutional racism can be as blatant as hiring practices that favor Whites over Blacks, or as subtle and complex as the higher incidence of diseases such as AIDS among certain minority groups (Hutchinson, 1992).

One of the most basic American institutions in which systemic racism exists is within the educational system. Not only are members of minority groups often denied access to educational opportunities, advancement, or curricula that best serve their needs, but educational practices further normalize and perpetuate White power and privilege through various forms of silence and denial. The silence which helps to perpetuate the status quo of inequality is experienced on both sides of the racial divide, although differently by those who are in power and those who experience racial prejudice. In either case, what is missing in our classrooms and curricula can make a profound impression on our students.

An examination of American history textbooks used in this country within the last hundred years reveals a fragmented chronology of our nation's past. Heroic acts of prominent White Americans are embellished and emphasized, while their brutal violence and injustice against indigenous peoples, Blacks, and other minority groups are virtually ignored. James W. Loewen (1995) states:

> The authors of history textbooks have taken us on a trip of their own away from the facts of history, into the realm of myth. They and we have been duped by an outrageous concoction of lies, half-truths, truths and omissions, that is in large part traceable to the first half of the nineteenth century. (p. 39)

In addition, the experiences of average men and women of color are largely omitted. Occasionally, prominent Black leaders or minorities who have accomplished great things are highlighted, but their stories are generally mentioned peripherally or as part of civil rights or Black history lessons covered once or twice a year. If discussion of the Black American experience is saved for one month, then what does this imply about the history taught every other month?

Not only are students developing a one-sided understanding of our history, but often their public school education lacks opportunities for open and honest dialogue about racism within the classroom and beyond. "When asked to reflect on their earliest race-related memories and the feelings associated with them, both White students and students of color often report feelings of confusion, anxiety and/or fear" (Iseke-Barnes & Wane, 2000, p.117). White students and teachers alike are hesitant to broach the subject of racism because they may feel nervous or unsure about how to proceed or how to deal with such a sensitive topic. As Rothenberg (2005) points out:

> Fear requires us to be honest with not only others, but with ourselves. Often this much honesty is difficult for many of us, for it would permit our insecurities and ignorances to surface, thus opening the floodgate to our vulnerabilities....Rather than publicly admit our weakness, we remain silent. (p.128)

Black students, for a different reason, often remain silent rather than confront or discuss racism as they experience it. Some feel so powerless to change the system that they do not believe it will do any good to even talk about the subject. One Black woman writes, "One thing that I struggle with as an individual when it comes to discussion about race is the fact that I tend to give up....I start to think 'He or she will never understand me. What is the point?'" (Quoted in Rothenberg, 2005, p.130).

Denial, like silence, has enabled White superiority to become so ingrained in our society and culture that many of us are not aware that it exists or the ways in which it provides for some, while isolating, shunning, and denying others. As Williams (1966) suggests, when a group of people enjoyed privilege for a considerable period of time, "there is a strong tendency for these people to feel that these benefits are theirs "by right" (p. 727). For this reason, when many Whites begin to be exposed to the multicultural ideas, they are in complete denial of the ways in which they personally contribute to racism. They cannot "see" the individual and institutional racism that has allowed them to benefit from a multitude of privileges not available to minority group members.

An example of this denial can be seen in a documentary, *American Dream at Groton* (Grubin, 1988). The film chronicles a group of high school students at an elite, predominantly White prep-school in Massachusetts. Many students from wealthy families share their educational and professional goals. Jo Vega, a Puerto Rican student from inner-city New York, shows her peers an art exhibit she has created. It shows the challenges, pain, and frustration many Puerto Ricans feel as they seek acceptance and success in a White-dominated society. Her striking artwork deals with racism, unemployment, alcoholism, and depression, and is clearly a project that she closely relates to. As she explains, one White student becomes visibly annoyed. He starts to berate her with questions: "Why do you make artwork about this stuff? If you are angry about something why don't you just bring it up at lunch and talk about it? Don't you think these are the same problems everyone faces? Everyone is put into a group, I am, and every group has its problems." Vega tries repeatedly to explain how Puerto Ricans as minorities experience institutional racism but her White peer continually interrupts her and dismisses her responses. He does not want to hear what she has to say because it would mean acknowledging the disparities within society. It is much easier for the White student to deny that these disparities exist than to consider honestly how he might benefit from his own Whiteness.

Public education has further allowed Whites to deny their participation in racism in this country. Just as textbook writers have consciously omitted significant segments of our country's history, they have also consistently denied responsibility on the part of White Americans for the oppression of others, through the creation of a distorted and mythical chronicle of the past. Gary Howard (1999) argues that "this selective perception of reality is a function of our refusal to acknowledge those truths that collide with the legitimizing myths of American specialness" (p. 59). In effect, the public education system in this country has consistently used denial to make heroes of White men and justify horrible acts of injustice against minorities.

Returning to the incident during my junior year of high school, I have come to see that the administration at my school was guilty of both silence and denial in its handling of the schoolyard scuffle. Administrators silenced the voices of the students involved because they lacked the courage to examine the complex issues related to racism. They believed that the best course of action was swift punishment of the White student because this was the safest and quickest way to distance themselves from dealing with the questions and complexity of racial tensions. Moreover, they were in denial about how they themselves contributed to these tensions with their response to the incident.

While I was angered by the administrative actions, I was completely unaware of my own cultural biases, misconceptions, and stereotypical beliefs regarding people of color. Back then, I believed, quite naively, that I in no way contributed to racism. I thought that I had a true understanding of what racism was and how it was used to oppress people. What I did not realize was that in subtle ways I, too, was guilty of using silence and denial to perpetuate racism. When I remained silent when someone told a racist joke, I thought I was making a statement, but the effect was avoiding confrontation and allowing racism to continue. The person telling the joke could easily assume, when I did not laugh, that I had not heard the punchline or did not "get" the joke.

Likewise, I myself have been in denial about the ways in which our culture has evolved based on White superiority, as well as about the ways that I as a White American, have benefited from this fact. My very narrow view of racism allowed me to live under a false sense of multicultural understanding in which I would pat myself on the back for being nice to Black people, as if I were doing them a favor. Additionally, I thought that being "colorblind" was the answer, when in reality I was actually failing to truly value different cultures as unique and worthy of understanding.

For me, becoming educated about White hegemony did not happen overnight. It was a lengthy process that included participating in discussions with my peers, reviewing multicultural literature, and examining my own attitudes, beliefs, educational experiences, and my own racial identity. Acknowledging what rights and privileges I took for granted as a White person was a major starting point in an ongoing journey toward multicultural understanding.

This journey is one that we as educators must take despite our own fears and reluctance. It requires us to question a system of which we are a part and which has served us well. Despite our desire to be culturally sensitive and inclusive to all of our students, an honest examination of our own Whiteness and its privilege may be difficult. It is easier to look to external and distant sources of racism and work to overcome them than to look within the institutions in which we operate and find success.

Reversing institutional racism is ultimately not about assigning blame, but about taking responsibility. After all it is not so much about individual acts as it is about systemic patterns. As members of the group that benefits disproportionately, we have a responsibility to clarify our perceptions of how power and privilege operate to the disadvantage of certain populations within our society so that we may find ways to actively engage anti-racism and recalibrate the scales of social justice and equality.

Next, we must make a concerted effort to break the cycle of silence and denial in our students' education. This means that we must choose textbooks and learning materials critically and present a more honest view of our nation's history in our teaching and bring as many perspectives to our students as possible, so that they may have the tools to form a more truthful and realistic understanding of their past.

And lastly, we must value our students' differences, whether they are racial, cultural, physical, or emotional, and teach our students the same respect for others' differences. Such a respect for others is also a respect for our own potential. As William F. Pinar (1993) points out:

> We are what we know. We are however, also what we do not know. If what we know about ourselves—our history, our culture, our national identity—is deformed by absences, denials, and incompleteness, then our identity—both as individuals and as Americans—is fragmented. (p. 4)

To avoid such a fragmentation, we need to help our students understand their own identity and how their own identity is influenced by and connected with those of their fellow Americans. As American public school teachers, we have a unique opportunity to re-shape the way young people experience, explore, and value diversity. After all, our students of today will be our institutional leaders of tomorrow.

Pedagogical Reflection V:
Self-Understanding and Engaging Others

Hongyu Wang

It still amazes me that some White Americans tell me with sincerity after they know that I am Chinese: "You people have a culture. We don't have a culture." Here, the use of "we" refers to Americans but actually means White Americans because, in their minds, "culture" belongs to ethnic others. The split between individual and culture is so deeply rooted that "we" hardly realize that the very notion of individualism dominating over culture is a cultural construct.

One of the activities I do in all my multicultural education classes is to ask students to bring to the class an autobiographical artifact related to their cultural identity. Such a simple assignment is not as easy as it seems. Some White students confess that they have to really think about what to bring and why it is culturally meaningful. My purpose is to produce a moment of pause so that the dualism of individual and culture can be questioned. It also proves to be beneficial—when done in the first half of the semester—for building a class community in which students know one another more closely. What is also interesting to me is that racial minority students or international students usually bring artifacts that are related to the bigger picture of their cultural roots, while many White students bring more personal artifacts that are related to their families or their own hobbies. Even though starting points are not the same, all have to stretch from a particular point to blend the personal and the cultural one way or another.

However, cultural self-understanding does not come automatically. It is hard work that comes through engaging with others in a mutually respectful way, especially for White students who are seldom challenged to think about their own cultural and racial identity in their daily lives. While culture is a much broader concept than race, the role of culture is invisible in the White culture to which individualism is essential. Just as the *White culture* is invisible, Whiteness itself is invisible. This invisibility, by default, becomes the standard to measure ethnic and racial others. As Tatum (1987) points out, "Whiteness was simply [an] unexamined norm" (p. 93). To understand and disrupt such a norm, White students have to be able to "see" it first. But the capacity to pause for a moment, turn around, and see the world differently requires the willingness to consider others' viewpoints that are different from or even opposite to one's own. In opening this part with the essay by Tracey Roberson and Stephani Brown, an interracial dialogue on Whiteness, I intend to highlight the necessity of understanding White identity in a multiracial group. Tracey's engagement with the Whiteness of David and with her own Whiteness is mediated through Stephani's lens. I also purposely locate this part at the end of the book to emphasize that critical self-understanding comes from engaging with others who are different. Sean Kinder's essay demonstrates well that his change is a result of engaging an Indian woman's story in Guatemala and experiencing his African American classmate's emotional reaction to the historical trauma of the race riot. Brian Payne's awakening also results from moving from a racial homogeneous city to living in a racially diverse city. As you can see, students' understanding of Whiteness is a major theme throughout this collection—not just in this part—but an interactive approach is the thread underlying many students' discussions.

As important as this mutual engagement between self and other is, transformation of subjectivity cannot happen without going back to unsettle the site of the self. Although there are cautious notes pointing out that focusing on Whiteness may obscure the necessity for privileging the voices from the margin, I believe the parallel focus on Whiteness along with minority perspectives must be highlighted in order to deal with racism at a deeper level. If understanding others does not transform self-understanding, mutuality of relationship cannot be fostered and racial others will remain as "others" who can be kept at a distance and objectified; thus the fabric of individualism, which has historically excluded others, will maintain intact. The cultural and relational embeddedness in which the White self is situated must be acknowledged, experienced, felt, and understood in order to challenge the racial norm. The pursuit for self-understanding is not new, but it is the racial self-understanding that challenges many students' taken-for-granted assumptions.

In White identity development, there are important moments when new thoughts and insights emerge. Just as it is easier to see others' privilege over our own, the moments that brought Whites' attention to the role of race may come from those occasions when they are underprivileged. It is interesting to see that three essays in this part (See Kristen Nelson's, Melanie Burgess', and Brian Payne's essays) describe situations where authors initially felt that their Whiteness was marginalized or mistreated. These instances demonstrate the emotional impact of racial issues, which White students usually experience only momentarily but which many minority students feel on a daily basis. Arguably, the situation of being marginalized can increase empathetic understanding. But there is a danger in fostering such empathetic responses on the part of White students because in doing so, the role of power in upholding Whiteness can stay unquestioned and the feelings of being wronged as Whites and as minorities can be assumed to be equal.

In examining these instances, one has to make efforts to see the bigger picture. Melanie is able to, for example, put her instance in the historical context of genocide of Native Americans, which influenced her American Indian classmates' reaction to her Whiteness rather than to her as a person. She is not stuck in the feelings of being bullied and does not use them to justify the colorblind approach, but such a level of awareness is achieved through a long process of intellectual and social experiencing and interacting. When students bring such instances into the classroom as an implicit argument for "reverse discrimination," educators are confronted with the challenge of guiding and moving them beyond those examples to understand the institutional and cultural practices of racism. Especially in a classroom where the majority of students are White, such a sharing of stories can solidify, rather than question, the unequal social and cultural system if Whites perceive themselves as the victim and refuse to see the role of White power—not available to racial others—in their own lives.

All essays in this part touch upon the issue of institutional racism to a different degree, and Kristen Nelson's insights into the functioning of White racism in silence and denial are quite telling. When racism is only understood as individual attitudes and behaviors—as many students tend to think in the beginning of their studies—many may take comfort in denying their responsibility for unraveling the knot of racism because they can safely say they are not racists. Understanding race not as a biological concept but as a social construct sometimes can play a similar role: Why don't we simply take the word "race" out of our dictionaries so there would not be any racism? The social, cultural, and political reality of race has to be confronted while problematizing the biological concept of race. Paradoxically, only through understanding the complicity of individual persons within the system can individuals take on social responsibility to make efforts against racial inequality.

The colorblind approach, the mainstream popular perspective on race, is also a popular belief of students in teacher education. Many of them equate an explicit reference to race as showing racism. What they don't realize is that "to be color blind is to be blind to White culture, and, thus, blind to one's own White privilege" (Rosenberg, 2004, p. 268). Pearl Rosenberg (2004) further points out that this claim of colorblindness also goes along with being (over)conscious of it, making pre-service teachers feel at a loss in a teaching environment where minority students' presence continually increases. Not working through the difficulty of one's own racial subjectivity, how can one relate to others who are racially different? Teachers' inability to reach out to racially different students is a symptom of not being able to understand their own racial self. Trying not to talk about it cannot hide the reality of racial difference.

In their struggles with the racial self, many students find Howard's (2006) narrations of his journey to understand Whiteness and to affirm a transformative White identity appealing. Many pre-service or in-service teachers care about their students and would like to help all students be successful, but they find it difficult to navigate in the river of diversity. White identity development approaches help them to locate where they are now and envision where they would like to go next. Kerri Bury's, Sean Kinder's, and Brian Payne's essays reflect such a conscious effort. While there are several models (Helms, 1990; Howard, 2006; Tatum, 1997) of White identity development, the progression line from adopting the colorblind approach to becoming racially conscious and further constructing a positive White identity is similar. I often ask students to focus on the transitional periods between developmental steps and think about what conditions can facilitate these transitions in order to foster the movement towards higher levels of multicultural thinking, feeling, and acting.

In such a progression, teacher educators need to be attentive to students' emotional responses and growth. While multicultural educators privilege certain emotions in cultivating social justice awareness, such as empathy (Howard, 2006), guilt (Todd, 2003), sympathy (Iyer, Leach, & Pedersen, 2004), or moral anger (Boler, 1999), what interests me most is how to help students accept emotions provoked in unlearning and not to be stuck in them. When difficult emotions are accepted rather than denied or pushed away, the intensity of those emotions can be softened to pave ways for integrating emotion, intellect, and relationality at a higher level. In such a process, shame and guilt can be transformed into responsibility, anger can be transformed into commitment, pain and sadness can be transformed into compassion, and empathy and sympathy can serve to get in touch with the interconnectedness of human life. Kerri Bury's essay particularly calls for multicultural educators' attention to the emotional labor in which we have to engage.

As I examine the trajectory of my pedagogy, I realize the shift in my own teaching approach during the past eight years of teaching multicultural education classes. From a more direct, confrontational tone to a more fluid waterway of confronting social inequality, I have been trying to develop approaches of teaching about difficult knowledge in a nonviolent way so that the root problem of control and domination in social hierarchy can be treated rather than reinforced. Such a nonviolent posture is more open to students' own processes of unlearning an invisibly normative Whiteness and forming an anti-racist White identity than to imposing anti-racism positions. Only nonviolence can undo the legacy of racial, gendered, class, and heterosexual violence, among other social violence. Challenging students' established perspectives and beliefs without forcing such a challenge is a pedagogical "aporia" that we as multicultural educators must live with in order to generate creative, situation-adaptive responses in specific teaching situations (Wang, 2005). Such an approach requires us to have a profound faith in our students' ability to unlearn the legacy of violence and further construct nonviolent Whiteness.

Here I would like to add a cautious note about the danger of treating Whiteness as a homogeneous social category, not only because of the incredible diversity within Whiteness but also because of the potential violence in the fixation on any social category (including the very term *multicultural education*). We need to be watchful of the essentializing tendency within multicultural education, which treats ethnic or racial groups as if each has some static and distinctive characteristics. In other words, the fluid and emergent nature of culture must be acknowledged to unlearn the mentality of control and mastery which produces social violence in the first place. I cannot emphasize enough that new openings are cultivated and not imposed, and fluidity of subjectivity and culture cannot be forced, but must be enabled. Just as White identity development is an ever-evolving process for these authors, my pedagogical work is a work in progress along a transformative journey of teaching, learning, and growth.

Part VI

Perspectives, Visions, and Praxis

24. Uncovering Racism:
Giving Voices to Uncomfortable Truths
Anita Ede

Racism lies deeply embedded within the fibers of society and the history of our society which we teach to future generations. The term "racism" may be defined as a set of beliefs and behaviors predicated on the assumption that one group is inherently superior to another on the basis of distinctive physical characteristics such as race (Bennett, 2003). Historically, some overtly racist practices were legitimized by Jim Crow laws such as those requiring non-White individuals to drink from separate water fountains, use separate rest rooms, eat in different restaurants, and sit in the back of the bus. Beginning in the 1960s, states began to repeal these laws and the overt, legally sanctioned practice of racism came to an end in the United States. The problem was solved—or was it? Although the legally sanctioned practice of racism was abolished, what remained was an insidious undercurrent of racism that still quietly bubbles beneath the surface—occasionally rising to the top but more often remaining obscured—shrouded within comfortable traditions. These comfortable traditions are well illustrated by the less-than-historically-accurate renditions of Christopher Columbus' and the Pilgrims' arrival in America, as taught to generation after generation of schoolchildren. At times, these comfortable traditions are also evidenced by silencing some traditions and giving voice to others through media coverage of events or lack thereof. The act of silencing sends a powerful message because the limited information becomes the basis of people's understanding. Young children unwittingly absorb and create their own racist judgments based on the ways in which people and events are depicted.

This essay chronicles an uncomfortable journey that begins with unquestioning acceptance of my own childhood images of Christopher Columbus and the Pilgrims. It winds its way through feelings of anger and doubt and leads to the uncomfortable realization that silence may be the most powerful "teacher" of all when it comes to the perpetuation of racism. In the end, I am left with a new lens through which to view the world—one that is clearer and leaves me more cautious.

Comfortable Acceptance

"Columbus sailed the ocean blue, in 1492..." Is there a child in our society who has not repeated these lines while preparing for his or her school's annual celebration of Christopher Columbus' "discovery" of America? As a young child, I prepared for this day by coloring pictures of a smiling and brave-looking Christopher Columbus. When I was older, I made *papier-mâché* replicas of his ships and sang patriotic songs in school-wide parades. Thus, the belief that Columbus was a heroic sailor who sailed halfway around the globe to discover a "new world" became an integral part of my world view.

Each November brought myriad activities related to the Pilgrims' arrival in America. Doors and walls were hung with posters of Pilgrims smiling benevolently. Little girls made white, construction paper Pilgrim caps and boys made tall, black Pilgrim hats with big yellow buckles. Movies and books depicted the Pilgrims' journey to America and their struggles after they arrived. Native Americans were portrayed as helpful and caring neighbors who appeared delighted to have the Pilgrims come and take over their land. Positive descriptions related to individual Native Americans, such as Squanto, were accompanied by the explanation that he had traveled to England and learned the language and customs of Great Britain. Regardless of the school or grade, the message was the same—compassionate and friendly Pilgrims came to the "wilderness" in order to live in religious freedom. These images from my childhood, unquestioningly accepted and cherished, helped to create a comfortable view of these historical events.

Anger

While taking a class in multicultural education as a doctoral student, I read James Loewen's (1995) book, *Lies My Teacher Told Me*. Initially, I saw his depictions of historical figures—Columbus and the Pilgrims in particular—as downright libelous given that they were no longer around to defend themselves. I felt angry that someone would want to besmirch these icons of my childhood. What made it even worse was that some of my classmates actually believed this "stuff." Didn't they recognize a calculated effort to sell books when they saw one? I vowed to keep my thoughts to myself and get through the class without making a scene by publicly accusing the author of making up the entire book. But once my initial anger subsided, an uncomfortable sense of confusion and imbalance took its place.

Doubt

Each time I came to class, I felt more and more confused by the discrepancy between my view of historical events and those promulgated by Loewen and some of my peers. I began to ask myself questions. Could I be wrong? Complacent? Uninformed? Uncaring? Was it possible to be forty-something and not have an accurate understanding of historical events that had always seemed so straightforward? These questions propelled me to begin my own research in hopes of validating my own beliefs and quieting the confusion that was making me so uncomfortable.

I began at the beginning—Christopher Columbus' "discovery" of America and made a discovery of my own—America did not require discovering. It had already been inhabited for thousands of years by a variety of Native American tribes. The West Indies, where Columbus and his men came to shore, was home to the Arawak civilization. Further research revealed other facts that were not a part of the Columbus Day celebrations of my childhood. Columbus' voyage was a well-planned trip that resulted from a written contract between Columbus and King Ferdinand and Queen Isabella of Spain. That contract gave him rights to ten percent of the profits from any goods he brought back to Spain, including "gold, silver, spices, pearls, and other articles and other merchandises" (Columbus at Granada, 1892, p. 4). Those "other merchandises" turned out to be Arawaks. On the day of his arrival in the West Indies Columbus wrote in his diary, "they [Arawaks] should be good servants...I, our Lord being pleased, will take hence, at the time of my departure, six natives for your Highnesses" (in Bourne, 1906, pp. 111–112). From his first voyage to the Indies Columbus took six Arawaks back to Spain to be sold as slaves. Columbus returned to the West Indies three more times—each time destroying villages; killing those who resisted; confiscating food, gold, and cotton; and returning to Spain with additional slaves (Zinn, 1900). Traditional accounts of Columbus and his men are certainly more comfortable than historically accurate versions; however they celebrate one individual [Columbus] while silencing an entire group of people [Arawaks] and relegating them to invisibility. Disheartened by my newfound knowledge of Christopher Columbus, I began to wonder if the friendly images of Pilgrims so often seen in textbooks and on Thanksgiving decorations and greeting cards were historically accurate, or simply more comfortable.

It did not take long to discover that the Pilgrims, or Separatists as they called themselves, were not the benevolent people of my childhood stories. Rather than clear their own land and build their own homes as I had previously believed, the Pilgrims laid claim to land that had previously been cleared by the Wampanoags and Patuxets, who had lost almost all of their members due to disease (Cheever, 1848). They simply changed the name of the already existing town from Patuxet to New Pli(y)mouth (Cheever, 1848). The Pilgrims' disposition towards their Native American neighbors is well-illustrated in a journal entry made by the governor of New Pli(y)mouth, William Bradford: "The good hand of God...favored our beginnings... sweeping away great multitudes of the natives...that he might make room for us" (in Johansen, 2006, p. 120–121). Rarely mentioned is the fact that the Pilgrims dug up Native American graves and stole artifacts that might be useful to them (Loewen, 1995). This image of the Pilgrims is far less comfortable than the one traditionally offered, and I am left to question why the voices of the Native Americans living in New Pli(y)mouth were silenced—and at what cost.

Uncomfortable Realizations

Discovering the fact that entire cultures were relegated to silence in traditional portrayals of Christopher Columbus' and the Pilgrims' arrivals in America was a disconcerting experience. I was surprised and embarrassed by my own naïveté and began to wonder why the silence existed. Who benefits from it?

As Winston Churchill said, "History is written by the victors," and the traditional versions of these historical events were indeed written by those who had the power to do so. They had access to writing tools, a printing press, newspapers, and books, which means that they had the means by which to "get the word out," something that was not the case for the Native American tribes at that time. The lack of historical accuracy can be attributed to any number of factors—not the least of which may be shame and embarrassment over less-than-stellar behavior. Most individuals like to portray themselves and those they support in the best possible light. It may be that historians of Columbus' time preferred to show him in the best light, which meant excluding the Arawaks from the accounting. The same could be said of the Pilgrims' settlement of New Pli(y)mouth. Of course one could also question the motives of the historians—was it not their duty to record history as accurately as possible? Was there an element of racism in early accounts of these events? No one will ever know historical facts for sure, but I am troubled by the reality that the same versions of Columbus and the Pilgrims are still perpetuated today. Silencing all of the "unpleasantness" may make the event more pleasant, but silence implies that those who are silenced are insignificant. We have to ask: Why is a particular group of people unworthy of recognition? How do children internalize the sanctioned images of different groups? What is the impact of silencing the unpleasant at school on students' perception of the world? Now I am able to see the cycle of racism which had been hidden from me.

Viewing the World through a New Lens

Empowered by the clarity of a new lens through which to view people and events, I turned to the world around me and was immediately struck by discrepancies in the news coverage of three female soldiers in the Iraq war. The news coverage of three female soldiers captured in 2003 exemplifies how media can bestow importance on a single individual while maintaining a virtual silence towards others. Have you ever heard of Lori Ann Piestwa? Chances are you have not. Private first class Piestwa was the *first* American woman to die from injuries she received during her capture in the Iraq war. She was a twenty-three-year-old Hopi Native American, and she left behind two young children (Mitchell, 2003). The return of this hero's body to the United States went largely unnoticed. Shoshana Johnson, a thirty-year-old African American, was the *first* female prisoner of war in American history. She was shot in both ankles and held captive for twenty-two days in Iraq in 2003 (Lander, 2003). This hero's rescue and subsequent return to the United States went mostly unnoticed as well.

However, media coverage of twenty-year-old Jessica Lynch, a Caucasian soldier, was entirely different from that given to Lori Piestwa and Shoshana Johnson. Hers was a media event. Private first class Lynch broke both her legs when her unit was ambushed in 2003 and she was held in an Iraqi hospital for nine days until her rescue by the U.S. military. This hero's rescue and subsequent return to the United States were intensely covered by the media. In fact, video cameras recorded her rescue, her transport to a field hospital, her transport to an army base hospital in Germany, and her return to the United States. Twenty-four hour news stations ran footage of Pfc. Lynch over and over again. Newspapers and magazines clamored for interviews and ran feature stories about her. Lynch's return to her home town of Palestine, West Virginia was marked by a parade through town, which the media eagerly broadcast. She was interviewed countless times both in print and on television. Her book deal, alone, was for over one million dollars, and then there was the made for television movie… (Italie, 2003).

I am deeply troubled when I view the discrepancies in the amount of media coverage these three soldiers received because the coverage itself sends messages about who is deemed "newsworthy" and important, and who is NOT. All three of these soldiers deserve our admiration, yet all the contributions but those of Jessica Lynch went largely unnoticed. The silence surrounding the stories of Lori Ann Piestwa and Shoshana Johnson speaks loudly. What conclusions will be reached by young children who spend more than two hours each day watching television (Rideout, Vandewater, & Wartella, 2003), or teenagers who watch as many as twenty hours of television per week (Media Literacy Fast

Facts, n. d.)? Media is not necessarily a bad thing—but it needs to be recognized as a powerful teacher because of its ability to convey messages not only overtly by what is said, but also covertly by what is left unsaid.

The Journey Continues

This uncomfortable journey is by no means over, for I am constantly viewing the world through lenses just polished and am finding things that make me question "facts" and wonder about events that once appeared beyond question. I search under and between the lines for traces of those who are not visible and ask, "Why not?" As an educator, I encourage my students to ask "Why not" questions. When all are visible and none are silenced, racism will no longer lurk in the shadows.

25. An Examined Life: The Journey of Becoming a Multicultural Educator

Sandra L. Bequette

> I am convinced there is a prior and equally compelling need for White people, particularly White educators…to look within ourselves and align our deepest assumptions and perceptions regarding the racial marker that we carry, namely Whiteness. We need to understand the past and present dominance, face how we have been shaped by myths of superiority, and begin to sort out our thoughts, emotions, and behaviors relative to race and other dimensions of human diversity.
>
> —Howard, 2006, p. 6

The issue of diversity in our schools currently presents a challenge. School districts complying with the No Child Left Behind legislation must demonstrate progress with all students, including English Language Learners, poor and minority students, and students with disabilities (Haycock, 2006). Schools are attempting to meet these mandates by aligning standards, providing tutoring, and implementing stringent testing practices. While student achievement has improved in some districts, research suggests a wide achievement gap of at least two grade levels remains between minority students and White students (Howell, 2006). Furthermore, White-Clark (2005) finds that "by the twelfth grade, the gap has widened even further with these students lagging nearly four years behind" (p. 24). The achievement problem becomes even more alarming when we consider that currently more than one-third of public school children in American classrooms are minorities and that the percentage of minority students might be near 50 percent by 2025 (White-Clark, 2005).

White-Clark (2005) proposes that cultural differences between students and teachers are a major reason behind the achievement gap. It is well acknowledged that despite the dramatically increasing racial diversity in student bodies, teachers are predominantly White. Howard (2006) suggests that there may be a relationship "between the over-representation of White teachers in our classrooms and the underperformance of children of color in our nation's schools" (p. 4). He recommends that White teachers embark on a transformational journey to become multicultural educators. This journey requires both an inner and outer transformation as educators examine the very frameworks of their lives. Nieto (2004) also emphasizes that becoming a multicultural educator requires first becoming a multicultural person. Answering their calls, in this essay, I reflect on what has shaped my life in order to continue my journey of becoming a multicultural person and educator.

Learning More about Pluralism

Nieto (2004) recommends that educators become involved in experiences that lead to understanding pluralism. Resources such as books and other materials are also helpful. She cautions that learning about pluralism can be difficult because the majority of people have been raised in a monocultural environment. In examining my own experiences, though, I realize that I was one of the first students to experience diversity in public education when mandatory busing began in my school district in Wichita, Kansas, in the early 1970s. Being exposed to difference at an early age has helped me to relate to people of color. However, I did not understand the White privilege existing in my own surroundings. Only in thinking back now do I recall that many of my minority peers did not do as well in the classroom, particularly the Black boys. I also remember my elementary school lunchroom where the bussed students all ate free, cold lunches. There were always oranges in the lunches—every single day.

When I was a first-year teacher, I was immediately thrown into a situation of diversity as students of various racial backgrounds filled my classroom. In my teaching experiences, I was baffled by some of their behaviors. However, I did not consciously see this confusion as an issue of Whiteness. Rather, I viewed it more as problems that the child had, not understanding that I was perpetuating White dominance by viewing my perspective as "correct" (Howard, 2006). To truly embrace pluralism, I must challenge my own assumptions about the world, which includes questioning the invisible privilege of Whiteness.

During my graduate work, I have read multicultural works and also engaged in discourse with students from different backgrounds, countries, and experiences. Learning about and from people different from myself has been a vital factor in developing my multicultural perspective. This learning, along with my classroom experiences, has allowed me to advance from monoculturalism toward pluralism. However, the journey isn't complete but is an ongoing process of growing toward greater awareness.

Seeing Reality from a Variety of Perspectives

As I look back at my years of teaching, in most cases, it is my students of diversity who stand out, and perhaps who taught me the most. I remember

Stephen, a Hispanic student in my kindergarten class, and his refusal to connect with me as a White person. He taught me how to deal with the complexity of race and to form an educational relationship with minority children. Such a situation requires the ability to see reality from a variety of perspectives. As Nieto (2004) points out, "Because we have often learned that there is only one 'right answer,' we have also developed only one way of seeing things. A multicultural perspective demands just the opposite" (p. 384).

Not many teachers understand such a demand. For instance, a fellow White teacher did not allow her students to speak their native language. She complained when the Hispanic mothers wanted to eat breakfast with their children. Others protested about having to send home letters in Spanish, saying, "They live in America. They need to learn English." We need to change such attitudes. One year I had five non-English-speaking students in my classroom and no training to teach them. They, in essence, taught me how to teach and called into play the use of relationships to build trust not only with the students but their families. I have never felt such educational pride as when these five children succeeded and surpassed even my expectations.

Perhaps my ability to connect with my students, especially those that might struggle a bit in the classroom is related to my sensitivity to what it meant to be on the outside, not belonging. Perhaps this understanding comes from my childhood home life when I had to learn to "read" my mother's moods as she battled with mental illness. Or as an older child, when I was often the one left out due to my inability to fit in with my peers. Later on, through a friendship with my adopted daughter's birth mom, I learned about social class and how the many things I took for granted were unattainable for her. This engagement with others different from me helped me form a "lens of otherness" (Howard, 2006, p. 38). As a teacher, I have always tried to see life in the classroom through my students' eyes. However, it wasn't until I confronted my own racial biases that I realized that I often did not acknowledge the cultural lives of my students.

Confronting Our Own Racism and Biases

I can honestly say that I had never confronted my own racism until my last teaching assignment. For so long, implicit racism was alive in my classroom—I just never "saw" it. Color blindness was one example, as I believed that by treating my students the same, I was showing respect. However, while attempting to be nondiscriminatory in how I treated my students, I did not affirm the very differences that made them culturally unique. In my own teaching, I have always felt I taught "through a child's eyes." I remember my childhood so well and the joy learning brought me. I strive to bring that joy into every classroom I work in. However, through reflection, I realize I have not always taken into account the complexities of children's lives. I need to question my own view of childhood and recognize students' own voices as they are.

Nieto (2004) suggests that educators question who is doing the accommodating in interactions with minority students and families. She calls for mutual accommodation as "teachers and schools, as well as students, need to modify their behaviors in the direction of a common goal: academic success with cultural integrity" (p. 374). Because my perspective was defined by my Whiteness, I did not understand what people of color had experienced in order to live in American society. We have asked them to accommodate to our White ways for too long. In confronting and changing the White power in my own classroom, I have to learn to meet my students more than halfway. I have learned that minority students and their families had reason to distrust me. To truly teach, I have to give *more* to overcome the imbalance established by my White predecessors. Encouraging all students to use their own languages, experiences, and develop their own identities in the classroom enables everyone to grow, including the teacher.

In developing a multicultural perspective, I am anxious to enter a classroom again, knowing my philosophical outlook will affect everything I say or do. I can no longer be part of the problem, only the solution. Racism is seldom explicit; rather, it lurks behind school funding, selection of curriculum, even literature titles. As Nieto (2004) argues, the school should become a site "that legitimates talk about inequality" and promotes dialogues about racism (p. 348). I am committed to speaking out when I see inequality occurring and working to bring about a diverse learning environment for all of my students.

Part of being a multicultural educator is to understand one's own cultural being. Howard (2006) cautions that "an unexamined life on the part of a white teacher is a danger to every student" (p. 127). Change does not happen overnight. We must allow our fellow White educators to see racism and grow beyond it. Our classrooms have changed drastically and will continue to be transformed into multifaceted learning environments. Perhaps the most important lesson that I have learned is that dismantling racism in our educational system will not be easy. However, acknowledging the problem and that I am part of it will lead to accepting responsibility for change, ultimately leading to transformation. Inspired by "a vision worthy of a lifetime of work" (Howard, 2006, p. 139), I continue my journey as a transformative multicultural educator with a renewed commitment.

26. The Glass Closet: Silencing Classroom Dialogue

Lauren Skvarla

Espousing the tenets of critical pedagogy, many educators strive to bring the voices of disenfranchised youth to the arena of educational debate. Teachers are attempting to develop a curriculum which actively promotes social change and involves the voices of marginalized students. The theoretical discourse of critical pedagogy is essential in the ongoing debate regarding numerous educational issues including student testing, curriculum development, staff development, and school finance. However, consideration of issues surrounding teachers' sexual orientation is too often approached hesitantly in the field of education.

A Teacher Like Jennifer

A colleague of mine, a first-year teacher, had decided to share something difficult with me. Unable to make direct eye contact with me, Jennifer paced the classroom. But I already knew what she was about to say, and I knew I could never divulge her secret. Jennifer was a young, enthusiastic, dedicated teacher, who was about to reveal she was a lesbian. In the small midwestern town in which we taught, I worried about what loomed ahead for her in the coming year. Jennifer strove to bring the voices of disenfranchised youth to the forefront. However, many teachers, teachers like Jennifer, are themselves marginalized—relegated to teach in a glass closet.

Though the boundaries for discussing homosexuality are widening, examining the role of homosexual educators in public schools can bring discomfort and even hostility. The rhetoric of religious groups and conservative political organizations further fuels the debate with hatred and misinformation. The Traditional Values Coalition, an inter-denominational public policy organization speaking on behalf of over 43,000 churches, fervently spreads the fear of homosexual educators. In a 2003 special report, the organization predicted the adulteration of public school students. "As homosexuals continue to make inroads into public schools, more children will be molested and indoctrinated into the world of homosexuality. Many of them will die in that world" (Sheldon, 2003, p. 1). Within this hostile climate, gay and lesbian teachers' decisions to identify their affectional orientation in the public school sphere are problematic.

Within this antagonistic climate of unsubstantiated accusations, Jennifer began her teaching career. An idealist, Jennifer entered education with the hope of expanding her students' awareness of the inequities of class, race, gender, and sexuality that permeate our society. She looked forward to engaging her students in meaningful discussions. However, she soon realized that the desire for authentic interaction with her students came with a price she was unwilling to pay.

The Fear of Harassment

Closeted educators wanting to engage in critical pedagogy through a dialogic relationship often hesitate to take part in meaningful conversations with their students, although such an engagement with students is crucial to liberatory pedagogy (Freire, 1998). According to Freire (2000), the teacher and student—as partners—must "engage in critical thinking and the quest for mutual humanization" (p. 75). However, the desire for authenticity with students brings tremendous risk. Kissen (1996) identified fear as the overwhelming concern for educators contemplating self-disclosure. This fear that silences homosexual educators also silences classroom dialogue and the possibility of democracy, individual freedom, and social justice for both teachers and students. For many gay and lesbian teachers, the fear that their affectional orientation will be exposed is unremitting. Though Jennifer confided in me, throughout the year, she avoided conversations with her students and colleagues about her personal life or any issue concerning homosexuality.

The pervasive fear of harassment from students and administrators is a central issue for educators considering disclosing their sexuality to students. In 1999, two openly gay teachers in Michigan claimed they had been discriminated against and subjected to harassment because of their sexuality. The board of education accused the two teachers of promoting their personal lifestyle by displaying a Gay History Month bulletin board which had been intended to promote safety and respect. Though the men received an apology in arbitration, it became clear that the school's stated mission of "respect for all" in actuality meant respect for heterosexuals only (School District, 2001). These two teachers were simply attempting to recognize a segment of the nation's population, as most schools do for Black American, Native American, and female heroes. The consequences they suffered appear as a warning to any teacher who might contemplate disclosing other than a heterosexual orientation.

Kissen (1996), interviewing gay and lesbian teachers, heard stories of students using innuendo and intimidation against teachers. Closeted teachers were constantly aware that this form of harassment, from students leaving notes to spraying a painting wall, could prompt questions from parents or an investigation into their sexuality by the administration. In a sincere note to a student returning to the district, a teacher named Lydia wrote, "I heard you were back. It would be great to see you. Drop by the school sometime," and was promptly accused by the girl's mother of making advances (Kissen, 1996, p. 13). Before she quit her job, the union representative reprimanded her, saying, "You are not supposed to be friends with kids" (p. 14). Fear that any indication of their sexual preference could result in harassment from students, parents, or administrators is preventing educators from authentic dialogue with their students and is detrimental to their fostering tolerance, trust, and acceptance (Shor, 1992).

The Fear of Termination

An equally distressing concern that gay and lesbian teachers confront is the fear of termination. In an anonymous letter to *The Advocate*, a gay teacher expressed his decision to stay closeted even within the liberal milieu of Massachusetts:

> As a high school teacher and soccer coach at a high school in Massachusetts, I'm afraid that if I come out as a gay man in a forum this public, I will risk losing my job. You see, although Massachusetts is one of the most forward-thinking states in the nation when it comes to providing protections for gay and lesbian students, it—like most states—has done little to make schools a safe place for gay and lesbian teachers. (Anonymous, 2000)

Across the Midwest, with its increased prevalence of religious fundamentalism, homosexual educators are subject to an even greater threat of termination. For homosexual educators, the fear of losing employment has intensified with the rise of the religious Right. During the emergence of the gay and lesbian rights movement in the 1970s, fundamentalist Christian groups became increasingly alarmed that American society was degenerating from its foundational moral traditions (Lugg, 1997). The increased visibility of homosexuals in society made the religious Right proclaim that homosexuals were infiltrating schools, spreading their disease, and recruiting unsuspecting children into their ranks. This hostility was, in part, a reaction to the political gains homosexual activists were achieving. Historian Joan Nestle explains, "We were seen as a danger in terms of education, in terms of social policy. Though in a way, it was recognition of our growing social power" (Quoted in Lugg, 1997, p. 7).

By 1978, the fervor of the religious Right to rid public schools of homosexuals led California State Senator John Briggs to introduce an Initiative, Proposal 6, which included the following statement:

> The state finds a compelling interest in refusing to employ and in terminating the employment of a schoolteacher. . . who engages in public homosexual activity and /or public homosexual conduct directed at, or likely to come to the attention of, school children or other school employees. (Harbeck, 1997, p. 64)

Though supported by Anita Bryant and conservative religious leaders, Prop 6 was defeated with the aid of an unlikely opponent, Ronald Reagan. With his eye on the Republican presidential nomination, Reagan knew he would need the support of teachers and their unions to secure a victory in 1980, and the passage of Prop 6 could alienate these potential voters. The proposition was defeated, but the campaign of the religious Right to rid the schools of homosexuals continued. In April of 1978, Oklahoma legislators presented a bill identical to Prop 6, which was overwhelmingly supported and passed into law (Harbeck, 1997). It would take until 1985 for opponents of the law to bring their case before the Supreme Court. With the Court's split decision, both sides claimed victory. The personal freedoms of educators continue to be in danger. The political and social climate of the new century has only refueled the zeal of religious groups.

Religious groups bent on removing these teachers from public schools often attempt to scare administrators into firing gay and lesbian teachers. The Christian Coalition of Maine in 2000 reported, in a statewide mailing to administrators, the increased incidence of child molestation by homosexuals, though such claims have been discredited. The letter explicitly threatened administrators who were aware of homosexuals on their staff. "'Knowingly employing homosexual teachers after receipt of this study places you in a precarious legal situation.' The letter suggests that school officials could face 'serious civil—and perhaps even criminal—liability' if a gay teacher molests a student" (Religious Group, 2000). The prevalence of scare tactics validates educators' anxieties that their next evaluation by the administration may result in termination. As long as organizations in the guise of religious faith spread aspersions and threaten lawsuits in the name of morality, gay and lesbian teachers who desire to interact in honest dialogue with students jeopardize their own economic security.

The Effects on Teaching

Gay and lesbian teachers who conceal their lives in the school environment because of the oppressive fear that threatens them on a personal and financial level live within a glass closet. Because of the underlying harassment and prejudice that can occur in public schools, they are denying themselves the full rewards of teaching by choosing to create a façade of heterosexuality. The effects can only be detrimental. It is not possible for homosexual educators to develop collaborative relationships with students when they must lie or ignore essential elements of their own lives. When teachers are forced into the classroom closet, opportunities to promote tolerance and dismantle stereotypes are lost. The necessity for deception limits the possibility of teaching toward transformational goals that include justice and equality. Prior to coming out, a teacher from Phillips Exeter Academy expressed her emotions on being silenced:

> With devastating simplicity   I learned
> complex RULES of BEHAVIOR, developing elaborate forms
> of   EVASION   SECRECY   DENIAL   and HALF-TRUTHS
> in which the FAILURE to SPEAK becomes in itself
> a FORM OF OPPRESSION....
> In other words   I learned to be pretty GOOD   LIAR....
> The ability to DISGUISE sex-u-ality is both
> a GIFT and a CURSE
> a FREEDOM   and   a BURDEN.
> For when you PASS you lose the opportunity to DEFINE
> YOURSELF
> Because you are NOT BEING yourself...
> (Robinson, 1994, p. 79–80)

The emotions she expressed represent homosexual teachers' authentic understanding of the issues that surround their career choice. The ease, for many educators, of living within a glass closet conceals the loss of empowerment they experience.

Not shying away from exploring gay themes in the classroom, a Massachusetts teacher believed hiding his sexual identity has inhibited his relationship with his students. Reflecting on his pedagogy, he explained, "The hallmark of a good teacher, however, is not a gay-inclusive lesson plan but limitless compassion. While I offer my students a lot of support, my being in the closet puts limits on that compassion" (Anonymous, 2000).

As statistics reveal the alarming rate of suicide among homosexual youth, gay and lesbian teachers "long to show their students that gay adults can lead happy, productive lives" (Kissen, 1996, p. 57). The silencing of homosexual teachers precludes the development of a community of support for gay youth. The diversity and pride within the GLBT community is unknown in the public school. Reflecting on the isolation of homosexual youth, Kissen (1996) writes, "They may go through their entire adolescence with no image of themselves other than the negative ones projected by mainstream American culture" (p. 57). This should be a critical issue with all educators, but homosexual teachers could foster a dialogue if they were allowed to be honest. "In a critical classroom, the teacher does not fill students unilaterally with information but rather encourages them to reflect mutually on the meaning of any subject matter before them" (Shor, 1992, p. 85). As teachers stay in the closet, they lose the opportunity to both share and exemplify for their students the positive contributions and diversity of the gay and lesbian community.

Perceived as a straight male because of his athleticism and risk-taking exploits, a gay coach reflected upon his influence on students: "But I can't help thinking that by remaining in the closet at school, I'm also showing them that there is something inherently wrong with being gay. As much as the students recognize that I am different from other teachers, they don't know what makes me different" (Anonymous, 2000). Gay and lesbian teachers who are fearful of voicing their perspectives openly become distressed when they cannot take an active role in confronting the numerous inequities homosexual youth experience in school without jeopardizing their own perceived heterosexuality. To protect their hidden identities, some may even go so far as to acquiesce in hateful acts toward gay and lesbian students. A Denver teacher recalled the experience with a closeted lesbian teacher:

> A student was chased out of the high school with three baseball bats. . . I talked to a lesbian teacher, and she said, "Well, he was just so flamboyant about everything.". . . She is totally closeted lesbian teacher telling a student who is openly gay that he deserves to be [assaulted] because he's here rattling the system. (Kissen, 1996, p. 58)

The teacher's own fears of being exposed led to her malicious assessment of an intolerant and brutal act. Students who may be questioning their identity, students who are called "faggot" or "dyke" by their fellow classmates, or students who simply may want to honestly express their adolescent angst, too often are unable to connect to a gay or lesbian teacher who is hiding behind a glass wall of silence.

Breaking a History of Silence

For many young educators, the public school is not a safe environment in which to disclose their affectional orientations; however, many older educators remember the lack of visibility of gays and lesbians in past decades and encourage younger educators to come out to their students and colleagues:

> A school with an openly lesbian or gay teacher is a better school. It is a school where truth prevails over lies; it is a school where our nation's rhetoric about equality moves

one step closer to becoming a reality. As gay and lesbian teachers win our freedom, we help to free our students, our colleagues, and our communities of the burden of bigotry, which has, for too long, taught some members of families to hate their own sisters, brothers, mothers, and fathers. We are the true upholders of family values. (Jennings, 1994, p. 14)

The long fight for the rights of gays and lesbians cannot yet be celebrated inside public schools; however, for those who dare to move through the door of their secrecy, the journey, though difficult, has been liberating.

School principal Mark French's coming-out on a Nickelodeon special called *My Family Is Different* was a non-issue for most of the students and parents in Maple Grove, Minnesota. In response to a few derisive comments suggesting that gay faculty threaten children's innocence, French explained, "I don't believe [my revelation] means the loss of innocence for our children. It opens up their minds and it opens up the opportunity to talk about topics such as discrimination, intolerance, acceptance, harassment and name-calling, and violent behavior against groups of people" (Blotcher, 2004). It is exactly this form of communication that is required for knowledge to build. Freire (1998) argues that a dialogic relationship—communication and intercommunication among active subjects who are immune to the bureaucratization of their minds and open to discovery—is indispensable to knowledge (p. 99).

By the end of May, Jennifer and I had been informed that, because of budgetary restrictions, neither of us would have a teaching position the following year. As we walked out of the school together on the last day, I reflected on the journey each of us had taken that year. Jennifer had maintained a safe distance from her students for the entire year, never really building a strong rapport with them. I had voiced my opinion about almost any subject my students had the nerve to bring up—I also believe I made connections that will keep me in touch with some of those young students for years. As we headed to our cars, I knew that Jennifer was not going to actively look for a new position and was considering changing careers. Until administrators, parents, and whole communities reflect upon the consequences of bigotry and hatred toward homosexuals, some of our best teachers, teachers who just happen to be homosexual, teachers like Jennifer, will continue to be silenced.

27. Educating Young Adults through Social Justice Literature

Tiffany Ballard

Albert Einstein once wrote, "The world is a dangerous place to live in, not because of the people who do evil, but because of the people who allow it to happen." While teaching various English classes in a rural city in Oklahoma, I try to negotiate a space in my classroom through multicultural education that does not allow evil to happen. One way to do so is through teaching social justice literature which addresses different and multiple layers of social difference. Regarding the educational use of literature in the classroom, Nieto (2004) points out, "With older students, focusing on multicultural literature that depicts the reality of women and men of many groups is an effective strategy" (p. 402).

Social justice literature is extremely difficult to teach in a rural town where high school students already have a defined voice with regard to their beliefs. Their voice is largely influenced by their not-so-diverse background. In my classroom, I strive to be what Howard (2006) describes as a transformatist educator, one who is continually responsive to negotiate the murky waters of multicultural education and meet the challenges that are presented in educating young adults. In this essay, I discuss the aspects of relationships, dialogue, and caring, and the role of emotions in a variety of teaching approaches that have transformed my social justice literature curriculum into an experience for my students that they may not otherwise have.

For this essay, I will focus on one piece of literature, Harper Lee's (1960) *To Kill a Mockingbird,* even though I use a variety of literature in each class. Lee's novel focuses on the issues of gender, social class, and race, all from the point of view of a young, White, middle-class girl named Scout. The setting is a small, southern town in the 1930s, where an African American man is wrongly accused of raping a White woman. Scout's father, Atticus, is the lawyer for the African American male and teaches Scout lessons about life, prejudice, and how to exist in an unfair world.

Teaching about social injustice through literature and multicultural education practices may cause, as Edgerton (1996) points out, students' resentment and resistance, but working through these difficulties is essential for genuine education to happen. Using literature in the classroom helps to fill in the gaps left by textbooks. Reading literature not only allows multiple perspectives to be presented in the classroom, but also creates room for dialogue in the curriculum. Freire (1970) believes that "without dialogue there is no communication, and without communication there can be no true education" (p. 93). In dialogue between students, the negative emotions associated with a particular perspective can emerge, leading to uncomfortable sensations. The uncomfortable dialogue leads the students to find their "voices" and further their self-understanding. In fact, Wang (2008) states,

> In multicultural education, novels, auto/biographies, and films can be used effectively to move students beyond their own world and into other people's lives to experience the impact of social injustice. In this process, students' emotions are touched and further articulated into new words to describe the world differently. (p. 12)

The students then personally participate in creating a safe space for dialogue and education to happen.

One way I encourage dialogue in my classroom is through questioning before and after reading sections of the book, using the "before questions" to discover already-formed beliefs. After the reading, I use the same questions as a starting point and challenge the students to discuss deeper thoughts and ideas concerning their beliefs. Through the communication with me and their classmates, new perspectives and insights emerge, changing their initial ideas. The students keep journals in which they examine their memories, ideas, and connections. Interestingly, several students use current magazine and newspaper articles along with their critical self-reflections through the lens of the novel.

Through dialogue, relationships are formed within the classroom among students and between student and teacher. Fleener (2002) argues that relationship is key to curriculum dynamics. Developing relationships is the first thing I do in my social justice curriculum, for it is the driving force to a non-violent classroom. The classroom can be a place where students feel comfortable in discussing emotionally charged subjects or a place where they feel bullied and not valued, which creates an atmosphere of hostility. Howard (2006) suggests that to become a transformationist, a teacher needs to be honest, have empathy, become an advocate for students, and take action in the classroom. All four areas together create a powerful educator, within and outside of the classroom, but more importantly, they help the educator form the relationships needed for a healthy environment in which to tackle sensitive subject matter.

Listening to and genuinely caring about others is a common thread in my curriculum. Fleener (2002) mentions that by looking through another lens, we can gain another dimension of knowing. The motif of walking in another's shoes or stepping into the skin of another is essential to *To Kill a Mockingbird*, which can help students personally connect with the world in order to change the world. This is the first novel I use in my social justice curriculum with the hope that my students can connect with Scout's transformation and see a bigger world for their own transformation. Freire (1970) emphasizes that only through committed connections can authentic learning happen in the classroom. One exercise that my students do during the reading of Lee's novel is rewriting through the perspectives of the characters in the novel. Seeing through these characters' eyes asks students to see different viewpoints and feel what others feel so that they can journey *with* the character of their choice. Through the character of Atticus and his soft gentle teachings, my students and I can learn how he fought for social justice when the social norm of the time was injustice.

Freire (1970) calls such a curriculum—where students are encouraged to take risks in thinking, to ask questions, and to be curious—a liberating education. This liberating education allows the students to "develop their power to perceive critically the way they exist in the world with which and in which they find themselves; they come to see the world not as a static reality, but as a reality in process, in transformation" (p. 83). As a result, students critically reflect on themselves. The students look at themselves in the mirror, seeing the reflection of their ideas and beliefs, shifting in perspective, and finding their new voices. Looking inward is an uncomfortable, learning, reflective practice, but necessary in the social justice curriculum to unravel social dominance. Students begin to see themselves as empowered and intelligent people who can use their voices for change.

A variety of instructional approaches need to be used to keep students engaged in the curriculum of difficulty. Affirming the differences in learning styles is a start in acknowledging and viewing multiple perspectives. Using Dunn and Dunn's (1992) learning style theory, I encourage students to be creative and learn new and difficult information in their preferred style of learning. To help students feel connected to the learning process, I engage students' active learning on a daily basis. Glennon (2004) argues that active learning "is a broad umbrella. It covers such pedagogical strategies as cooperative learning, independent learning contracts, role-playing, discussion groups, and the like" (p. 31). Collaborative learning techniques enable each individual student to make meaningful connections with literature through "real-life" assignments. For example, one useful assignment toward the end of the reading of the novel is a group activity to examine the types of prejudice happening today. The groups present their findings to the class in some artistic or technological medium. They create collages, write songs, or make a PowerPoint presentation. There are many different ways of presentation to make connections between the novel and today's life, and through the lively class discussions students teach one another.

Another interesting in-class instructional method is to role-play different scenarios of prejudice written by the students. After their scenarios are played out for the class, I bring in scripts written by friends of different race, gender, and age groups about real-life events that have happened to them. As a class, we compare our scenes with theirs, discussing how or why their views are similar or different. This activity, rather than imposing social justice knowledge, opens up alternative landscapes, provokes students' critical self-reflection, and brings the themes of the novel to another level of understanding and social action.

In addition, a successful instructional approach in helping to form relationships and community within the classroom is the "quick write," an idea of the National Writing Project. A "quick write" is just that, writing over a specific topic that is done quickly. As the students share their quick writes, a community can emerge. Quick writes are useful in teaching social justice literature because they can bring out the individual student's thoughts, opinions, and life stories in a relatively spontaneous manner. I select the topics in different parts of the text. For example, one of the quick write topics in teaching *To Kill a Mockingbird* is the limitations Scout feels from being a girl, a type of prejudice often discussed in literature for adolescents. This topic works well to demonstrate both sides of the issue of gendered prejudice and how high school students view gender differences. Nieto (2004) states, "Making these discussions an explicit part of the curriculum . . . helps [students] tackle racism and other biases in productive rather than negative ways" (p. 404). In this way, the discussions are monitored but not silenced. Students feel safe in using the literature as a lens to share fears, hurts, and confusions.

Praxis, another of Freire's (1970) notions, is the backbone of my ideas concerning pedagogy: "Human activity is theory and practice; it is reflection and action" (p. 125). Reflection is a key factor in diversity and multicultural education. Through the teaching of literature, I have been challenged to reflect upon my teaching practices and my core beliefs about social injustice and to change my pedagogy practices. As Freire states, "The teacher cannot think for her students, nor can she impose her thought on them" (p. 77). As teachers, we bring into our classrooms our histories, our biases, our cultures, our fears, our educational journeys, and our relationships. Engaging praxis, I not only negotiate between curriculum and the needs of my individual students with the hope of decreasing biases and prejudices in my classroom, but I also deepen my own self-understanding. I write a teaching journal entry each week, reviewing my thoughts of each lesson—what worked or what did not work—and my ideas for change the next time. Most importantly, I write down my connections with students, the discussions and points brought out by students, and more ideas for guiding students to a deeper, critical thought process.

One of the difficulties that I encounter in teaching social justice literature is that I cannot reach every student. At the end of each curriculum unit, I have dialogues with the students through conversation and writing. At times I become disgruntled when I realize I did not reach all students with the literature. An example is a typical "American" female student in a ninth grade English class. She had blond hair, blue eyes, a family resembling the "American dream," and was very intelligent. I was concerned and disappointed to hear her proclaim that she was a racist and would continue to be a racist no matter how much literature she read in her classes. I was stunned. After reevaluating my lesson plans and my classroom theory and practice, I eventually realized that even though I had not changed her perspective, I might have planted a seed or she would not be protesting so adamantly. Wang (2008) discusses the students' flight and how "recognizing such a flight and guiding students gently back to what they fear requires pedagogical patience, insights, and creativity" (p. 12). Through all stages of the social justice curriculum, I had directly challenged her White bias and her "own positionings about race, culture, and power" (Johnston, 2003, p. 234). Moreover, just as Johnston (2003) states, "I failed to take account of their lack of experience of or preparation for dealing with issues surrounding cultural difference" (p. 237), I sometimes forgot how my students lacked diversity experiences. Precisely because of such a lack, it is important that I utilize literature to expose students to different worlds and increase their experiences of life different from their own. And precisely because of the student's refusal to learn, I must continue my efforts to challenge students to learn difficult knowledge.

In future endeavors with the social justice curriculum, I want to try something similar to Wang and Yu (2006) and Johnston's (2003) idea of reading two pieces of literature with heroes and heroines coming from different backgrounds, presenting different perspectives. As Johnston (2003) observes, this parallel reading might enable students to "become aware of the contrasting voices of the text and to be more critical of their own reading positions" (p. 237). In his class, he not only uses *To Kill a Mockingbird* but also *Roll of Thunder, Hear My Cry* whose hero is an African American girl. Students' responses to these two novels reveal that the relationship between the reader and the text is a complicated process mediated by the reader's own racial positioning, and that such a relationship itself can produce another layer of reading and understanding for both teacher and student. This idea intrigues me.

Using social justice literature in the classroom is a commitment and a journey. It is not a one-size-fits-all curriculum, but it is a curriculum that deserves a place in every school. Freire (1970) maintains that a true revolutionary leader has the power to liberate both the oppressed and the oppressors. I want to be a revolutionary leader whose classroom demonstrates the principle that every human being is worthy of respect and dignity. I want to model through my curriculum of social justice literature and my treatment of students that every human being must have empathy for others who are different from themselves.

28. Culture and the Literary Canon

Martin Meadows

Within dominant cultures, traditions exist that create subtle gender and racial biases. The tradition can be admirable and fulfill a need within the society, but the structure of the tradition aids in the creation of a single powerful culture and acts to control the influence of other cultures. The American literary canon is an example. "Canon" implies that, like the writings of the Christian Bible, this literary canon is sacred. Yet the list is actually an abstraction. It has no physical existence. Although a variety of scholars, writers, and personalities have generated lists of what they consider great writings, no single list has been declared "The List." The list of authors and works changes as it moves from professors of language to high school teachers to well-read citizens. If the canon is such an abstraction, why is it an issue of cultural power? The canon becomes much more limited as it forms the core of literature books in high schools, colleges, and universities, and the core list becomes *de rigueur* of study in survey courses of literature. The result is that the great majority of college students study a literary core that has only recently started to expand beyond its focus on White European culture. The dominant culture in America promotes a mono-cultural education, maintaining and reinforcing the racism and sexism within the canon. This essay argues that canonization, treating literature as object, creates a mono-cultural literature, and that there is a dynamic relationship between literature and culture.

Traditional Perspectives of Culture and Canon

The traditional view perceives the literary canon as a static representation of American culture; as one reads the works of the literary canon, one gains knowledge of the culture and its essential values (see Bennet, 1914; Adler, 1940; Hirsch, 1987; & Cheney, 1987). Lynne Cheney, a former chair of the National Endowment for the Humanities, presents the narrowest view of the literary canon in *American Memory* (1987). Cheney (1987) argues that knowing the classics of Western culture enables students to "realize our human potential," the "essence" of humanity, and it is a duty of education to provide this knowledge (p. 6). The lack of knowledge of these writers, Cheney claims, will destroy our sense of nationhood (p. 7). However, Cheney's canon recognizes only the European/Western civilization. It is a canon that Robert Scholes (1985) describes satirically as "pre-selected by culture, laid down like fossils in the sedimented layers of institutional tradition" (p. 58). Cheney's narrow vision frames the canon as defending the Anglo-centric culture against the attacks of the non-dominant cultures.

A slightly broader representation of the traditional view is found in E.D. Hirsch's (1987) *Cultural Literacy: What Every American Should Know*. Hirsch argues, as his subtitle conveys, that the American culture operates with expectations that its most successful members possess a shared knowledge. Like Cheney, he contends that Americans who do not possess that knowledge are unable to participate effectively within the society of the United States. Hirsch suggests that it is not necessary that students read a particular work, but that they must be aware of particular vocabularies, phrases, and ideas presented in the work. In the appendix, Hirsch creates "The List" of words and phrases, including an extensive list of authors, artists, places, and others aspects of culture. However, Simonson and Walker (1988) see a White, male, academic, Eastern U.S., Euro-centric bias in the long list.

Hirsch, Kett, and Trefil (2002) partially address this issue with the creation of *The New Dictionary of Cultural Literacy*. This more extensive list includes many of the omissions noted by Simonson and Walker, although authors Kate Chopin and Albert Camus are missing. Expanding the list suggests a problem inherent in making such canonical lists: Why are particular works or authors included and others not? Broadening the scope of authors and works to be more inclusive is not effective when there is no clear basis for selecting them. At the heart of the problem is that this dictionary appears to present knowledge as a series of objects to be numbered and listed. However, knowledge is not a series of objects but a process of thinking that is constantly developing and changing.

Cheney and Hirsch both view the construct of knowledge as fixed, and their perception of American culture and the literary canon also is neutral and static. Kaplan and Rose (1990) criticize *American Memory* for its narrow and imperialistic perception of culture and suggest that Cheney has forgotten American diversity. Cheney and Hirsch find this diversity menacing: If the perception of who and what represents American culture changes, both the current culture and the literary canon are threatened because change will bring an end to the literary canon and therefore to the culture as they know it. For traditionalists, this struggle for power over the canon is of the greatest importance.

However, their own fear reveals the flaw in their arguments and points in an alternative direction where the dynamic relationships between the American culture and the literary canon achieve recognition. If changing the canon affects the culture and if changing the culture affects the canon, their interactive relationship operates as a bi-directional system and this involves a different construct of thinking. As Capra (1996) notes, "systems thinking is 'contextual' which is the opposite of analytical thinking" (p. 30). Analytical thinking falls into an either-or pattern. For Cheney and Hirsch, American culture appears in only one form, and the literary canon reflects that form. Any other form, for them, must not be American culture. This perception creates an imaginary culture where the relationship between the canon and culture is unchanging. Although both secondary-level and university-level educators have frequently discussed opening the canon to women and minorities, the most important discussion is discovering the nature of the relationship between culture and the canon. This relationship is best described as a dynamic system, to which I will return in more detail in the last section.

Critiques of Traditional Perspective: The Multiplicities of Culture

Traditionalists perceive the American identity as embodied in the classical canon as existing over hundreds of years, but as Guillory (1993) notes, "social identities are themselves historically constructed; they mean different things at different historical moments" (p. 17–18). Crèvecoeur examined the idea of American identity in *Letters from an American Farmer* published in 1782 and, in describing it, created the concept of mingled races as a "melting pot." However, Crèvecoeur was speaking of the mingling between Southern Europeans and Northern Europeans. Until recently, Americans descended from Europeans presented as varied a culture mix as the current cultural mix of Latinos, Asians, Blacks, and Native Americans. The Irish, Italians, Poles, Swedes, Germans, and others shared a common continent and not much else. They differed in language, customs, and religions (not only Judaism and Christianity, but also numerous, and at times widely differing, denominations of Christianity). As various large ethnic groups of Europeans immigrated to the United States, each group suffered from the stamp of "foreigner" in American society. Through the twentieth century, Irish were stereotyped as lazy, Polish as ignorant, Germans as traitors, and Italians as Mafia hit men.

Yet, American Literature textbooks have reflected the myth of a homogeneous culture. A little over a half century ago, Jones and Leisy's (1945) revised and enlarged anthology called *Major American Writers* included only two women, Emily Dickinson and Ellen Glasgow, and no Black or Latino authors. The list of authors in the Fourth edition of *Adventures in American Literature*, published in 1952, included only a few Negro spirituals, and no Black writers except for one selection by James Weldon Johnson. In addition, less than 10 percent of the authors listed were women.

Recognizing a more diverse group of authors does not dilute the culture, but we need to acknowledge that American culture has always been much more diverse than presented in the early twentieth century textbooks. Modern textbooks have expanded their representation of Native American, Asian, and Hispanic American authors, and increasing the representation of women and minorities is likely to help present other faces of American culture. Recognizing that women and minority authors are also a part of the literature of America acknowledges that "the reality around us and the concepts that we use to recognize it, race and gender among them, are cultural constructions" (Schwenk, 1996, p. 2). Culture is not a monolithic structure with one face but a structure of many faces, and the canon of American literature must reflect such many faces. This reflection should take place in both high school English and college literature classes.

Cheney and Hirsch assume that the culture and the canon reflect specific, long-standing values of American society. As Gregory Jay (1997) explains, the concern of traditionalists is not that the other works are trivial, but "that academics are producing *a body of different truths* that threaten certain traditional value systems" (p. 31; italics in the original). This assumption that a long-standing value system exists is misleading. Lawrence Levine (1996) reports a study conducted in 1928 by Ferner Nuhn which found that in American colleges in the early twentieth century, Italian, Spanish, German, and French literature courses each accounted for more offerings than did American literature courses. Colleges in the early twentieth century focused on European and Ancient Greek civilizations but often did not include courses in American literature. Not until after WW II, Jay observes, did colleges become oriented toward American literature. The shifting nature of courses in colleges suggests that cultural literature shifts much more frequently than we acknowledge. These shifts suggest that, rather than one basic set of truths, cultural literature involves a shifting set of values.

Multiculturalism and the Literary Canon

The crux of the traditionalist approach to culture and the literary canon lies in the treatment of the canon and culture as a distinct, independent object, instead of a dynamic system that requires a multicultural approach. For the traditionalist, adding or subtracting works from the canon alters it and makes it into something that no longer identifies the best works of literature.

This reduction of American culture ignores the complex relationships between text and culture. Robert Dunne (1992) argues that texts have a dialectical relationship with their respective cultures. For example, Charles Dickens' novels create images of the industrial society taken from his culture. Even as he criticizes the society, he is creating for future generations of readers images of the culture of industrialization he is criticizing. Literature creates images of cultural values and reflects these images back into the culture even when the intent is to condemn the values. While a mono-cultural education may place a text within the framework of a specific era, it ignores the interaction between the culture and the literature and, as a result, the multiplicity of the culture disappears. A multicultural education in literature explores the dynamic relationship between the literature and the culture and reveals their various facets.

Another element of the complex relationships within the framework of the literary canon includes recognizing the culture of readers. Northrup Frye (1968) distinguishes between knowledge of literature and value in literature. He says, "In knowledge, the context of the work of literature is literature; in value judgment, the context of the work of literature is the reader's experience" (p. 311). If value in literature is reader-based, a cultural relationship with the literary canon cannot be limited to the qualities of the literature.

The importance of the interaction of readers and text has been clearly established, especially by the works of Louise Rosenblatt (1978) and Robert Probst (1988). Awareness of this interaction means that changes in readers result in changes in the relationships readers have with texts. Levine (1996) describes the changes in the student population of American colleges over the last part of the twentieth century, when the minority population grew from 6 percent in 1960 to over 25 percent by 1988. In 1960 women earned 35 percent of the bachelor's degrees and 10 percent of the doctorates conferred, but in 1990 the numbers were 54 percent and 37 percent, respectively (p. xvii). Thus it is unreasonable to expect the same reaction to literature in 1990 as in 1960, given the change in readers. Yet a mono-cultural education ignores the changes and considers the student of 1990 as the same student of 1960.

While the changes in gender are significant, the movement away from the White European male image is not in one direction, but in multiple directions generated by increases not only in women students but also in ethnic groups. Just as the label "European" is an overly simplistic cultural label, the same can be said for other ethnic labels. Levine (1996) explains that when we look closely at any one ethnic group, "what looked like a culture becomes a series of cultures" (p. 155). He notes as an example that Japanese Americans include the

Issei, born in Japan and legally barred from becoming United States citizens; the *Nisei,* born and raised here and thus citizens by birth; the *Kibei* born here but raised in Japan and thus legally Americans and culturally Japanese; as well as those who lived in cities and those who live on farms; those who struggled to maintain the old ways and those who hungered for acculturation. (p. 155)

Levine argues that the same can be said of any other group. Native Americans are members of a variety of tribes, each with a culture independent of the other. Hispanics come from a multitude of backgrounds and have descended from different nationalities. Caucasians have also descended from a great variety of cultures and nationalities. Yet the common perspective is to see only the larger group, causing the subgroups to disappear under the umbrella of similarity. Therefore, to understand the relationship between the literary canon and culture, we need to consider the multiplicities within each culture, however it is defined. Jay (1997) further points out that the multiple dimensions of cultural groups are made even more complex by economic, social, and political changes in readers, not just by changes in gender or ethnicity.

These multiple dimensions within each group create a bewildering number of interactions between reader and literature. The general cultural group provides one image and then each subgroup reflects an image unique to itself. A multicultural education approach that recognizes the multiple faces of the literary cultures and promotes dynamic, interactive relationships between different cultures and within each culture holds the greatest potential for depicting a system view of canon and culture that clearly represents the variety of cultures found within the literature.

A multicultural approach makes visible the faces and cultures that have been hidden under the dominant culture. In establishing the canon, the dominant culture has worked to deny the literature of the non-dominant cultures, making it almost invisible. This invisibility also appears in the treatment of students as unchanging and in the invisibility of subgroups within a culture. If minority cultures are invisible, how can there be a relationship between cultures? Without relationships, there is no possibility for dialogue and discussion, and the generative potential of a system is lost. The loss of relationships harms the entire system by creating a false image of American society and generating a false sense of reality. By making other cultures visible within the academic subject, not only do we recognize their existence, but we also more realistically describe our society and literature.

In this approach, a multicultural education is not extraneous, separate and distinct from academics. Instead, schools integrate multiculturalism with academic matter to reinforce and expand the understanding of both. Looking closely at the dynamics of canon formation reveals the tremendous role of culture. From the selection of works for textbooks to the effect upon individual readers, we can see how the dominant culture tries to close off the representation of the non-dominant cultures. However, such a narrow-minded, mono-cultural approach cannot capture the dynamics of either the literary canon or the society; neither can this approach meet the needs of a multicultural society. An open system view asks us to allow multiplicity to play its creative role.

Bringing Cultures to Life

Although the focus of this work has been on English literature, other areas of academics would have similar benefits from integrating multicultural education. The interaction between culture and the literary canon also exists in the interaction between culture and other academic studies. When the multicultural dimension in academics is not visible, non-dominant cultures have disappeared from education. The treatment of academic subjects as separate from issues of culture misrepresents the subject matter and limits our understanding of the world around us. An organic view of culture and academics encourages us to recognize that a multicultural education interacts dynamically with academics. The recognition of this condition does not just further our understanding of cultures. It also furthers our understanding of the subject matter and of the interactions of history, arts, mathematics, and other disciplines with the various cultures and the dynamic relationships that exist between subject matter and cultures.

Notes

1. This essay is a revision of chapter three of my Master's Thesis (2006), *The Literary canon as a dynamic system of chaos and complexity theory* and my class writings on multiculturalism.

References

Adler, M. (1940). *How to read a book*. New York: Simon & Schuster.

ACTFL (2005). *The year of languages*. Retrieved December 7, 2004, from http://www. Actfl.org

Albert, R. D. (1995). The intercultural sensitizer/culture assimilator as a cross-cultural training method. In S. M. Fowler & M. G. Mumford (Eds.), *Intercultural sourcebook* (pp.157–167). Yarmouth, ME: Intercultural Press.

Allgood, I. (2001). The role of the school in deterring prejudice. In C. F. Diaz (Ed), *Multicultural education for the 21ˢᵗ century* (pp. 184–200). New York: Longman.

Alosh, M. (2000). *Ahlan wa Sahlan*. New Haven and London: Yale University Press.

Angelou, M. (1994). *The complete collected poems of Maya Angelou*. New York: Random.

———— . (1997). *I know why the caged bird sings*. New York: Bantam Books. (Original work published 1969)

Anonymous. (2000, April 11). Teaching from the closet [Electronic version]. *The Advocate*. Retrieved November 15, 2004, from http://www.advocate.com/html/stories/809/809_anon_persp.asp

Anzaldúa, G. (1999). *Borderlands*. San Francisco: Aunt Lute Books.

Aoki, T. T. (2005). *Curriculum in a new key*. Mahwah, NJ: Lawrence Erlbaum.

Apple, M. (1990). *Ideology and curriculum*. London: Routledge.

———— . (1999). *Power, meaning and identity*. New York: Peter Lang.

Ayers, W. (2001). *Fugitive days*. Boston, MA: Beacon Press.

Baars, B. J. (1997). In the theatre of consciousness. *The Journal of Consciousness Studies, 4*(4), 292–309.

Banks, J. A. (2006). *Cultural diversity and education*. Boston: Pearson.

———— . (2008). *Introduction to multicultural education* (4ᵗʰ ed.). Boston: Pearson.

Banks, J., & Banks, C. (Eds.). (2005). *Multicultural education* (5ᵗʰ ed.). Hoboken, NJ: Wiley.

Belenky, M. F., Clinchy, B. M., Goldberger, N. R., & Tarule, J. M. (1986). *Women's ways of knowing*. New York: Basic Books.

Bennet, A. (1914). *Literary tastes*. Retrieved April 2, 2006, from Project Gutenberg http://www.gutenberg.org/dirs/etext03/taste10.txt

Bennett, C. I. (2003). *Comprehensive multicultural education* (5ᵗʰ ed.). Boston: Allyn and Bacon.

Berlak, A. C. (1996). Teaching stories. *Theory into Practice, 35*(2), 93–101.

Block, A. A. (2001). Ethics and curriculum. *Journal of Curriculum Theorizing, 17*(3), 23–28.

Bloom, B., Mesia, B. B., & Krathwohl, D. R. (1964). *Taxonomy of educational objectives*. New York: David McKay.

Blotcher, J. (2004, July 23). Teaching by example [Electronic version]. *The Advocate.* Retrieved November 11, 2004, from http://www.advocate.com/html/stories/ 868/868_french.asp

Boler, M. (1999). *Feeling power.* New York: Routledge.

Boler, M., & Zembylas, M. (2003). Discomforting truths. In P. P. Trifonas (Ed.), *Pedagogies of difference* (pp. 110–136). New York: Routledeg Falmer.

Bourne, E. G. (Ed.). (1906). *The Northmen, Columbus and Cabot.* New York: Charles Scribner's Sons.

Brune, A. (2002, March 18). Tulsa's shame. *The Nation, 274*(10), 11–15.

Camarota, S. A. (2007). Immigrants in the United States, 2007: A profile of America's foreign-born population. Retrieved December 5, 2007, from http://www.cis.org/articles/2007/ back1007.pdf

Capra, F. (1996). *The web of life.* New York: Anchor Books Doubleday.

Carnes, M. (2004, October 8). The liminal classroom. *The Chronicle of Higher Education, 51*(7), p. B6.

Cassidy, M. B. (1988). *Taking students abroad.* Brattleboro, VT: Pro Lingua Associates.

Central Intelligence Agency. (2005, November). *World factbook.* Retrieved June 27, 2008, from https://www.cia.gov/library/publications/the-world-factbook/geos/xx.html

Chalmers, D. M. (1981). *Hooded Americanism* (3rd ed.). Durham, NC: Duke University Press.

Chan, C. S., & Treacy, M. J. (1996). Resistance in multicultural courses. *The American Behavioral Scientist, 40*(2), 212–221.

Chan, E., & Boone, M. (2001). Addressing multicultural issues through teacher stories. *Journal of Critical Inquiry into Curriculum and Instruction, 3*(2), 36–41.

Cheever, G. B. (1848). *The journal of the Pilgrims at Plymouth.* New York: John Wiley.

Cheney, L. (1987). *American memory.* Washington D.C.: National Endowment for the Humanities.

Chizhik, E. W. (2003). Reflecting on the challenges of preparing suburban teachers for urban schools. *Education and Urban Society, 35*(4), 443–461.

Chomsky, N. (1987). The responsibility of intellectuals. In J. Peck (Ed.), *The Chomsky reader* (pp. 59–82). New York: Pantheon Books.

Clabaugh, G.K. (1995). Positive discrimination. *Educational Horizons.* Retrieved December 10, 2006, from http://www.newfoundations.com/Clabaugh/CuttingEdge/ PositiveDiscrimination.html

Columbus at Granada. (1892, April 17). *New York Times.* Retrieved June 28, 2008, from http://query.nytimes.com/gst/abstract.html?res=9905E7DB1438E233A25754C1A9629C9 4639ED7CF

Costo, R. (1974). There is not one Indian child who has not come home in shame and tears. In M. Wasserman, *Demystifying school* (pp. 192–93). New York: Praeger.

Cox, W. E. (2004). Reflections of one who was there. In The Editors of Black Issues in Higher Education with J. Anderson & D.N. Byrne (Eds.), *The unfinished agenda of Brown v. Board of Education* (pp. xvii–xxiv). Hoboken, NJ: John Wiley & Sons.

Cross, W.W., Jr. (1995). The psychology of Nigrescence: In J. G. Ponterrotto, J. M. Casas, L. A. Suzuki, & C. M. Alexander (Eds.), *Handbook of multicultural counseling* (pp. 98–115). Thousand Oaks, CA: Sage.

Cushner, K. (2003). *Human diversity in action.* New York: McGraw-Hill.

David, G. C., & Ayouby, K. K. (2005). Studying the exotic other in the classroom. *Multicultural Perspectives, 7*(4), 13–20.

Davis, A., & Jackson, J. (1998). *Yo, little brother ….* Chicago: African American Images.

De Waal, E. (1998). *Living with contradiction.* Harrisburg, PA: Morehouse.

Delpit, L. (2006). *Other people's children* (2nd ed.). New York: The New Press. (Original work published 1995)

Derrida, J. (1992). *The other heading.* Bloomington, IN: Indiana University Press.

Doll, M. A. (1995). *To the lighthouse and back.* New York: Peter Lang.

Donne, J. (1994). *The complete poetry and selected prose of John Donne.* New York: Modern Library.

Dörnyei, Z., & Csizer, K. (1998). Ten commandments for motivating language learners. *Language Teaching Research, 4,* 203–229.

Dougherty, L. (1999). *Understanding race.* Princeton, NJ: Films for the Humanities.

Dunn, R., & Dunn, K. (1992). *Teaching elementary students through their individual learning styles.* Boston: Allyn and Bacon.

Dunne, R. (Feb, 1992). Avoiding labels. *College literature, 19*(1), 136–141.

Dyer, R. (1997). *White.* London: Routledge.

Edgerton, S. H. (1996). *Translating the curriculum.* New York: Routledge.

Edwards, B. (1986). *Drawing on the right side of the brain.* New York: Simon and Schuster.

Ellsworth, S. (1982). *Death in a promised land.* Baton Rouge: Louisiana State University Press.

Erikson, J. M. (1988). *Wisdom and the senses.* New York: Norton.

Estes, M. E. (1942). Historical survey of lynching's in Oklahoma and Texas. Unpublished master's thesis at the University of Oklahoma, Norman.

Estes, C. P. (1992). *Women who run with the wolves.* New York: Ballantine Books.

Fantini, A. E. (1999). Comparisons: Towards the development of intercultural competence. In J. K. Phillips & R. M. Terry (Eds.), *Foreign language standards* (pp.165–217). Lincolnwood, IL: National Textbook Company.

Fine, M. (2004). Witnessing whiteness/gathering intelligence. In M. Fine, L. Weis, L. P. Prutt, & A. Burns (Eds.), *Off white* (2nd ed.) (pp. 245–256). New York: Routledge.

Fleener, J. (2002). *Curriculum dynamics.* New York: Peter Lang.

Fowler, J. W. (1981). *Stages of faith.* San Francisco: Harper and Row.

Franklin, J. H., & Ellsworth, S. (2001). History knows no fences: An overview. In *Tulsa Race Riot: A report by the Oklahoma Commission to study the Tulsa Race Riot of 1921*(pp. 21–35). Available through the Greenwood Cultural Center, 322 North Greenwood, Tulsa, Oklahoma 74120.

Freire, P. (1998). *Pedagogy of the heart.* New York: Continuum.

——— . (2000). *Pedagogy of the oppressed.* New York: Continuum.

——— . (2004). Pedagogy of the oppressed. In D. J. Flinders (Ed.), *The curriculum studies reader* (pp. 125–133). New York: RoutledgeFalmer.

——— . (2005). *Pedagogy of the oppressed.* New York: Continuum. (Original work published 1970)

Frye, N. (1968). On value judgments. *Contemporary Literature, 9,* 311–318.

Gallavan, N. P. (2006). Helping teachers unpack their "invisible knapsacks." *Multicultural Education, 13*(1), 36–39.

Gardner, D. (1995). *When racial categories make no sense.* Retrieved December 11, 2005, from http://www.sinc.sunysb.edu/Stu/lmarfogl/project/race_gerdner.htm

Garrod, A., & Larimore, C. (Eds.). (1997). *First person, first peoples.* Ithaca, NY: Cornell University Press.

Gates, E. F. (2003). *Riot on Greenwood.* Eakin Publications.

Gilligan, C. (1993). *In a different voice.* Cambridge, MA: Harvard University Press.

Glennon, F. (2004). Experiential learning and social justice action. *Teaching Theology and Religion, 7*(1), 30–37.

Goble, D. (1997). *Tulsa: Biography of the American city.* Tulsa, OK: Council Oaks Books.

Gough, N. (2003). Thinking globally in environmental education. In W. F. Pinar (Ed.), *International handbook of curriculum research* (pp. 53–71). Mahwah, NJ: Lawrence Erlbaum.

Grande, S. (2004). *Red pedagogy.* Lanham, MD: Rowman & Littlefield.

Grubin, D. (Producer). (1988). *American dream at Groton* [Film]. New York City: Smithsonian World.

Guillory, J. (1993). *Cultural capital.* Chicago: University of Chicago Press.

Harbeck, K. (1997). *Gay and lesbian educators.* Boston: Amethyst Press.

Hart, L. A. (1998). *Human brain and human learning.* Kent, WA: Books for Educators.

Haycock, K. (2006). No more invisible kids. *Educational Leadership, 64* (3), p. 38–42.

Helms, J. E. (Ed.) (1990). *Black and White racial identity.* Westport, CT: Greenwood Press.

Hesford, W. S. (1999). *Framing Identities.* Minneapolis, MN: University of Minnesota Press.

Hirsch, E. D. (1987). *Cultural literacy.* Boston: Houghton Mifflin.

Hirsch, E. D., Kett, J., & Trefil, J. (2002). *The new dictionary of cultural literacy.* New York: Houghton Mifflin.

Hirsch, J. (2002). *Riot and remembrance.* Boston: Houghton Mifflin.

hooks, b. (1994). *Outlaw culture.* New York: Routledge.

Howard, G. (1999). *We can't teach what we don't know.* New York: Teachers College Press.

————— . (2006). *We can't teach what we don't know* (2nd ed.). New York: Teachers College Press.

Howell, A. (2006). Report points to progress in closing achievement gap. *Crisis, 113* (2), 9.

Huebner, D. (1975). Poetry and power. In W. Pinar (Ed.), *Curriculum theorizing* (pp. 271–280). Berkeley, CA: McCutchan.

————— . (1999). *The lure of the transcendent* (V. Hillis, Ed.). Mahwah, NJ: Lawrence Erlbaum.

Hutchinson, J. (1992). AIDS and racism in America. *Journal of the National Medical Association, 84*(2), 119–124.

Ikeda, D. (2005). Foreword. In N. Noddings (Ed.), *Educating citizens for global awareness.* New York: Teachers College Press.

Institute of International Education. (2007a). International student enrollment in the U.S. rebounds. Retrieved December 5, 2007, from http://opendoors.iienetwork.org/?p=113743

Institute of International Education. (2007b). U.S. students studying abroad at record levels. Retrieved December 5, 2007, from http://opendoors.iienetwork.org/?p=113744

Iseke-Barnes, J., & Wane, N. (Eds.) (2000). *Equity in schools and society.* Toronto: Canadian Scholars' Press.

Italie, H. (2003, September 4). Jessica Lynch agrees to $1 million book deal. *Oakland Tribune.* Retrieved on October 16, 2003, from http://findarticles.com/p/articles/mi_qn4176/is_20030904/ai_n14556606

Iyer, A., Leach C. W., & Pedersen, A. (2004). Racial wrongs and restitutions. In M. Fine, L. Weis, L. P. Prutt, & A. Burns (Eds.), *Off white* (2nd ed.) (pp. 345–361). New York: Routledge.

Jakubowski, L. M. (2001). Teaching uncomfortable topics. *Teaching Sociology, 29*(1), 62–79.

Jay, G. S. (1997). *American literature & the culture wars.* Ithaca, NY: Cornell University Press.

Jennings , K. (Ed.) (1994). *One teacher in 10.* Boston: Alyson.

Johansen, B. E. (2006). *The native peoples of North America.* Fredericksburg, PA: Rutgers University Press.

Johnson, R. C. (1997). Heart of darkness. Retrieved October 18, 2004, from http://worldatwar.net/chandelle/v2/v2n3/congo.html

Johnston, I. (2003). Reading and resisting silent spaces of whiteness in school literature. In E. Ludt & W. Hurren (Eds.), *Curriculum intertext* (pp. 227–238). New York: Peter Lang.

Jones, H., & Leisy, E. (1945). *Major American writers.* New York: Harcourt, Brace and Company.

Kanza, T. (1979). *The rise and fall of Patrice Lumumba.* Cambridge: Schenkman.

Kaplan, C., and Rose, E. C. (1990). *The canon and the common reader.* Knoxville, TN: University of Tennessee Press.

Kermode, F. (2004). *Pleasure and change.* Oxford, NY: Oxford University Press.

King, M. (2004). *Quotations from Martin Luther King, Jr.* Bedford, MA: Applewood Books.

Kissen, R. (1996). *The last closet.* Portsmouth, New Hampshire: Heinemann.

Kohli, W. (1991). Postmodernism, critical theory and the "new" pedagogies. *Education and Society, 9,* 39–46.

Ladson-Billings, G. (2001). *Crossing over to Canaan.* San Francisco: Jossey-Bass.

Land, R. (2005). Wounded (soul)diers in the classroom. In M. C. Brown II & R. R. Land (Eds.), *The politics of curricular change* (pp. 105–127). New York: Peter Lang.

Lander, M. (2003, April 19). A nation at war. *New York Times.* Retrieved on October 16, 2003, from http://query.nytimes.com/gst/fullpage.html?res=9C05E3DF53AA2575C0A9659C8B63&sec=&spon=&pagewanted=1

Lawrence, S. M., & Tatum, B. D. (2004). White educators as allies. In M. Fine, L. Weis, L. P. Prutt, & A. Burns (Eds.), *Off white* (2nd ed.) (pp. 262–272). New York: Routledge.

Lee, H. (1960). *To kill a mockingbird.* New York: Warner Books.

Lee, M. W. (Producer). (1994). *The color of fear* [Motion Picture]. United States: Stir Fry Productions.

Lerner, G. (1993). *The creation of feminist consciousness.* London: Oxford University Press.

Lesage, J., Ferber, A. L., Storrs, D., & Wong, D (2002). *Making a difference.* Lanham, MD: Rowan & Littlefield.

Levine, L. (1996). *The opening of the American mind.* Boston: Beacon Press.

Levine, M. P., & Pataki, E. (2004). *Racism in mind.* Ithaca, NY: Cornell University Press.

Li, X. (2002). *The Tao of life stories*. New York: Peter Lang.

Loewen, J. (1995). *Lies my teacher told me*. New York: Touchstone.

Lugg, C. (1997, October 31). No trespassing. Paper presented at the UCEA Annual Convention, Orlando, Florida.

Malloy, A. M. (2006). *Fiery formation of global citizenship in higher education: Teacher as the Vessel*. Unpublished doctoral dissertation, Oklahoma State University.

Matus, C., & McCarthy C. (2003). The triumph of multiplicity and the carnival of difference. In W. F. Pinar (Ed.), *International handbook of curriculum research* (pp. 73–82). Mahwah, NJ: Lawrence Erlbaum.

Maxwell, B. (2002, March 24). There's no place like the south. *St. Petersburg Times Online*. Retrieved June 27, 2008, from
http://www.sptimes.com/2002/03/24/Columns/There_s_no_place_like.shtml

McAulay, M. (n.d.). *The Soweto riots*. Retrieved October 22, 2004, from
http://www.ccds.charlotte.nc.us/History/Africa/save/mcaulay/mcaulay.htm

McCarthy, C., Crichlow, W., Dimitriadis, G., & Dolby, N. (Eds.) (2005). *Race, identity, and representation in education* (2nd ed.). New York: Routledge.

McIntosh, P. (1998). White privilege and male privilege: A personal account of coming to see correspondences through work in women's studies (1988). In M. L. Anderson & P. Collins (Eds.), *Race, class, and gender: An anthology* (pp. 94–105). Belmont, CA: Wadsworth.

McIntosh, P. (2005). Gender perspectives on educating for global citizenship. In N. Noddings (Ed.), *Educating citizens for global awareness* (pp. 22–39). New York: Teachers College Press.

McKern, S. (1979). *Redneck mothers, good ol' girls and other southern belles*. New York: Viking Press.

Meadows, M. (2006). *The literary canon as a dynamic system of chaos and complexity theory*. Unpublished Master's thesis, Oklahoma State University, Stillwater.

Media Literacy Fast Facts (n.d.). *Teen health and the media*. Retrieved January 29, 2004, from
http://depts.washington.edu/thmedia/view.cgi?section=medialiteracy&Page=fastfacts

Meer, F. (1990). *Higher than hope: The authorized biography of Nelson Mandela*. New York: Harper Perennial.

Menchú, R. (1998). *I, Rigoberta Menchú: An Indian woman in Guatemala* (Elisabeth Burgos-Debray Ed. & Intro. Ann Wright, Trans.). London: Verso.

Michelson, E. (1996). Usual suspects: Experience, reflection and the (en)gendering of knowledge. *International Journal of Lifelong Education, 15*(6), 438–454.

Miller, J. L. (2005). *Sounds of silence breaking*. New York: Peter Lang.

Mitchell, M. (2003, November 15). Three soldiers' tales show racial divide. *The Tulsa World*, p. A21.

Morain, G. (n.d.). *The culture quest*. Paper presented to graduate students in Language Education, University of Georgia, Athens.

Morrison, T. (1988). Unspeakable things unspoken. *Michigan Quarterly, 28*(1), 1–34.

Munro, P. (1998). *Subject to fiction*. Philadelphia, PA: Open University Press.

Myers, A. (2004). *Tulsa burning*. New York: Walker and Company.

Nakata, Y. (1997). Turn off the stereo(type). In A. E. Fantini (Ed.), *New ways in teaching culture* (pp. 206–207). Bloomington, IL: Pantagraph Printing.

National Standards in Foreign Language Education Project. (1996). *Standards for foreign language learning.* Lawrence, KS: Allen Press.

Newman, R. (1998). *African American quotations.* Phoenix, AZ: Oryx Press.

Nieto, S. (1999). *The light in their eyes.* New York: Teachers College Press.

———. (2004). *Affirming diversity* (4th ed.). Boston: Pearson/Allyn and Bacon.

Nieto, S., & Bode, P. (2008). *Affirming diversity.* Boston: Pearson Education.

Noddings, N. (1984). *Caring.* Berkeley: University of California Press.

———. (2002). *Starting at home.* Berkeley: University of California Press.

———. (2005). *Educating citizens for global awareness.* New York: Teachers College Press.

Nossiter, A. (2001, November 11). Something Tulsa forgot. *New York Times.* Retrived August 28, 2008, from http://query.nytimes.com/gst/
fullpage.html?res=9A06E7D61030F932A25752C1A9679C8B63

Obidah, J. E., & Teel, K. O. (2001). *Because of the kids.* New York: Teachers College Press.

Ogletree, C. J., Jr. (2005). Remembering May 31, 1921. *Sentinel,* LXXI (14), p. A4.

Oklahoma State University, College of Education. (n.d.). *Strategic plan.* Retrieved October 30, 2008, from http://system.okstate.edu/planning/plans/stw_edu_AreaPlan-CollegeofEduction.php

Olson, N. (1989). *Decoding the cultural context.* Unpublished doctoral dissertation, University of Georgia, Athens.

Paley, V. G. (2000). *White teacher.* Cambridge, MA: Harvard University Press. (Original work published 1979).

Patrick, E. J. (1999, July 09). *The Tulsa, Oklahoma Race Riot of 1921.* Retrieved October 19, 2004, from http://www.exodusnews.com/HISTORY/History007.htm

Pettigrew, T., Fredrickson, G., Knobel, D., Glazer, N., & Ueda, R. (1982). *Prejudice.* Cambridge, MA: Harvard University Press.

Pinar, W. (1975). *Curriculum theorizing.* Berkeley, CA: McCutchan.

———. (1993). Understanding curriculum as a racial text. In Cameron McCarthy & Warren Crichlow (Eds.), *Race, identity, and representation in education* (pp. 61–70). New York: Routledge.

———. (1994). *Autobiography, politics, and sexuality.* New York: Peter Lang.

———. (1995). Introduction. In M. A. Doll, *To the lighthouse and back* (pp. 1–7). New York: Peter Lang.

———. (2004). *What is curriculum theory?* Mahwah, NJ: Lawrence Erlbaum.

Pinar, W. F., & Grumet, M. R. (1976). *Toward a poor curriculum.* Dubuque, IA: Kendall/Hunt.

Pipino, M. F. (2005). Resistance and the pedagogy of ethnic literature. *MELUS, 30*(2), 179–190.

Pitt, A. (2003). *The play of the personal.* New York: Peter Lang.

Probst, R. E. (1988). *Response and analysis.* Portsmouth, NH: Heinemann.

Religious group attacks gay teachers [Electronic version]. (2000, April 14). *The Advocate.* Retrieved November 15, 2004, from http://www.advocate.com/html/news/041400/
041400news02.asp

Rhone, A. (2002). Effective teaching techniques to overcome teacher resistance. *Contemporary Education, 72*(2), 43–46.

Rideout, V. J., Vandewater, E. A., & Wartella, E. A. (2003, Fall). Zero to six. *Kaiser Family Foundation.* Retrieved March 24, 2006, from http://www.kff.org

Roberts, A., & Smith, K. I. (2002). Managing emotions in the college classroom. *Teaching Sociology, 30*(3), 291–301.

Robinson, C. (1994). You cannot tell by looking at me. In K. Jennings (Ed.), *One teacher in 10* (pp. 78–85). Boston: Alyson.

Ross, D. (2003). *Greenwood: Ruins, Resilience and Renaissance.* Available through the Greenwood Cultural Center, 322 North Greenwood, Tulsa, Oklahoma 74120.

Rosenberg, P. M. (2004). Color blindness in teacher education. In M. Fine, L. Weis, L. P. Prutt, & A. Burns (Eds.), *Off white* (2nd ed.) (pp. 257–272). New York: Routledge.

Rosenblaat, L. (1978). *The reader, the text, the poem.* Carbondale, IL: Southern Illinois Press.

Rothenberg, P. (2000). *Invisible privilege.* Lawrence, KS: University Press of Kansas.

———. (2005). *White privilege.* New York: Worth Publishers.

Sadker, M., & Sadker, D. (1986). Sexism in the classroom. *Phi Delta Kappan, 67*(7), 512–515.

Scholes, R. (1985). *Textual power: Literary theory and the teaching of English.* New Haven, CT: Yale University Press.

School district reprimanded for violating gay teachers' rights [Electronic version]. (2001, December 6). *The Advocate.* Retrieved November 15, 2004, from
http://www.advocate.com/news_news.asp?id=1879&sd=12/06/01

Schwenk, K. (1996). Introduction. In W. Siemerling, & K. Schwenk (Eds.), *Cultural Difference and the literary text* (pp. 1–9). Iowa City: University of Iowa Press.

Sheldon, L. (2003). Homosexuals recruit public school children. Retrieved November 18, 2004 from http://www.traditionalvalues.org/pdf_files/
TVCSpecialRptHomosexualRecruitChildren.PDF

Shor, I. (1992). *Empowering education.* Chicago: University of Chicago Press.

Simonson, R., & Walker, S. (1988). *Multi-cultural literacy.* St. Paul, MN: Graywolf Press.

Sleeter, C. E. (2000). *Culture, difference, and power.* New York: Teachers College Press.

———. (2005). How white teachers construct race. In C. McCarthy, W. Crichlow, G. Dimitriadis, & N. Dolby (Eds.), *Race, identity, and representation in education* (2nd ed.) (pp. 243–256). New York: Routledge.

Smith, D. G. (2003). Curriculum and teaching face globalization. In W. F. Pinar (Ed.), *International handbook of curriculum research* (pp. 35–51). Mahwah, NJ: Lawrence Erlbaum.

Starratt, R. J. (1994). *Building an ethical school.* Washington D.C: Falmer Press.

Steinberg, S. R. (2001). *Multi/intercultural conversations.* New York: Peter Lang.

Steinberg, S. R., & Kincheloe, J. L. (2001). Setting the context for critical multi/interculturalism. In Shirley R. Steinberg (Ed.), *Multi/intercultural conversations* (pp. 3–30). New York: Peter Lang.

Swisher, K., & Schoorman, D. (2001). Learning styles. In C. Diaz (Ed), *Multicultural education for the 21st century* (pp. 55–70). New York: Longman.

Tagore, R. (1995). *Creative unity*. Delhi: Macmillan India Limited press. (Original work published 1922)

Tatum, B. D. (1997). *"Why are all the black kids sitting together in the cafeteria?" and other conversations about race*. New York: Basic Books.

Todd, S. (2003). *Learning from the other*. Albany: State University of New York Press.

Trifonas, P. P. (2003). *Pedagogies of difference*. New York: RoutleFalmer.

Trompenaars, F., & Hampden-Turner, C. (1998). *Riding the Waves of Culture* (2nd ed.). New York: McGraw-Hill.

The Tulsa Race Riot Commission (2001). *Tulsa Race Riot: A report by the Oklahoma Commission to study the Tulsa Race Riot of 1921*. Available through the Greenwood Cultural Center, 322 North Greenwood, Tulsa, Oklahoma 74120.

Tutu, M. D. (1999). *No future without forgiveness*. New York: Doubleday.

Wallis, H. (Producer). Glenville, P. (Director). (1964). *Becket* [Motion Picture]. United States: E & M Enterprising.

Wang, H. (2004). *The call from the stranger on a journey home*. New York: Peter Lang.

———. (2005). Aporia, responsibility, and im/possibility of teaching multicultural education. *Educational Theory, 55*(1), 45–59.

———. (2008). "Red eyes." *Multicultural Perspectives, 10*(1), 10–16.

———. (in press). The temporality of *currere*, change, and teacher education. *Pedagogies: An International Journal*.

Wang, H., & Yu, T. (2006). Beyond promise. *Multicultural Education, 13*(4), 29–35.

Ward, M. A. (2005). *Incoming college freshmen's perceptions of racial, religious, and sexual orientation groups*. Unpublished doctoral dissertation, Oklahoma State University, Stillwater.

Weiler, J. (2000). *Codes and contradictions*. New York: State University of New York Press.

White-Clark, R. (2005). Training teachers to succeed in a multicultural classroom. *Education Digest, 4*, 23–27.

Williams, R. M. (1966). *Prejudice and society*. Upper Saddle River, NJ: Prentice Hall.

Wilkerson, M. (Producer). (2000, May 31). *The Tulsa lynching of 1921*. United States: Cinemax.

Zavadny, C. (2004, May 4). Language enhances students' prospects. *The Daily O'Collegian*, 7.

Zinn, H. (1980). *A people's history of the United States*. New York: Harper Collins.